A-LIST ANGELS

ALSO BY ZACK O'MALLEY GREENBURG

3 Kings: Diddy, Dr. Dre, Jay-Z and Hip-Hop's Multibillion-Dollar Rise
Michael Jackson, Inc: The Rise, Fall, and Rebirth of a Billion-Dollar Empire
Empire State of Mind: How Jay-Z Went from Street Corner to Corner Office

A-LIST ANGELS

How a Band of Actors, Artists,
and Athletes Hacked Silicon Valley

Zack O'Malley Greenburg

Little, Brown and Company
New York Boston London

Little, Brown and Company
Hachette Book Group
1290 Avenue of the Americas, New York, NY 10104
littlebrown.com

First Edition: March 2020

Little, Brown and Company is a division of Hachette Book Group, Inc. The Little, Brown name and logo are trademarks of Hachette Book Group, Inc.

The publisher is not responsible for websites (or their content) that are not owned by the publisher.

The Hachette Speakers Bureau provides a wide range of authors for speaking events. To find out more, go to hachettespeakersbureau.com or call (866) 376-6591.

ISBN 978-0-316-48508-1
Library of Congress Control Number: 2019956544

10 9 8 7 6 5 4 3 2 1

LSC-C

Printed in the United States of America

For Danielle, who's number one on my A-list

CONTENTS

A-LIST ANGELS

INTRODUCTION

On a warm October night at trendy Boston eatery Deuxave, Ashton Kutcher lowers the brim of his Los Angeles Dodgers cap and tucks himself behind a pillar the size of a refrigerator. The *Dude, Where's My Car?* star is in town for the Forbes Under 30 Summit, along with 6,000 young entrepreneurs. I've just profiled him in a cover story for the aforementioned magazine; as we exchange greetings, his eyes dart around the room, suggesting a desire to at least briefly avoid detection—not by autograph seekers but by the stream of startup founders hounding him for investment.[1]

Kutcher and his business partner, U2 and Madonna manager Guy Oseary, launched a $30 million fund called A-Grade in 2010 and grew it to $250 million in just a few years by investing in Uber, Shazam, Airbnb, Pinterest, and more. "Once you learn how to identify a snow leopard," Kutcher tells me, "it's pretty easy to see a snow leopard coming along."[2]

This is just one chapter in the story of Hollywood and Silicon Valley's lucrative collision. Look out across the entertainment landscape, and you'll find that the world's top actors, artists, and athletes now own slices of the country's hottest tech companies: Beyoncé (Uber), Kevin Durant (Postmates), Serena Williams (Coinbase), Jared Leto (Robinhood), and Jennifer Lopez (Acorns), just to name a few. Many of those early investments ballooned in value as start-ups turned into billion-dollar companies on paper or with the help of public markets. U.S. venture capital firms, or VCs (a term also used to describe individual venture capitalists), are now pouring some $100 billion into startups annually in hopes of finding the next billion-dollar startup.

Mammoth institutions have historically been the only ones with easy access to such companies, apart from a handful of high-net-worth individual investors—or angels, in venture-world parlance. Now a group of A-listers has found a way to join professionals in the bonanza, often at discounted rates and sometimes even for free, parlaying evanescent fame into long-term fortunes. It's the culmination of a decades-long shift in which entertainers have gone from wage laborers—often exploited by wealthy bosses—to owners of diversified investment portfolios and a chance to control their own financial futures.

For the purposes of this book, we'll focus on several individuals in the vanguard of this trend. Foremost among the A-List Angels is Kutcher, an Iowa-born college dropout turned Hollywood superstar with a penchant for making savvy startup investments. NBA Hall of Famer Shaquille O'Neal is the lone member of the group with an MBA, having received that degree after blazing a trail by investing in Google back in 1999, before it went public. Then there's Nas, the hip-hop legend who made his first big splash by championing and investing in lyrics site Rap Genius (now Genius) before adding stakes in others, including Dropbox and Ring; like Shaq, he cashed in on the latter when Amazon bought it for $1 billion in 2018.

These forerunners opened the doors for a diverse range of investors in the entertainment world, many of whom also shared their stories for this book. DJ and producer Steve Aoki told me about accumulating stakes in startups from Airbnb to SpaceX; NFL legend Tony Gonzalez recounted earning as much from selling his fitness app to Fitbit as he did during his peak playing years; Sophia Bush detailed how she turned her career as a television star into a chance to invest early in companies like Uber.

Less famous but equally influential are three operators who helped bring about the A-List Angel phenomenon behind the scenes. Guy Oseary grew up in Israel and moved to Los Angeles as a youngster, catching on as the manager of Madonna and U2 before teaming with Kutcher to start A-Grade. Troy Carter spent several years managing Lady Gaga before turning his focus to companies like Spotify. Rounding out the crew is Ben Horowitz, the hip-hop aficionado and cofounder of venture firm Andreessen Horowitz, which Nas and other entertainers have followed into countless major investments—among the Silicon Valley elite, nobody has done a better job at securing mutually beneficial relationships with A-List Angels.

In about a decade, these investors have racked up a tremendous track record, graduating from early roles as angels or entrepreneurs to, in many cases, running funds of their own. They've often shared the best investment opportunities with one another, helping scores of startups grow into multibillion-dollar behemoths while generating an unprecedented sort of wealth for the creative class. Not bad for a group with only a couple of college graduates among them.

"A big part of entrepreneurship is being willing to do every job in the company," says Carter. "I do think there's a level of hustle, whether you're [someone] like myself and Guy who were party promoters, just where you're willing to get your hands dirty...being able to bring that level of grit to the table for entrepreneurs, I think they respect it."[3]

Carter and his compatriots showed how a group of imaginative outsiders could cash in on the greatest wealth-creation engine of the twenty-first century: the venture capital–fueled tech boom that followed the Great Recession. Yet the historical links between technology, artistry, and fame date back to the Industrial Revolution, when advances in printing helped pave the way for British poet Lord Byron to widely distribute his work and become arguably the first modern celebrity.

Later, before the turn of the twentieth century, Thomas Edison's inventions paved the way for modern movie stars and an even wider means of disseminating content. From the early days of Hollywood's studio system, actors' pay was relatively low. Midcentury superstar James Cagney once got a raise by threatening to leave Warner Brothers for medical school. Aside from rare exceptions like Babe Ruth, pro athletes had to work odd jobs in the off-season to make ends meet. And musicians had it perhaps worst of all, with some of the greatest groups signing away their copyrights for almost nothing. For athletes, actors, and artists, careers were often short—and, once these public figures were past their prime, their moneymaking opportunities declined sharply.

"We get old, and then we're like everybody else," Nas tells me. "We came here to give art. It's fun to get the perks that come with it, and we have a great time. But at the end of the day, look what happened with Elvis."[4]

Indeed, as with countless stars before him, the King's coffers were rapidly dwindling when he passed away in 1977. Compensation began to change for the better across the board in the 1980s, when two Michaels—Jordan and Jackson—started branching out beyond basketball and music, negotiating multimillion-dollar deals with Nike and Pepsi, respectively. Jordan's sneaker royalties offered a new playbook for monetizing fame that hip-hop stars soon adopted, paving the way for the branding boom of the 1990s. Soon, rappers turned moguls from Diddy to Jay-Z were making far more on their onetime side hustles (clothing lines, liquor deals, sneakers) than from the sale of recorded music.

The first tech bubble offered a hint of something more significant: a chance to convert fame and creative chops into stakes in uncorrelated companies, as William Shatner did by accepting equity instead of cash for shilling Priceline.com in the late 1990s. But that trend disappeared in the wake of the turn-of-the-millennium dot-com bust. A few Hollywood investors who'd been dabbling in Silicon Valley got wiped out back then, among them Oseary. "I lost everything I ever made," he says.[5]

Even as a new wave of startups emerged and social media erupted in earnest, Hollywood remained skeptical, missing myriad chances to invest; some of those who jumped back in after the dot-com bust got smacked down again during the Great Recession. Yet most tech-world operators had always functioned with a long-term outlook, taking small salaries with large equity guarantees. They dreamed of getting rich in the event that their startups got sold or went public, even if macroeconomic conditions looked dire in the short term. Entertainers still wanted to get paid large sums of cash up front, even if it meant forgoing a shot at a bigger payday down the line.

"How they got paid was very different than how we wanted to pay," says Heidi Roizen, an industry veteran who worked as an Apple executive before moving on to venture firm Draper Fisher Jurvetson (DFJ), an early investor in Twitter, Tumblr, and SpaceX.[6]

The struggle between those who created content and those who built the platforms upon which it would be displayed reached an inflection point at the turn of the millennium, when musicians noticed that their work was being distributed for free via services like Sean Parker's Napster and Travis Kalanick's Scour. Even though those companies eventually pivoted beyond recognition—or got sued out of existence—their founders resurfaced just a few years later at two of the most influential startups of all time: Facebook (Parker) and Uber (Kalanick). As Hollywood types started sniffing around startups again with the idea of buying in, both sides had to overcome their previous prejudices.

"When I first started investing, it was a big gap, which we turned into a drawbridge between Silicon Valley and Hollywood," says Carter. "The Valley had the stereotype of L.A. as antiquated, litigious dinosaurs who would never change. L.A. had this perception of the Valley as pirates [who] didn't respect content."[7]

Hollywood and Silicon Valley ultimately had more in common than they realized. Successful players in either world generally had to follow a similar path: come up with a deeply compelling idea, then sacrifice everything—time, money, sleep, relationships—to see it to completion. In a way, U2 began as a startup just as Facebook did. It's only fitting that Bono invested in the social network before it went public.

As creators grew their audiences through Facebook and Twitter, simultaneously boosting the fortunes of the services themselves, a debate sprung up over the merits of content versus platform. "A bunch of these early tech products grew and got very large just because they were great technology," says Josh Elman, an early employee at both Twitter and Facebook who later became a venture capitalist. "How much is it that coolness and the trendsetting...versus just great technology?"[8]

The past decade has seen Hollywood become instrumental in Silicon Valley startups, and vice versa—from actress Jessica Alba's consumer goods outfit the Honest Company to indie musician Jack Conte's Patreon, a service that allows creators to release content directly to a community of paid subscribers, each boosted by well over $100 million in funding from the venture capital world. Still, starting tech companies of their own didn't change how these individuals thought about the value of creativity.

"Unequivocally, the internet is an empty shell without the people that fill it with all the things that we love to read and watch and listen to," says Conte. "We actually say at Patreon, internally and externally, 'We are nothing without our creators.'"[9]

Companies from Patreon to Airbnb wouldn't exist—at least not in their current incarnation and scale—without the help of venture capital firms. Like baseball teams or record labels, these giants roll the dice on dozens or even hundreds of prospects in an effort to find those rare few capable of capturing the world's imagination.

These firms' rainmakers, usually called general partners, invest money for wealthy individuals known as limited partners and take a management fee of about 2 percent, as well as a piece of profits in the neighborhood of 20 percent (the hedge fund business is structured similarly). It's a steep price, but buying into a fund allows investors to take advantage of savvy general partners' expertise and breadth of opportunity (also known as deal flow), resulting in a chance to pour cash into many different startups rather than putting all their eggs into one risky basket.

Entrepreneurs take money from these firms for a simple reason: starting a business is usually a cash-intensive affair, and most people who come up with a great idea often don't have the resources for bootstrapping (startup lingo for self-funding). Founders eventually need to quit their day jobs, hire staff, rent office space, and often manufacture physical objects, among other things. Typically, they begin by raising a round of investment from risk-tolerant angels (who must certify themselves "accredited investors," meaning they have annual income in excess of $200,000 or assets of more than $1 million).

Generally, high-rolling angels willing to invest in fledgling companies—often without any revenue, let alone profit—aren't easy to find. That's where venture capital firms tend to come in.

Either way, getting checks isn't easy: about 97 percent of startups never get funded.[10] The small fraction of startups that do obtain some form of early investment, generally termed a seed round, proceed to a more formal funding event called a Series A; subsequent rounds are labeled Series B, Series C, and so on. Along the way, startups tend to shift their focus from acquiring users toward becoming profitable with the aim of getting bought out by another company or going public.

The top Silicon Valley venture capital firms get first dibs and invest only in a small subset of this group (regular investors can't get in until companies go public, generally after many years of growth, at which point the biggest returns have already been gobbled up by VCs). Whereas a baseball player who only reaches base two times out of ten won't stick in the majors, a hit rate of 20 percent is perfectly acceptable for VCs, and one grand slam can make up for dozens of strikeouts. Pouring resources into unprofitable companies that have a chance of becoming a billion-dollar "unicorn" (we now have "decacorn" and "centicorn" to signal greater orders of magnitude) comes with the territory. So does the possibility of losing everything. But the payoff can be enormous: take Sequoia Capital, which has invested tens of billions in companies from Apple to Zappos now worth north of $3.3 trillion combined.

"[That's] the business model of Silicon Valley," says DFJ's Roizen. "You lose money for a long time, and then you make a shit ton of money."[11]

For entertainers, the exchange of coolness, creativity (and, sometimes, cash) for equity proved to be a far wiser formula than shilling a product for a flat fee, creating lasting wealth in a way that the brand extensions of the 1990s and early 2000s couldn't. Using fame to build a clothing line or eponymous sneaker is impressive. But leveraging it to get a piece of Uber and Airbnb—companies worth tens of billions of dollars—is something else, especially as such startups choose to delay IPOs longer and longer.

"Find a way to make yourself valuable from an equity perspective, and then the potential upside is on you," says Kutcher. "I'd rather bet on me every time that I can give a brand lift than basically give the upside back to the company."[12]

In other words: entertainers have a chance to profit much more by getting a piece of the companies they endorse than by accepting cash for their time. Under this arrangement, stars get an edge by accumulating stakes in the young companies disrupting the world economy, while startups gain new users and cachet by leveraging the social followings and Rolodexes of their famous investors. Big venture firms have vast amounts of cash to throw around and can't concern themselves with five- and six-figure investments in early-stage startups. For founders, the alternative is often fundraising from smaller firms or from angels who don't bring any significant connections to the table.

"Celebrities really have to put a lot of work in for a small check size," says Michael Ma, Joe Montana's partner on the seed-stage fund Liquid 2 Ventures, founded in 2015. "[Founders are] not taking advantage of the celebrity investor, but getting a really good deal there."[13]

Hollywood and Silicon Valley have plenty of similarities, including a number of unfortunate ones. Both suffer from a lack of diversity, with women and minorities drastically underrepresented, especially in the executive ranks. The worlds of entertainment and tech have also shared widespread issues of sexual harassment and assault, as many observers learned in recent years. And yet the convergence has shaken things up to an extent, bringing a rainbow of investors and entrepreneurs into the startup universe—helping to put a dent in demographics that skew heavily toward white males.

Along the way, entertainers have earned a chance not only to profit from selling their work but, in some cases, to grab pieces of the platforms upon which their work is distributed. "The real story is what happened in this awkward transitional phase where all the artists believed that art was never going to be how you made money, ever again, and they freaked out," says D. A. Wallach, the rocker turned Spotify artist-in-residence who first convinced Carter and others to invest in the streaming service. "And they all chased tech because they believed that it was where they could leverage the brand equity they had built in entertainment to make money."[14]

Over the course of my decade-plus covering media and entertainment at *Forbes*—and chronicling the earning power of superstars as editor of our annual Celebrity 100 issue—I've been sitting front row with a notebook as the first crop of A-List Angels emerged. My efforts began with a 2012 cover story called "Justin Bieber, Venture Capitalist" after the singer's manager, Hollywood power broker Scott "Scooter" Braun, helped him grab equity in Spotify and other startups. A couple years later, I wandered Rome with Katy Perry, who'd just landed a stake in Popchips; in 2016, I ubered around Los Angeles with Kutcher and Oseary, getting the full story of A-Grade for the first time.

In between, I've also reported on startup investments by the likes of Michael Jordan, Jennifer Lopez, Kevin Hart, Usher, and Mark Wahlberg. My first three books explored how Jay-Z, Diddy, Dr. Dre, and Michael Jackson monetized their fame. I've also got some Hollywood experience myself, having played the title role in the 1992 film *Lorenzo's Oil* as a child (though it didn't lead to any early investments in modern-day unicorns).

This book is based on my conversations with more than 100 people sitting at the intersection of entertainment and tech, including my interviews with A-List Angels like Kutcher, Shaq, and Nas over the years or specifically for this book—in many cases, both. The coming pages also feature extensive exchanges with behind-the-scenes players such as Oseary and Carter; investors at venture capital firms from Greylock to Lightspeed; and executives and founders at startups like Acorns, Genius, and Robinhood (if you need help keeping track of the maelstrom of people and company names, flip to the glossary on page 201).

For the average reader, discovering how rich and famous creators get richer and more famous might be enraging, as most deals described in the coming pages simply aren't available to the typical person. Sure, you can avoid leaving equity on the table: for instance, if your employer matches 401(k) contributions of up to 3 percent of your paycheck and you're not taking advantage, you are ignoring a fountain of free assets. But unless you're someone like Shaq, nobody is going to tap you on the shoulder and ask you to invest in Google before it goes public, nor will entrepreneurs line up outside your home offering you free equity in their startups in exchange for a couple of promotional tweets.

The strategies used by these A-List Angels are instructive in other ways. Kutcher and Oseary generated an 8.5x return with their first fund by applying a certain investment philosophy: look for companies solving a real problem (Uber shaking up the plodding yellow cab industry and the very idea of even owning a car) and consider unglamorous sectors (human resources, not jet sharing). Kutcher is the rare example of a celebrity who generally does the legwork himself, rather than relying on trusted advisors (which he sometimes does, too). Both everyday humans and celebrities would be wise to start with a mix of low-fee index funds and professional advice before dabbling in anything more exotic.

"Eisenhower said the greatest leaders are the ones smart enough to hire people smarter than them," says Shaq. "I got a lot of people who really know what they're looking at."[15]

As the relationship between Hollywood and Silicon Valley has evolved, so has the role of creators involved in startups. Stars often got what they paid for when accepting free equity, as they learned with failed companies like Viddy (an Instagram knockoff) and BlackJet (Uber for private jets). Entrepreneurs also learned that celebrities with skin in the game—especially the sort that was purchased, even at a discount, but not given—tend to make better partners. What began as a cheap and sexy way to attract an audience is now, in many cases, less about gaining users and more about making connections between little-known companies and huge corporations—or other celebrity investors. Joe Montana knows that as well as anyone.

"I meet with our companies in the beginning, but, realistically, my role is more as they get down the line, as they get a little bit older," he says. "They're looking for intros to some of the larger organizations like Visa, American Express. That's where my contacts come in, enable me to put them in touch with the Whole Foods guy or whatever it might be. Even if I don't have a contact, a lot of times I can get a callback."[16]

At its heart, this is a story about a group of historically underpaid workers who finally grabbed their rightful piece of the means of production. It's also an inspiring tale of a class of laborers—once known for accumulating cash quickly and frittering it away, or getting swindled out of assets by unscrupulous handlers—finding a way to turn short-term earnings into something that can last.

"Wealth is passed down from generation to generation," Chris Rock once noted. "You can't get rid of wealth. Rich is some shit you can lose with a crazy summer and a drug habit."[17]

The A-List Angels' efforts are fueling a shift in generational wealth that's already changing the complexion of the upper echelons of American society. Jay-Z is a billionaire; Dr. Dre and Diddy are knocking on the door. As Beyoncé, a centimillionaire many times over in her own right, noted on the song "Boss": "My great-great-grandchildren already rich / That's a lot of brown children on your *Forbes* list."

This is the story of the group behind that transformation.

CHAPTER 1

Employees Only

Forty-five floors and seven feet above the boardwalk in Atlantic City, Shaquille O'Neal gazes from his Ocean Casino Resort penthouse suite down to the seaside HQ2 day club with a mighty mix of satisfaction and anticipation. In between Shaq and the water, brightly colored little planes skim the ocean just as diminutive point guards once scurried below him on a basketball court. In a half an hour, he'll be front and center downstairs at HQ2 in a relatively new role: DJ.

Spinning records professionally is the latest addition to Shaq's list of titles, which, in addition to Hall of Fame basketball player, includes wrestler, podcaster, pitchman, talking head, sheriff's deputy, mixed martial artist, and venture capitalist. That last title is motivated by an emotion most wouldn't associate with the 325-pound former NBA star.

"Fear," Shaq tells me, almost solemnly, in his husky bass voice. "Seventy-five percent of all athletes go broke two years after they're playing.... I went back, got my master's in business, and my doctorate. Watched guys like Magic and Jordan, and I've watched them very, very close. People said, 'You gotta invest, you gotta know what you're investing in.'"[1]

To that end, Shaq ultimately accumulated more degrees than any of his fellow A-List Angels—and stacked plenty of cash. He earned some $300 million in his two-decade basketball career and as much as $27.7 million in a single year.[2] He also managed to find time to work as an actor (playing the titular 5,000-year-old genie in the film *Kazaam*) and as a rapper (he released four studio albums).[3] Even after all of that, Chris Rock pointed out a fact that reflected an unsettling reality about money and race in America. "Shaq is rich," the comedian famously said in 2005. "The white man who signs his check is wealthy."[4]

That seemed to be the case during Shaq's playing days, anyway. Since then, he has methodically gone about turning riches into wealth, in part by amassing stakes in startups. He began with Google in the late 1990s, years before its IPO. He continued with investments in Vitaminwater and Ring, both of which later sold for ten-figure sums; Shaq also accumulated pieces of Uber and Lyft well ahead of their multibillion-dollar IPOs. His fortune has since been estimated in the hundreds of millions, though he won't get into detail on precise amounts.

"My mother would be disappointed if I talk about numbers," he says. "It makes it seem like bragging, and I don't want to do that." But, like an increasing number of his peers, he confirms that even as a retired athlete, his best years in the venture capital world can sometimes rival the best years of his playing career.[5]

And Shaq's prescient investment in Google showed one path to building lasting wealth for entertainers, many of them people of color, that would serve as the beginnings of an antidote to the dynamic described by Chris Rock—and something of a blueprint for other A-List Angels.

Shaq may have been a pioneer in the monetization of fame—burnishing his investing credentials with recent outlays into entities like the NBA's Sacramento Kings—but there have been celebrities since the beginning of recorded history, generally actual monarchs. And it's worth exploring the evolution of fame in order to understand how today's stars are cashing in on it.

The modern notion of celebrity didn't come into view until the advent of the printing press in the mid-fifteenth century, as technology helped creativity scale up in the Western world. While the Industrial Revolution swept through Europe, rakish British poet Lord Byron captivated the populace with his writings (and the salacious tales surrounding his personal life) en route to becoming what many consider to be the first true superstar.

"I know the precise worth of popular applause, for few Scribblers have had more of it," Byron once wrote in a letter to his publisher. "They made me, without my search, a species of popular Idol."[6] Even then, the fates of celebrity, creativity, and technology seemed intertwined: in the early 1840s, Byron's daughter, Ada Lovelace, published an algorithm for a yet-to-be-invented computer. Because of this, many consider her the world's first programmer.[7]

The advent of the motion picture nearly a century later offered a way in which creators' images, not just their words, could be broadcast far and wide. Much of the early film ecosystem ran on technology created or co-invented by Thomas Edison, who controlled patents for everything from cameras to printers to the machines that perforated physical film. Largely as a result, the early movie industry sprouted up in Edison's New York–New Jersey stomping grounds at the dawn of the twentieth century.

Edison's dominance caused many filmmakers to head west, where patent enforcement was more difficult: any infringement case concerning technology used in California had to be filed in the Golden State, a logistical nightmare for an East Coast operation prior to the Jet Age. In 1910, director D. W. Griffith put Hollywood on the map when he shot the town's first production, a 17-minute silent film called *In Old California*. Shortly thereafter, the U.S. government broke up Edison's monopoly in the film business.

"The patents kept on being shown to be not adequate, in terms of controlling the technology," says Yale film studies professor Charles Musser, who points out that California provided more than just a refuge from Edison. "The West Coast offered a number of advantages. One was good weather almost all year round, another was scenery. The other was the expense of living in L.A. was cheaper than living in New York."[8]

Within just a few years, Hollywood became the center of America's growing film industry. Silent films gave way to "talkies," and a handful of stars launched independent production outfits; others milked considerable sums from the emerging studio system. Charlie Chaplin landed a million-dollar contract ($18 million today) for eight two-reel comedies (each roughly the length of a modern half-hour sitcom).[9] Then, in 1919, he teamed with Griffith and a pair of fellow stars—Douglas Fairbanks and Mary Pickford—to create United Artists, a studio owned by and for actors. But they weren't able to release films as rapidly as (or establish a distribution network capable of competing with) their erstwhile employers. By the middle of the century, United Artists' founding members had all either sold their stakes or died; the studio subsequently changed hands numerous times, gradually morphing away from its original mission.[10]

Hollywood's biggest names remained mired in financial mediocrity as the years rolled on. Academy Award–winning actor James Cagney was earning $1,250 per week in the early 1930s and grew displeased when he found that Dick Powell—like Cagney, a musical film actor who'd go on to play gangster roles later in his career—had been clocking $4,000. He threatened to leave the silver screen to study medicine at Columbia University; a doctor's salary presented a valid challenge to an actor's in those days, and his employer knew

4

it. After Cagney filed a suit in 1932, Warner Brothers gave him a new contract that guaranteed him $3,000 per week, ramping up to $4,500 by 1935.[11]

After World War II, miserly studios often limited the earning potential of Hollywood's returning heroes. MGM tried to force Jimmy Stewart to make up the five years he'd spent in Europe before receiving a new deal; after a contentious back-and-forth, the studio concluded that his previous contract had expired, and Stewart didn't work for a year. For his next gig, he had to settle for a small independent production: *It's a Wonderful Life*.[12]

The only star who came close to fully capitalizing on his fame in the first half of the twentieth century was Babe Ruth. Back then, athletes were contractually bound to their teams by a series of club options.[13] Ruth's first deal with the Boston Red Sox, inked in 1914, guaranteed an annual salary of $3,500 for three years,[14] or $88,000 in today's dollars.[15] Soon after the Sox shipped him to the Yankees following the 1919 season, the swaggering Ruth, legendary for his appetites—culinary, automotive, sexual—had cemented himself as the best player in baseball, as well as its most bankable star off the field, with the help of business manager Christy Walsh. In 1926, a year in which he earned a $52,000 playing salary, Ruth landed a $100,000 contract to perform in a twelve-week vaudeville tour after the season, plus an additional $75,000 or so to headline the Hollywood flick *Babe Comes Home* (1927), one of several star turns.[16]

Ruth wasn't successful in all his outside business ventures: a Manhattan haberdashery dubbed Babe Ruth's Shop for Men lasted just six months, while a snack called Ruth's Home Run candy bar got shot down by the U.S. Patent Office after a complaint by the makers of Baby Ruth (named after President Grover Cleveland's daughter).[17] Yet Ruth's ancillary income gave him leverage when he negotiated with the Yankees. After the team refused to raise his pay to $100,000 ahead of the 1930 season, Ruth reminded owners that he was "good for $25,000 a year for life even if I quit baseball today." The Yankees promptly upped his salary from $70,000 to $80,000, more than four times their next highest paid player (for those scoring at home, that was pitcher Herb Pennock, who made $17,500).

Ruth "had all the leverage in the world for marketing promotions and for the Yankees," says longtime Dodgers executive Robert Schweppe. "Star ballplayers got endorsements. Other guys, you got what was there."[18]

When asked how he felt about receiving a bigger salary than President Herbert Hoover in the midst of the Great Depression, Ruth famously—and perhaps apocryphally—replied, "Why not? I had a better year than he did."[19] Ruth may have earned more than Hoover, but today's annual minimum in all three major sports is higher than the U.S. presidential salary. And for most big names in baseball and beyond, midcentury endorsement deals offered a fraction of what stars now receive.[20]

Some tried to go the independent route. Marilyn Monroe, who'd been historically underpaid, tried starting her own production company in the mid-1950s. But Monroe found she couldn't finance films on her own and eventually agreed to a deal with Fox that paid her $100,000 per movie; on her final film, the unfinished *Something's Got to Give*, her co-star Dean Martin took home five times her pay.[21]

Though many midcentury stars managed to improve their circumstances—notably Elizabeth Taylor, who received $1 million to star in *Cleopatra* (1963)—compensation hadn't caught up with celebrity. The bottom line: as long as a studio, record label, or Major League Baseball team "owned" the talent, wages remained low. Perhaps the best example: the Beatles, who got stuck with an early record deal that paid them a penny per record sold; their songwriting pact was just as bad.[22]

"We didn't care what it was," says Paul McCartney. "We were

just like any other writers; we wanted to get published. It turned out to be basically a slave contract; no matter how successful we made the company, we didn't get a raise."[23]

Up the coast a few hundred miles from Hollywood, Silicon Valley would eventually become the epicenter of today's tech boom—and play a crucial role in turning creators into owners—but the first gold rush in Northern California took place in the nineteenth century. The search for nuggets 100 miles east boosted San Francisco's population from 1,200 to 300,000 in just three years. In the 1870s, the state of California unwittingly set itself up to encourage distant tech bubbles by passing a law prohibiting companies from suing their former employees for jumping to a competitor, a contrast to the more burdensome regulations on the East Coast.[24]

Ty Cobb may have been the only connection between Silicon Valley and the entertainment world in the early days. The notoriously nasty baseball Hall of Famer retired to a mansion in Atherton, California—a town more recently home to Ben Horowitz and his legendary barbeques—where he spent much of his retirement trading stocks with the help of a Wall Street ticker installed in his home. He didn't leverage his fame to get free equity, but he invested wisely in the publicly traded startups of his day: by the time he died in 1961, he was worth $12.1 million.[25]

"Coca-Cola was a new drink on the market in 1918," he noted. "Wall Street didn't think much of it. I gambled the other way....It brought me more than $4 million as time went by."[26]

Northern California proved to be fertile territory for groundbreaking innovation in the following years. The vacuum tube—which allowed for the amplification of sound and paved the way for the modern music industry—was invented in Palo Alto; during

World War I, Silicon Valley engineers designed the first radios. There wasn't always a gender imbalance in the tech world: myriad midcentury women followed in the footsteps of Ada Lovelace in the development of programming, among them Grace Hopper, the mathematics PhD and U.S. Navy rear admiral behind one of Harvard's first supercomputers.[27]

As the United States fell behind the Soviet Union in the midcentury space race, President Eisenhower set up the Advanced Research Projects Agency (now known as DARPA) to fund marvelous technological projects on par with the Russians' *Sputnik* satellite. Bob Taylor, the pipe-smoking Texan director of the agency's Information Processing Techniques Office, realized Eisenhower's creation was bankrolling three different computer research projects, each with a different communication system. So, in 1966, he convinced the agency's chief to move $1 million out of the ballistic missile defense budget and into connecting them via what became known as the ARPANET, a network that many believed could provide reliable communications in the event of nuclear war. More importantly, it would go on to serve as the forerunner to the internet.[28]

Taylor funded a number of other crucial projects, including a particularly noteworthy moon shot by Stanford researcher Douglas Engelbart. Born in 1925, Engelbart served in the navy and then went to work in Silicon Valley at the Ames Research Center, now part of NASA. Much like Lovelace, Engelbart envisioned a machine that hadn't been invented yet, one capable of storing humanity's information in a universally accessible way, and made it his life's mission to further that cause.

"One day, it just dawned on me—BOOM—that complexity was the fundamental thing," he once said. "And it just went click. If in some way, you could contribute significantly to the way humans could handle complexity and urgency, that would be universally helpful."[29]

Engelbart's solution: to will something like this into existence. Few believed he could do it, including his own supervisor at NASA. But he had an ally in Taylor, who in turn harbored Texas-sized ambitions for a demo of the project ("Spend what you need, but don't do it small," he told Engelbart). The final cost to put everything together was somewhere around \$175,000—about \$1.3 million when adjusted for inflation.[30]

By the time Engelbart unveiled "The Mother Of All Demos" in 1968 at an early San Francisco computer conference, he'd amassed a setup that consisted of off-the-shelf hardware with about one one-thousandth the computing power of a modern iPhone, software created from scratch, and the first-ever mouse. Engelbart demonstrated his creation's capabilities—videoconferencing with a colleague down in Silicon Valley, collaborating on a document, embedding audiovisual elements—to a gobsmacked crowd that gave him a standing ovation once he finished his ninety-minute presentation.[31]

Taylor left government agency life in 1969 and taught for a year at the University of Utah before resurfacing at Xerox's new Palo Alto Research Center. At PARC, his team created an early personal computer known as the Alto, which pioneered the use of the virtual desktop that dominates today's landscape. But for all the promise of PARC, Xerox never ran away with the personal computer category, thanks largely to the lack of imagination shown by its brass back east.[32] As a New York executive once told Taylor: "The computer will never be as important to society as the copier."[33]

Cash-rich companies willing to support the plucky startups that would usher in the Information Age sprouted up in the Valley during the middle of the twentieth century. Early entrants modeled themselves after investment banks like Rothschild and J. P. Morgan, which shied away from the spotlight (in part because they often funded wars—sometimes both sides of the same one), quite the opposite of Hollywood's usual any-publicity-is-good-publicity model.[34]

The venture firms that appeared in the 1960s and '70s, backing early manufacturers of the semiconductors and chips needed to fuel the computing revolution, were similarly impenetrable, but racked up revolutionary results. Venrock, which started as the venture arm of the Rockefeller family, became one of chipmaker Intel's first investors in 1969; several of today's premier firms got their start shortly thereafter, becoming the talent scouts of Silicon Valley.

Of course, not all people with bold ideas walk away with scads of cash. Baseball legend Curt Flood made three All-Star teams, but it was his impact off the field that earned him immortality in the sport. Traded to the Philadelphia Phillies in 1969, Flood refused to report to the team. "I do not feel that I am a piece of property to be bought and sold irrespective of my wishes," he wrote in a letter to commissioner Bowie Kuhn. "I believe I have the right to consider offers from other clubs."[35]

Flood's statement was a direct challenge to the reserve clause, the stipulation that had previously been a part of major professional sports contracts and bound players to their teams through a series of club options. Players could technically still negotiate, but since they weren't allowed to become free agents and sign elsewhere at will, power rested almost entirely with the teams.

"It goes back to no leverage," says Schweppe. "You were just in a situation of really nowhere you can go. Unless you were a superstar, and then you could possibly do a holdout, but you couldn't really break through many ceilings in terms of being able to make more money."[36]

In the midst of the dispute, Flood sat out the 1970 season, retiring after a woeful performance upon his return in 1971, no doubt due in some part to the abuse hurled at him by fans and even some players. Flood's case went all the way up to the Supreme

Court, which ruled against him. But when an arbitrator ruled in favor of another player in 1975, the reserve clause flickered away; ace pitcher Jim "Catfish" Hunter became the first modern superstar free agent that year, and the Yankees inked him to a five-year, $3.75 million deal that featured a $1 million signing bonus.[37]

Flood's example made waves in baseball and rippled across the sports landscape, setting into motion a movement that would begin to challenge the dominance of management over labor.[38] The shift also had implications for the racial dynamics Chris Rock called out decades later with his bit on Shaq: despite the fact that, in aggregate, the majority of pro athletes in the three major U.S. sports are people of color, there wasn't a single black principal owner until 2002. Today, Michael Jordan is the only African American majority owner among the ninety-two teams in the NFL, NBA, and MLB.[39]

Jordan went from rich to wealthy thanks mostly to off-the-court endeavors beginning early in his career. In the mid-1980s, he signed a seven-year, $18 million deal with Nike, negotiating a royalty on every Air Jordan sneaker sold. Jordan became the ultimate influencer decades before Instagram existed, using nationally televised basketball games as billboards to showcase Nike's latest offerings. Buoyed by Air Jordan (and Spike Lee–directed commercials starring the shoe's namesake), the company doubled its sales to $1.7 billion from 1987 to 1989, with Jordan receiving a cut that would set him on his way to billionaire status.[40]

But for most athletes and entertainers through the end of the twentieth century, hefty paychecks didn't always translate to long-term wealth, let alone even medium-term financial security. As Nas once put it in an interview with me: "Money doesn't make you rich all the time."[41]

Even as revolutionary ideas exploded out of its midst, Silicon Valley itself remained a collection of pleasant yet unremarkable suburbs. To this day, sleepy Sand Hill Road—the central artery that runs through Palo Alto, Menlo Park, and Woodside—is home to many of the country's top venture firms. They're clustered in office parks that, aside from ubiquitous Tesla charging stations, are mostly indistinguishable from just about any other affluent enclave in America. (Says DFJ's Roizen: "It's a rather dull place.")[42] Silicon Valley's no-frills attitude stretched to the broader startup world—Jeff Bezos famously furnished Amazon's early Seattle offices with desks made out of doors because they were cheaper than the actual desks for sale at Home Depot.

"Our joke used to be you get funding, and the first thing you do is throw a million-dollar party and buy all Herman Miller furniture, that's a sure sign of a company that's gonna be out of business," Roizen explains. "Don't put your money on looking important or having fancy offices, or paying everyone astronomically large salaries, because it all needs to go in the company because of the payoff in the future."

Over time, there have been a few exceptions to Silicon Valley's drab ethos, perhaps most notably Steve Jobs. The Apple cofounder dropped out of Reed College and landed a job as a solderer at Atari in the mid-1970s, quickly developing a reputation as a brash and brilliant youngster with a penchant for Eastern philosophy and psychedelic drugs (he also didn't shower much). Jobs enjoyed rock and roll—and he recognized the Bay Area's role in helping to create it.

"Rock and roll really happened [here]," he once said, citing Jimi Hendrix, Janis Joplin, and Jefferson Airplane. "You also had Stanford and Berkeley, two awesome universities drawing smart people from all over the world and depositing them into this clean, sunny, nice place where there's a whole bunch of other smart people."[43]

Steve Wozniak was one such brainiac—for him, even physical recreation ideally involved technology (I once interviewed Woz about his passion for Segway polo, though not for this book). He grew up down the street from Jobs in Sunnyvale, taking a job at Hewlett-Packard before creating the Apple I in 1976 and cofounding Apple Computer with Jobs. After launching the company out of Jobs's garage, the duo upgraded to an office in Cupertino. Hardware junkie Wozniak provided the technical know-how, while Jobs brought the marketing savvy: when it came time to design the Apple II, Jobs went to the mall and studied a Cuisinart for inspiration. Unlike most of his peers, he understood the computer would soon be a household appliance, not just a trinket for hobbyists. With a sleeker, more tightly integrated design, the Apple II went on sale for $1,298 in 1977 and moved 100,000 units within three years.[44]

As time went on, Jobs had more and more encounters with creators in the music world, both professionally and personally. He dated singer Joan Baez in the 1980s and befriended Bono in the 2000s. He even got into several legal tussles with the Beatles over his company's name and its similarity to Apple Corps, the moniker of the entity founded by the Fab Four in the late 1960s to guard their commercial interests.[45]

"Someone made him a street sign and it's the intersection of Technology and Liberal Arts," recalls Andy Miller, a former Apple executive who now owns a minority stake in the NBA's Sacramento Kings alongside Shaq. "That's what [Jobs] thought Apple had always done. He didn't want to hire the awesome coder, he wanted to hire the awesome coder who was an awesome guitarist."[46]

Still, back in the 1980s, the entertainment industry felt a lot farther away than the several hundred miles between Cupertino and Century City. "I can't remember a time when it ever occurred to me to even think about Hollywood...it may as well have been Mars," says Roizen. "Apple was perhaps the first consumerish brand in technology; I think Steve occupied a different place, but most of the rest of them, nobody knew who the hell they were. We were not famous people, nobody gave a shit about us."[47]

Jobs and Wozniak came to embody two stereotypes of what Silicon Valley success looked like: the mercurial, charismatic genius running the company and the awkward, brainy tinkerer behind the scenes. Hollywood tended to reinforce these very white, very male images with mid-1980s films like *Revenge of the Nerds* and *WarGames*. According to *Brotopia* author Emily Chang, that's part of the reason women started to disappear from Silicon Valley. Female students received nearly 40 percent of all computer science degrees the year the Macintosh made its debut; three and a half decades later, the number sat at just 22 percent.[48]

The 1980s marked a turning point in the financial fortunes of artists. Michael Jackson—who'd long labored under oppressive recording contracts as a member of the Jackson 5, where he'd earned pennies per album sold—released his solo smash *Thriller*, which would go on to sell 100 million copies worldwide. He demanded and received a groundbreaking $2 per record royalty, launched his own clothing line, and even released a sneaker with LA Gear. Jackson also landed a $5.2 million endorsement deal with Pepsi, the highest such fee ever received by a musician to that point.[49]

Jackson would later earn a reputation as a spendthrift, but he made a few shrewd investments—the best of which happened, in part, at the accidental guidance of Paul McCartney. "In the mid-1980s, Michael Jackson and I were hanging out, and he asked me for career advice.... 'Be careful about your songs—own your work—and get into song publishing,'" McCartney remembers telling him. "And he said, 'Oh, I'm going to get yours!' I kind of laughed; I didn't think he was serious. But he was."[50]

In 1985, Jackson plowed his *Thriller* profits into buying the ATV music publishing catalog for $47.5 million. The purchase included the rights to some of the Beatles' biggest hits, which they'd let slip away early in their careers before they knew anything about contracts. The ATV deal would prove to be Jackson's savviest, with his holdings eventually increasing by an order of magnitude, and then some. But it was his apparel arrangement that offered a new way to monetize his own fame, a model that hip-hop acts adopted throughout the decade.

One night in 1986, a single question asked onstage at Madison Square Garden set into motion a fundamental change in the way musicians made money. Soon after trailblazing hip-hop act Run-D.M.C. hit the stage, one of the group's members asked the audience to remove their shoes and lift them high. The crowd complied and the act played "My Adidas" as thousands of shell toes soared toward the rafters, much to the amazement of the German footwear executives sitting in a skybox, guests of Run-D.M.C.'s manager. Flabbergasted, they quickly awarded the group a million-dollar deal for their own shoe line, and the lucrative alliance between hip-hop and advertisers was born.

For the most part, though, entertainers remained increasingly well-paid employees, though still not owners. By the end of the 1990s, Hollywood stars from Harrison Ford to Mel Gibson were topping $50 million in annual pay, with athletes like Shaq and Tiger Woods close behind. In music, the wave of large U.S.-style arenas opening up in post-Soviet eastern Europe and increasingly wealthy countries in Asia and South America boosted top acts like the Rolling Stones, U2, and Madonna to nine-figure annual grosses. These stars usually got paid by a familiar formula.

"'We pay you enough so that we then get the rights to do everything else we can with it' is sort of the Hollywood model," says venture capitalist Josh Elman. "The Silicon Valley model is 'You come and spend a few years trying to turn this thing from something good into something great.'"[51]

Entertainers continued to experiment with new forms of monetization. Boxing legend George Foreman fired up his first Lean Mean Fat-Reducing Grilling Machine, helping him earn double-digit millions annually long after his athletic prime. David Bowie securitized himself in the form of Bowie Bonds tied to his music catalog, trading a decade of annual payouts for a $55 million advance. Martha Stewart founded her eponymous lifestyle company that same year and took it public in 1999, briefly becoming a billionaire.

Jay-Z and Diddy launched clothing lines of their own and by the late 1990s were doing hundreds of millions in annual revenue. But such ventures sometimes fell prey to the whims of the broader market and to the fickleness of fame. While Jay-Z and his partners went on to sell his Rocawear brand for $204 million in 2007, Diddy sold his controlling stake in Sean John for just $70 million in 2016, no doubt less than he would have gotten if he'd sold at the height of his recording career, when the streetwear category was on fire. Silicon Valley offered the prospect of a lasting alternative.

"If you get the software company right and the platform right, that can live on for a long time and be worth billions," says Elman. "Whereas almost every piece of content that Hollywood ever makes decays in value over time."

Back in Atlantic City, a throng of tipsy, sunburned, scantily clad revelers release a collective whoop as Shaq makes his way to the stage, a large gold Superman medallion hanging from his neck. He proceeds to delight the day club crowd with a mix of tunes by artists ranging from electronic star Skrillex to fellow rapper-turned-investor Jay-Z.

Shaq does very little talking on the microphone during his set (except for an occasional potshot at his basketball frenemy Charles Barkley), though he does take a moment to savor the tomahawk steak brought out for him in the midst of his time on stage. "Shaq loves to eat," his manager tells me with a shrug, as we watch the spectacle from just behind the DJ booth.

After Shaq's performance, we follow him off the stage and down a hall that leads us through the hotel's innards, much to the delight of the janitorial and catering staff who greet the big man along the way. We hop into a cargo elevator and zip back up to his hotel suite, where Shaq's entourage of advisors and managers are still buzzing about. Indeed, the erstwhile basketball player and his team have little time to slow down amid his packed schedule: in just a few moments, he'll jet off to his next gig, a DJ set at Major League Baseball's All-Star Weekend.

Shaq leans on these advisors for gig planning and startup vetting alike. After years of angel investing, he has settled on a fairly simple formula: follow smart venture capitalists into credible companies created by dynamic founders, understand that most startups fail, and try to spread resources across a wide range of promising options. Like many of his peers, Shaq's method doesn't require digging through Microsoft Excel spreadsheets or spending inordinate amounts of time scouting startups on his own; rather, he relies on his team. "I'll give [investment ideas] to them," he says. "They'll look at it and then break it down with me."[52]

Still, for Shaq—and some of his fellow A-List Angels—coming to that level of understanding of the startup scene took some time, with a fair number of hard lessons learned along the way.

CHAPTER 2

Crash Course

Y ou serious?" asks Guy Oseary across the low-slung coffee table in his Beverly Hills office, after I ask him to take me back through the beginning of his professional journey.

"Way back," I reply. "Yeah."

Oseary came to the United States from his native Israel— the country with more startups per capita than any other in the world—some four decades ago as a grade schooler. Unlike many of his gregarious countrymen who populate the tech firmament, he'd much rather fold his lanky six-foot, two-inch frame into the background than tell his life story.

"That's insane," he says of my request.[1]

It's not an unreasonable ask for most, but perhaps for the notoriously press-shy Oseary, it is. And the ability to fade in and out of the picture can be a handy skill in his primary line of work, represented by visual clues covering his office. Above his curly salt-and-pepper coif, a mural stretches across the wall featuring images of twenty-one unique seats, each from a different arena. It's appropriate, given that Oseary manages two of the biggest live acts on the planet: Bono and Madonna.

Oseary first met Madonna after befriending the daughters of her then manager, Freddy DeMann, in Los Angeles. DeMann was so impressed with the teenaged Oseary's poise that when he launched a record label, he picked the youngster to be one of his first employees. Oseary didn't disappoint, signing superstar acts from Alanis Morissette to Muse before going on to an even more lucrative career as a manager and finally teaming with Ashton Kutcher and supermarket mogul Ron Burkle to form A-Grade.

"Let's start with what you really need," he says. "I'll fill you in on maybe when Ashton and I got together and then how we work with the tech community and then you go back and ask me."

"Okay."

"I was on a plane to Milan [in the 1990s] and the record company was doing really well," he begins. "On my way there, I read about a guy named Sky Dayton. He was my age and he was doing really well, started EarthLink...I was like, 'I gotta learn more about this guy.'"

When Oseary got back to California, he called Dayton.

"If you're impressed with my story, you should meet this guy Bill Gross," the entrepreneur told him. "He's the only guy in history to create three [separate] billion-dollar companies in one year."

Dayton connected Oseary to Gross, who'd launched a startup incubator known as Idealab in 1996. When Oseary finally went out to Pasadena to meet him, he found a scene that had a surprising amount in common with his record label world: creators and managers dipping in and out of rooms, developing and debating ideas, laying groundwork for revolutionary new products. Says Oseary: "I was immediately in love."

Two decades after Oseary's initial trip to Idealab, the incubator still thrums with the same vibrant energy that initially intoxicated him—thanks mostly to the kinetic charisma of its founder. Now in his early sixties, Gross greets me at the entrance of his Pasadena headquarters sporting an open windbreaker, as if to keep himself dry amid random squalls of inspiration. A pen peeks out from the pocket of his dress shirt, lest a wayward idea attempt to escape his clutches unchronicled. And as soon as he shakes my hand, we're off on a tour of his 34,000-square-foot facility.

Gross whisks me through the sprawling agglomeration of buildings—a collection of 1920s single-story brick offices he expanded by annexing the Korean restaurant next door ten years ago—and from the outset, it's clear that Idealab remains what Gross had always intended it to be: a company that makes companies. Concepts cascade out of his head faster than he can execute them himself; his Pasadena facility serves as both incubator and receptacle. As we stroll past conference rooms with names like Picasso, Jobs, and Yosemite, he points out the startups in all sorts of fields taking shape around us, from Edisun Microgrids (solar energy) to aiPod (driverless autos).

"Of every twenty ideas we prototype, nineteen of them we kill," he explains excitedly. "One of them, we take forward. We kill them either because they're too early…timing's not right, can't find a great CEO, don't have an angle that's proprietary, something differentiable. The one idea out of twenty, maybe, that we take forward, we'll then say, 'Okay, is it justifiable to spin out a separate company?'"[2]

If the answer is yes, Idealab invests $250,000 to get the company started and receives a chunk of equity. The incubator's Pasadena headquarters include everything a young company might need, from an in-house legal department and a CFO to human resources and a public relations team. There are more specialized options, too: in one corner, there's a machine shop for founders who need to build physical prototypes of their wares; in another, there are stacks of servers for startups with a heavy appetite for data; on the roof, there's a solar lab for outfits working on renewable energy.

Startups come together in pods scattered throughout the open layout, the smallest designed for five people to work comfortably together. They can take advantage of Idealab's shared amenities, from free parking to a cafeteria to the startup-essential game room. As a company grows, it can move into a bigger space, with the largest maxing out at a capacity of fifty employees. But no matter the size, each pod is very much in the mix with its neighbors, separated only by three-foot walls.

"I want everybody to see what's going on, even at not their own company, because there's no two companies competing with one another," says Gross. "By having other noncompeting companies nearby, you get to learn best practices from other companies. It's completely nonthreatening, because that company is not in your industry."

Gross got his start as an entrepreneur unusually early in life. During the energy crisis of 1973, while he was in high school, he sold more than 10,000 solar power kits via mail order after running advertisements in *Scientific American* and *Popular Science*. He put himself through Caltech with cash from that venture and from selling a patented high-end loudspeaker that he invented while in college. After graduating in 1981, he and his brother built a company that was acquired by Lotus for $10 million. Ten years later, Gross founded educational software publisher Knowledge Adventure to make learning games for kids; his brother came on as vice president of engineering.[3]

In 1993, the *Economist* ran a story on Knowledge Adventure's success, prompting a mysterious man to leave several messages for Gross, saying that he'd read the article and wanted to arrange a meeting. After six months, Gross finally phoned him back—and discovered the caller he'd been ignoring was Steven Spielberg's financial advisor. Gross's response: "Well, why didn't you say that in the first place?"[4]

A few days later, Spielberg sat down with Gross.

"My son Max uses your products and loves them," the director explained. "I love what you're doing. I really am passionate about education software."

Gross took him on a tour of the building, and, like Oseary after him, Spielberg was hooked.

"This is incredible," he said. "Not only do I want to invest, I want to make a product with you."

"What kind of product would you want to make?" Gross asked.

"I want to make a product that lets kids play with movie clips and get a sense of what it's like to think through a cinematic sequence."

"Well, how are you going to do that?"

"I'll figure out a way," Spielberg replied. "Here's my idea. I'll be the overall director. I'll get a cinematographer. I'll get some actor friends of mine to participate. We'll go to shoot some footage. I'll narrate it, but I'll tell kids what is happening in each...what I'm trying to achieve visually. Then I'll let them make their own storytelling by cutting the footage up and putting it in any order that they want."

"That sounds incredible," said Gross. "Let's do it."

Spielberg invested in Knowledge Adventure—one of the earliest examples of a celebrity putting money into a tech startup—and began following what would become the playbook for such partnerships, using his Hollywood connections to bring value to the project. He brought in famous friends Quentin Tarantino and Jennifer Aniston to work on what would become the filmmaking computer game *Steven Spielberg's Director's Chair* (for free, as a favor to him). They found a decommissioned prison on the 110 Freeway near downtown Los Angeles and shot for a week. Tarantino worked the camera, Aniston did the acting, and Spielberg directed. The game shipped a year later; in 1995, Vivendi bought Knowledge Adventure for $90 million, according to Gross.

Spielberg's involvement had provided a valuable boost, and he was rewarded handsomely. As the director and the inventor grew closer, Spielberg saw creativity in how Gross approached entrepreneurship—and Gross spotted a business model in the way Spielberg handled his film empire. The two would get together once a month at Spielberg's Amblin Entertainment headquarters, an adobe bungalow situated in a wooded oasis on Universal's lot in Burbank. Their meetings followed a similar pattern: Gross would arrive and wait in a conference room for Spielberg, who'd be pulled in from another meeting to brainstorm ideas before moving on to his next appointment.

"His day was basically moving from idea to idea, contributing his passion...but then handing off to other people to go carry products forward," Gross recalls. "I said, 'That's what I want to do, but for businesses.' That was my inspiration for Idealab. I wanted to be able to go around, work with different people, share the ideas, but then have them go off and carry them out. Every once in a while, direct one myself—sort of like he would do."

Flush with cash from the Knowledge Adventure buyout, Gross started Idealab in 1996, promising himself he'd work on the experiment for at least a year if he could raise $2.5 million to seed ten startups. He quickly hit that sum, parceled out in batches of $500,000 from investors including executives from Compaq and First Round Capital, which later became one of Uber's early funders. The most enthusiastic backer may have been Spielberg himself.

"I'd like to be one of your first investors," he told Gross upon hearing about the plan for Idealab, quickly committing $500,000. "Oh yeah, you gotta bring my friend in, too."

"Who's your friend?"

"Come meet me over at the Peninsula."

Shortly thereafter, Gross cruised down to the Beverly Hills hotel to see Spielberg for lunch and found Michael Douglas sitting with him—ready to invest another $500,000.

"I don't know anything about this," the actor admitted, according to Gross. "But if Steven's in, I'm in."[5]

Gross's lunch partners represented the two major flavors of celebrity investor that would emerge at the intersection of Hollywood and Silicon Valley: Spielberg, the rare hands-on type who put money mostly into what he knew, and Douglas, the kind who understood the gaps in his own knowledge and only invested if he could follow a trusted guide.

By the mid-1990s, Oseary's entry into the startup world was still a couple of years off, but the link between the realms of entertainment and startups was growing stronger. Hollywood producer Howard Rosenman, known for his work on films from *Buffy the Vampire Slayer* to *Call Me by Your Name*, remembers going to a party in Hollywood and hitting it off with a heavyset man surrounded by models and actresses.

"What do you do?" asked Rosenman.[6]

"I'm in computers."

"You should stay in computers, because I hear you can get very, very rich."

Rosenman still didn't know his name.

"Do you know Jeanne Tripplehorn?" the man asked.

"Yes, would you like to meet her?" replied Rosenman, who was managing the actress at the time. Two nights later, the three went to dinner at the House of Blues in West Hollywood. Rosenman's new friend, who went by the name Paul, immediately handed the maître d' a $100 bill.

"Listen, you don't have to do that," said Rosenman. "Just

mention my name, you can get in. Save your $100...you shouldn't be spending so much money."

Later that night, the man gave Rosenman his email address: paulallen@aol.com.

"I still didn't know who he was," admits Rosenman. "So I email one of my friends and I say, 'Do you know who this guy Paul Allen is? He lives in Seattle.' He said, 'Yeah, schmuck, he invented Microsoft with Bill Gates.'"

In 1994, *Forbes* declared Allen (who passed away in 2018) the sixteenth-richest person in America, with a personal fortune of $4 billion. Gates claimed the No. 1 spot and would famously declare "content is king" in an essay two years later, predicting "broad opportunities for most companies involve supplying information or entertainment."[7] But it was Allen who laid down gargantuan bets on Hollywood with his own cash. His first big investment came the following year: a $500 million outlay to help launch DreamWorks—the studio responsible for *American Beauty*, *Gladiator*, and *A Beautiful Mind*—with Steven Spielberg, Jeffrey Katzenberg, and David Geffen.[8]

By 1996, Allen was worth $7.5 billion, making him the third-richest man in America behind Gates ($18.5 billion) and Warren Buffett ($15 billion), and he deployed even more of that cash to bring Hollywood and Silicon Valley closer together. Allen started a short-lived annual tradition of uniting a couple hundred of the most prominent names in tech and entertainment—Gates, Spielberg, Mick Jagger, Barry Diller, Diane von Furstenberg, and many more—to cross-pollinate in some of the world's most exotic locales. For the first confab, Allen flew guests to the Hotel du Cap-Eden-Roc in the South of France, where events included elaborate meals, concerts, and even a masquerade ball.[9]

"It was the beginning of 'convergence,' which was his idea," says Rosenman, one of the attendees. "He knew, predicted, and fomented the marriage of content and digits.... Paul understood the nature of the business, that it's all about friendships and contacts. And he wanted to be known in the world."[10]

The second year, Allen flew everyone to Venice for a similar program; the third year, he convened the crew on his megayacht for a trip to Alaska. Former Apple executive Roizen was one of the lucky guests and remembers the Hollywood stars being more interested in meeting their Silicon Valley counterparts than vice versa ("The comment was made, 'Well, we have all the fame, but you guys have all the money,'" she recalls). But business conversations generally ended up back at the same place: Silicon Valley types were used to taking equity, while Hollywood veterans—who'd long ago graduated from working on spec—wanted cash.

Roizen encountered this phenomenon when she asked a few film industry stars to sit on the board of a company with which she was affiliated. "It was like, 'My name and my brand are important, and I want to be paid a hundred fifty thousand dollars a year to sit on your board,'" Roizen remembers. "You're like, 'Yeah, that's not how it works. How it works is you get paid nothing, and then if the company is successful, you get money.'"[11]

Allen's trips didn't necessarily lead directly to significant deals between Hollywood and Silicon Valley types, but they generated a framework of familiarity and mutual understanding. That would prove important in the coming years, as upstarts like Napster pitted the tech world against the creative community. In any case, the trips generated quite a few noteworthy anecdotes for the attendees. On the boat in Alaska, for instance, Rosenman noticed a man in glasses wearing a *Buffy the Vampire Slayer* jacket.

"He comes over to me, and he looks at me, and he says, 'Does the word 'duh' mean anything to you?'" says Rosenman. "He's quoting from my own movie—Bill Gates."[12]

Meanwhile, over at Idealab, three of the startup factory's first ten companies failed—but the remaining seven went on to raise additional funding, a terrific rate in the volatile startup world (generally speaking, more than half of startups that receive seed funding fail to raise another round). The performance enabled Gross to raise another $5 million to boost his growing portfolio. The earliest startups seeded by Gross included Citysearch, Tickets.com, eToys, and CarsDirect, all highfliers in the first dot-com boom.

"The second year, two of them were getting ready to go public," says Gross. "After the second year, we had so much success that that was able to fund everything going forward."

Oseary stepped into this milieu in 1998 after Dayton told him about Gross's company—then styled as "idealab!," mirroring the young manager's enthusiasm for the project. He recognized that musical acts are very much like tech startups. Their founders usually reach a point where they have to quit their day jobs and commit before whatever they're working on becomes profitable; in most cases, they need some amount of funding to create their products, which leads them to fork over equity or copyright ownership in exchange for the cash needed for expansion, usually from a venture capital firm or a record label.

Both sides had plenty to learn from each other, so Oseary started making regular trips to Pasadena to exchange information. He'd sit with Gross, who'd introduce him to startup founders; Oseary would use his experience in the entertainment business to give them advice on how to promote what they'd created.

"When I looked at these companies, I felt like the founders were the artists and they had their vision—they had their album, they had their songs, and they wanted help getting their music out there," he says. "I'd give them some advice on things that I knew. I was the only guy from our community driving up to Pasadena every month or so really trying to learn and help."[13]

Gross and Oseary gave each other tips, too. The Idealab founder showed his new friend the first BlackBerry, recently launched by a then obscure Canadian company called Research in Motion. Far from a smartphone, that earliest iteration was essentially a pager with a tiny keyboard and a little green screen, capable of displaying eighty characters at a time.

"This is really pretty incredible," Gross explained.[14]

"I can't believe it," Oseary replied. "Bill, that is a game changer."

Oseary then went and bought a hundred units and gave one to all his friends in the entertainment industry, including Spielberg.

"Why are you doing that?" Gross asked.

"Because if I give them that, and I have a connection with them, and I have their email address...I can stay more in contact with Spielberg than anybody else, because I gave him the thing," said Oseary. "Thank you, Bill, for giving me this idea."

The help flowed both ways. Gross, an audiophile since his early speaker-making days, found out that Oseary somehow didn't have a top-notch sound system at home. So he bought him one—featuring Bowers & Wilkins speakers and a Mark Levinson amplifier (a setup that generally costs tens of thousands of dollars)—and installed it in his house as a surprise.

By 1999, Oseary had become a full part of the Idealab crew. When Gross offered him a chance to make it official by investing, he went all in. "I decided to take every dollar I had on the planet Earth that I'd saved since I was fourteen or fifteen years old and put it into Idealab," recalls Oseary.[15] Adds Gross: "Guy always admired and saw this idea of investing in other talent...he was obviously very good with talent. But he wanted to be into the merger of tech and entertainment."[16]

Oseary invested just as tech stocks were really starting to heat up. The Nasdaq surged fivefold from 1995 to its 2000 peak as buyers snatched up any company with ".com" in its name, most of them boosted by early investments from tech giants and Silicon Valley firms. In 1999 alone, Pets.com, backed by Amazon, went public at a $290 million valuation;[17] online grocery store Webvan.com, propped up by funding from Sequoia, debuted at $7.9 billion; Priceline.com counted Paul Allen among its early investors—and closed its first day of trading at $9.8 billion, a fourfold increase over its initial offering price.[18]

Idealab's portfolio companies continued to shine as well, each performing better in its first day of trading than most stocks do over many years. Tickets.com jumped 75 percent in its debut and eToys.com leapt 280 percent; after Citysearch merged with Barry Diller's Ticketmaster Online, shares of the combined entity tripled in value upon their initial public offering. But another company turned out to be Idealab's biggest success—and could have been even bigger.

On February 28, 1998, Gross gave a TED-style talk unveiling a then controversial idea—paid search, or the practice of allowing advertisers to bid for positioning atop a list of search results—and a startup called GoTo.com that would focus on it. Within twelve months, the company was doing $100 million in revenue. The following year, Gross entered talks to merge with or buy another nascent power player in the search field: Google. The latter didn't have any revenue at that point and decided to try to license GoTo's technology. After acquisition discussions broke down, Gross threatened to sue, and Google eventually agreed to a settlement he says was worth $366 million in stock.[19]

"Bill Gross was the guy who basically invented Google AdWords," says Kutcher. "He's the guy that built the technology."[20]

Beyond Paul Allen's trips, a few other celebrities dipped their toes into the startup waters elsewhere in the mid- to late 1990s. Perhaps most famously, *Star Trek* actor William Shatner shilled for Priceline in exchange for stock. Although British tabloids reported that the decision eventually earned him $600 million, the company's chief called that number "an urban legend" in 2013, telling CNBC that Shatner sold his shares "at a relatively low price....But he's doing O.K. Don't worry about him."[21]

Other deals offered a tantalizing peek at the potential of uniting tech and talent, such as the pact signed by *South Park* creators Trey Parker and Matt Stone to craft animated shorts for Shockwave.com parent Macromedia, a web software provider. The deal marked a meaningful compromise between Hollywood and Silicon Valley— Parker and Stone settled for a piece of the company rather than a big advance, choosing to bet on the possibility of an IPO; Macromedia coughed up a $50,000-per-minute budget, outrageous for cost-conscious tech types, to execute their vision.

But for the most part, the worlds of platform and content remained far apart. Los Angeles–based Michael Yanover learned this firsthand when Macromedia dispatched him to bridge the gap between the two sides as other investors piled in, from venture capital giant Sequoia to Jim Clark, who cofounded Netscape with Marc Andreessen. Yanover would pull up at the airport by six o'clock every Monday morning, arriving at a desk in San Francisco two hours later and returning to L.A. by the end of the week. He couldn't believe the difference in attitudes on either side of his commute despite the compromises each had made in the negotiation process.

The Silicon Valley crew "didn't even care about their salaries," says Yanover. "They were calculating how much money they were worth based upon the valuation that was the last round of the company. It was all just like, 'We're all going to be rich.' Hollywood was like, 'I don't give a shit about these stock options. Don't even tell me about them. All I care about is how much money you're paying me, and how much of that is up front.'"[22]

Yanover's experience also revealed a key difference between Silicon Valley and Hollywood: the former valued technology first;

the latter prioritized content. So, in the case of the Shockwave deal, it seemed the Macromedia side believed the platform itself was the revolutionary part of the equation, while Parker and Stone thought it was their creations that would take the company into the stratosphere. Those two belief systems were about to go head-to-head.

As broadband internet achieved mainstream availability across much of the developed world throughout the late 1990s, techies and creators started to come into direct conflict over the price of content—with a handful of future billionaires playing lead roles. Uber cofounder Travis Kalanick dropped out of college in 1998 and founded Scour.net, a search engine for multimedia files that eventually drew an investment of millions from billionaire Ron Burkle and Michael Ovitz, cofounder of Hollywood superagency CAA.[23]

Napster, the file-sharing service founded in 1999 by Sean Parker and an online message board chum named Shawn Fanning, cannonballed into the pool party of the turn-of-the-millennium music business and enabled consumers to access a nearly unlimited buffet of music for free. Its founders followed what would become a familiar pattern: create a disruptive startup at a young age (Parker and Fanning were both in their late teens), get funding from Silicon Valley (Zynga cofounder Mark Pincus and venture capitalists Yosi Amram and Eileen Richardson all wrote six-figure checks to get Napster off the ground), move to California, and create a real corporate infrastructure around an idea.[24]

"You could just have your whole library on your computer, that was an incredible revolution," says Josh Elman, who at the time worked for the company behind RealPlayer, a program for listening to digital music. "The internet opens that up, but that kind of does break copyright."[25]

Parker and Fanning also faced a typical challenge: the power players in the industry they were disrupting didn't take kindly to change. Record labels had grown accustomed to charging $20 apiece for albums often laden with filler tracks,[26] reaching an all-time industry-wide high of $14.6 billion in revenue in 1999. Due in part to the arrival of Napster, that number had fallen by nearly $1 billion within two years.[27]

Then there was the matter of legality. Soon lawsuits flooded in from the labels, as well as artists including Metallica and Dr. Dre, alleging that Napster and its 20 million-plus users were stealing their work. The techies on the other side of the battle argued that they were merely providing a better platform for people to discover and listen to music. Two years after Napster's founding, an injunction shut it down; Travis Kalanick's Scour, which enabled a similar sort of access to content, was felled by a stunning $250 billion suit by thirty-three media companies. "We didn't realize we were creating enemies in the world of intellectual property," Ovitz later said. "That didn't bother Travis. It sure as hell bothered me."[28]

Napster has since been revived in various forms, none of them involving free file sharing or Parker. The experience, however, still provided him with some sort of value. "I kind of refer to it as Napster University—it was a crash course in intellectual property law, corporate finance, entrepreneurship," Parker said in 2011. "Some of the emails I wrote when I was just a kid who didn't know what he was doing are apparently in [law school] textbooks."[29]

Amid all of this, the stock market hurtled higher and higher. In March 2000, the Nasdaq reached 5,000, setting yet another new record. Many of its top stocks were propped up by average Americans turned day traders scooping up shares of companies they'd seen only in Super Bowl ads.[30] The U.S. Federal Reserve fueled the boom by keeping interest rates low, in part due to the uncertainty surrounding the "Y2K bug"—the long-rumored global computer glitch posited to occur when digital calendars flipped from '99 to '00. But when the millennium came and went without incident, the Fed started raising rates, cooling the overheated market.

Then tech-heavy Japan tipped into recession, followed by the April 2000 decision in the *United States v. Microsoft Corporation* antitrust case, which found Gates and Allen's company guilty of monopolization. The selling continued that month as investors cashed in stocks to pay for the previous years' capital gains tax bills. Priceline, whose shares had flirted with the $800 mark in 1999, was trading for the price of a ham sandwich by the end of 2000, while Pets.com went bust a year after its IPO and just two after its founding; Webvan crashed the following year after spending over $1 billion and leaving 2,000 workers jobless.[31]

Most market corrections punish good companies along with bad ones, and the popping of the dot-com bubble was no different. As the Nasdaq plummeted to 3,000 in 2000, then down past 2,000 in 2001—bottoming out just north of 1,000 in 2002—some of the most significant tech giants in history saw their shares savaged. Within a span of just a couple of years, Microsoft fell by more than half; Amazon went from trading above $100 to under $10.

Idealab wasn't immune, either—even though at the turn of the millennium, the outlook had been quite good. Gross was talking with Jamie Lee Curtis and Julia Louis-Dreyfus about partnering on some sort of ecommerce jewelry venture. He even reluctantly entertained the notion of his own IPO in 2000. "We didn't want to go public because our business is not predictable," says Gross. "But Goldman and other bankers were saying, 'Oh, you'd be so valuable as a public company…people want to invest in a company that's making companies.' They convinced us to do it."[32]

Gross went as far as actually filing for the IPO that March, but eventually withdrew in October after seeing that the market's rumblings were more than distant thunder. Investors were suddenly wary of just about everything, especially the sort of unproven tech companies that had become synonymous with the dot-com crash (needless to say, the plans with Curtis and Dreyfus were also dashed). By 2001, many of Idealab's biggest successes had been pummeled, while some (like eToys, worth billions just months earlier) had been annihilated altogether.[33]

"The love affair between Silicon Valley and Hollywood was officially over," says Yanover. "Hollywood had said basically, 'We know what we're doing. We're really good at it.' Silicon Valley said, 'We know what we're doing. We're really good at it. We don't want to get embroiled in this whole content thing or the celebrity thing.' The two sides went their separate ways."[34]

For Bill Gross, the dot-com crash was just another market cycle reaching its inevitable end; tech would come back, whether or not its more recent fans—including those from Hollywood— stayed invested. His startup factory had been battered but not broken, with hits like GoTo leaving more than enough cushion to stay afloat.

"People were preparing for like a nuclear winter of startups—in fact, some people said, 'Startups are over,'" Gross recalls. "I started Knowledge Adventure in 1991, when the Gulf War was going on. People said, 'The economy is terrible.' I said, 'I don't care about the economy. I'm going to do what's important to me.' . . . If you have a good idea, it doesn't matter what's happening in the world. I mean, eventually, people need things."[35]

Gross figured the economy would come back, as it has always done in the past. For Oseary, then in his late twenties, it was a different story. He'd poured his life savings into Idealab. The planned IPO would have given him a chance to cash out a seven-figure profit; instead, the offering evaporated, along with much of the value of his holdings.

"I really went all in on Idealab," Oseary tells me. "It was like, get in, and then four weeks later, it was already over. It was the weirdest thing. I didn't even know what happened. I got really beat up."[36]

Oseary even began to question why he'd gotten so focused on the startup world. "I couldn't believe that I had made this mistake," he reflects. "I went to Pasadena, I'm hanging out with all these guys. All of a sudden, I'm like, 'What was I doing? I was doing just fine in my own world.'"

One of the people who helped Oseary get through this period was Burkle, who'd started out as a box boy in his dad's grocery store. He'd gone on to make a fortune buying and selling super-market chains and launching private equity firm Yucaipa. Over the years, Burkle—now a shy, round-faced mogul in his sixties—became the ultimate insider, befriending big names from Diddy to Bill Clinton.[37]

The billionaire investor had seen his share of bubbles, but this was Oseary's first. For the young entrepreneur, the dot-com crash served as a lesson in the vicissitudes of the markets and, above all, on the importance of diversification. "So great that you learned it at this age," Oseary remembers Burkle saying.[38]

It wasn't long before the startup world came calling again, but Oseary wasn't interested. He passed on an opportunity to invest not only in Research in Motion but Glacéau, the parent company of Vitaminwater.

"I was just gutted," he recalls. "Had Idealab lasted another six months without imploding, I would've been on those other two deals and it wouldn't have even mattered."

Oseary may have been too burned-out to invest in Vitaminwater, but for several others in the entertainment world, it would turn out to be quite remunerative. And meanwhile, in Silicon Valley, one of Oseary's peers was busy building a career that would soon turn him into one of the most successful venture capitalists on the planet.

CHAPTER 3

Liquid Gold

These days, Ben Horowitz is best known as one-half of the venture firm Andreessen Horowitz—where he has the inside track on some of the world's most promising investment opportunities—but he's always been a bit of an outsider. Even as one of Silicone Valley's better-known venture capitalists, he'd rather cite hip-hop lyrics than Harvard Business School case studies when explaining business in his widely read books and blog.

So perhaps it shouldn't come as a surprise that the venture capitalist with a penchant for straight talk and occasional profanity has ended up investing alongside A-List Angels like Nas. Together with other stars, including Kutcher and Eminem, they helped fund hip-hop lyrics site Rap Genius and encouraged its expansion into a medium for annotating everything on the web. Horowitz also saw a way to add another layer of worth to creators' work.

"At the end of the day, we think there's tremendous value being added to the original text," he told me in 2012. "That's going to accrue to the original authors and publishers as well as to Rap Genius."[1]

Horowitz became accustomed to bouncing between disparate worlds long before he and Netscape cofounder Marc Andreessen launched their venture firm, and decades before his legendary barbeques united stars like Nas with Silicon Valley bigwigs. Born in the UK, Horowitz grew up in Northern California, where his father David Horowitz, then a Marxist intellectual, enmeshed himself with the Black Panthers before becoming disillusioned and turning into a far-right radical (the elder Horowitz is now known for throwing Twitter bombs like "Obama is an American traitor.")[2]

The younger Horowitz, who disagrees vehemently with his father's politics (yet still reportedly pays for his bodyguard during controversial speeches), went on a decidedly different track. After playing football in high school, he left the Bay Area to attend college at Columbia, where he and two friends recorded a hip-hop album under the name Blind Def Crew (somehow, the tracks haven't made it to major streaming services, although Horowitz annotated part of the group's oeuvre on Genius). As with Troy Carter, his career as a rapper ended—perhaps mercifully—at the dawn of adulthood, but his love for the genre remained a lifelong affair.[3]

Horowitz met Andreessen at Netscape and teamed with him to found a cloud computing company called Loudcloud in 1999. They raised $15 million from Benchmark at a $45 million valuation and got an unquantifiable boost from Horowitz's ability to bring a human element to the tech world. "In Silicon Valley, people always say that an extroverted engineer is one who stares at your shoes rather than his own," explained Greg Sands, a colleague from his Netscape days. "Ben was an engineer, which meant he had a bit of an awkward user interface, but perhaps his life as an outsider generated empathy. He could get people to work together."[4]

Within a couple of years, however, all the dot-com companies Loudcloud relied on for business were falling from the sky like so many frozen iguanas dropping from trees during a Florida cold snap. It wasn't long before Horowitz concluded that, in order to survive, he had to sell Loudcloud's core to a bigger competitor and pivot to the software business. Horowitz drew interest from Ross Perot's EDS and computer giant IBM, but his momentum stalled as negotiations began. With Loudcloud burning cash at a fiendish rate, he needed to find a way to sell quickly—so he flew to Los Angeles with his head of business development to seek advice from Michael Ovitz, the Loudcloud board member who cofounded CAA.

"Gentlemen, I've done many deals in my lifetime and through that process, I've developed a methodology, a way of doing things," Ovitz began. "Within that philosophy, I have certain beliefs. I believe in artificial deadlines."[5]

After the meeting, Horowitz took Ovitz's advice and gave EDS and IBM an ultimatum: they had eight weeks to get an offer together or there would be no deal. Seven weeks later, EDS came through with $63.5 million in cash for the heart of Loudcloud's operation. Horowitz hung on to the software business, which he rebranded as Opsware. It wasn't the bonanza Horowitz had envisioned when he first started the company, but given the pall that had fallen over tech investors in the meantime, it was much better than the alternative: filing for bankruptcy. And the Ovitz-Horowitz connection served as a reminder of what Hollywood and Silicon Valley had to offer each other, even as the dot-com crash brought the boiling love affair between the two sides to a simmer.

The collision of entertainment-world panache and tech-sector smarts helped Horowitz, but it would take longer to sink in for A-List Angels like Shaq, who didn't know the importance of equity in his early days. Not long after signing with the Los Angeles Lakers in 1996, the NBA Hall of Famer drove out to see Bill Gross. The Idealab founder suggested teaming up on a new company:

Big.com. He already owned the URL and wanted to create an Amazon competitor, envisioning Shaq as its public face.

"I wanted to do a deal where I gave him equity in the company," Gross told me in his Pasadena offices. "He was in here. Actually, he was in this chair. He said, 'I'm hungry. Can you go get me like six Double-Doubles at In-N-Out?'"[6]

According to the Idealab founder, cheeseburgers weren't the only compensation Shaq demanded. He wanted $20 million—in cash. Gross was willing to give him that much in equity, but the basketball star wouldn't have it. He figured his compensation for deals off the court ought to be more than his salary as a player, and the Lakers weren't paying him in equity (though of course that would have worked out better for him: the value of the franchise has increased many times over since then).

"He was excited for the same reasons we were, too, because we wanted to use the benefits of Hollywood marketing, entertainment branding, storytelling—all those things are some of the strengths of companies here in L.A.," says Gross. "That's an advantage that a company here could have compared to, say, a company in Silicon Valley, which really is more engineering-focused, but doesn't have the marketing and entertainment groups. Shaq wanted to do it for those reasons."

But the sticking point seemed to be compensation. Shaq's distaste for equity matched that of his Hollywood compatriots at the time. The basketball star attributes his stance, at least on his part, to inexperience. "When you're younger, you're trying to keep it all in cash....I was probably only making six, seven million dollars a year, so I needed all the cash," he says. "Once you accumulate a lot of cash, you can say, 'Okay, now I've got enough cash.'"[7]

Reportedly, part of the reason Shaq ditched his first team, the Orlando Magic—and left some money on the table—was the lure of Los Angeles, where he figured he could more than make up the salary difference with the help of his side hustles in film and music.

By 2002, he had won three consecutive NBA championships with the Lakers and his career earnings had exceeded $100 million on the court. Along the way, he felt more comfortable taking smart risks when they arrived. And, like any successful investor, he had an important ally on his side: luck.

"I got into Google by accident," he says. "I was in a restaurant playing with some kids."

The children just so happened to belong to a high-profile investor whom Shaq declines to name.

"He said, 'Shaq, I like you, I got something for you,'" the basketball star recalls. "I looked at it."

Shaq already knew about Google, and it seemed like a good business to him. He remembered hearing Amazon founder Jeff Bezos say that if you invest in things that make the world a better place, it'll always be a good deal. *A search engine, type in anything you want and it pops up? That's gonna be the business of the future,* Shaq thought to himself. After his agent introduced him to fellow Google investor Ron Conway—a pioneer of Silicon Valley angel investing, thanks to his early outlays in the search giant and others, including PayPal, Twitter, Dropbox, and Airbnb—Shaq plowed in some cash.[8] (Conway politely declined to be interviewed for this book.)[9]

Bill Gross invested in Google, too—in much more roundabout fashion than Shaq. Idealab had survived the dot-com crash by relying on its war chest, depleted but still considerable, as companies around the tech sector evaporated. "We said, 'Okay, well, we're not going to go public, but let's just make great companies,'" Gross recalls. "'Let's look at every industry, and see where are their big problems that need solutions, where entrepreneurship can help them.'"[10]

In his first few years at the helm of Idealab, Gross had learned two valuable lessons: first, to give the people running his portfolio companies more room to control their own destiny, and, second, to not fall in love with his own ideas. He set up a new rule stipulating that if Gross couldn't find another firm willing to invest in one of his ideas alongside his incubator, he'd pull the plug.

One startup that made the cut was photo management software outfit Picasa. Gross launched the company in 2002, when he saw that digital cameras were about to take off. Google did, too—but initially had no image search function in its vaunted web crawler. Shortly before going public, the company reached out to Gross to see about making a deal; he was able to extract a swath of stock worth tens of millions at the time, and orders of magnitude more today.[11]

Google went public on August 19, 2004, jumping 18 percent in its first day of trading; neither Gross nor Shaq would reveal the precise valuation at which they got into Google, but they were well ahead of regular investors who purchased shares at the search giant's debut. Within a decade, every $1 invested had turned into $15.[12] Shaq had figured out one of the key advantages of his fame: leveraging celebrity to get in on winning companies before they're publicly traded.

"It was presented to me, I knew it was gonna hit," Shaq explains. "And I said, 'Wow, I'll try it.' My only regret is that I wish I would have bought more."[13]

But for the most part, Hollywood had soured on Silicon Valley in the wake of the dot-com crash. So, as tech stocks started to recover, with Google and its ilk taking off again, the entertainment industry was largely left on the sidelines of the new boom.

If Shaq was the most fearsome player in the NBA during the early 2000s, his equivalent in the world of full-time rappers had to be Curtis "50 Cent" Jackson. The musclebound former drug dealer crashed into the mainstream conversation with his 2003 multiplatinum album, *Get Rich Or Die Tryin'*, and within three years he'd generated half a billion dollars in sales across an empire that included recorded music, publishing, touring, sneakers, apparel, video games, and his own record label.

By the time he glowered out from the cover of *Forbes* in 2006, he'd taken to cruising New York in a $200,000 black Chevy Suburban featuring bulletproof windows and a bombproof undercarriage, the same model frequently used by U.S. military personnel in Iraq. 50 pocketed $41 million that year alone—but was eyeing more than cash. Buried toward the end of the story was a proclamation that revealed his proclivities: 50 predicted that the flavored water he'd been shilling in exchange for equity would one day be bought by Coca-Cola.

"I'm creating a foundation that will be around for a long time, because fame can come and go or get lost in the lifestyle and the splurging," he said. "I never got into it for the music. I got into it for the *business*."[14]

Vitaminwater was the beverage in question; 50 had received a piece of its parent company, Glacéau, in exchange for his support. The total amount, later reported at 5 percent, seemed ample compensation for the rapper as he launched his own Formula 50 flavor and became the face of the brand. 50's manager, the late Chris Lighty, had arranged the deal with Rohan Oza, then the VP of marketing for Vitaminwater.[15]

Oza didn't seem to have all that much in common with 50 on paper. Born to Indian parents, he grew up in Africa, earned his MBA at the University of Michigan, and got his start selling candy—working at M&M's purveyor Mars. 50, on the other hand, grew up in a crack-wracked corner of Queens; with little formal education, his first job was selling cocaine on the streets of New York. Oza eventually ended up in Coca-Cola's Powerade division, and that's where his kinship with 50 kicked in.

"I wasn't very good at following the rules," Oza explains, insisting that—like 50—he intimidated too many people with his brash style. He made the jump to Glacéau in 2002 and within two years had decided his brand needed a hip-hop artist as its face. Weighing 50 and Jay-Z, Oza decided to first reach out to the former, given that both the rapper and the beverage company came from Queens. When they started talking numbers, Oza told 50 he couldn't pay him much; the rapper said he'd happily bet on himself by taking equity.[16]

Soon 50 was starring in television commercials that raised both his profile and Vitaminwater's. In one, drinking Formula 50 magically gives 50 Cent the ability to conduct a Beethoven symphony at a fancy concert hall. "Since he began drinking Vitaminwater Formula 50, he feels he's up to the task," an announcer proclaims, as 50 directs the string section to perform a remix of his hit "In da Club."

He wasn't the only celebrity with this sort of arrangement. Glacéau approached Shaq with the idea of doing commercials, but when the basketball player revealed his price, he received a hard no. As Shaq recalls, "They said, 'We can't pay that much, 'cause we're paying 50 Cent.'" Several years before, Shaq might have scoffed at such a negotiating tactic. Instead, he kept listening, and soon Glacéau made an offer. Shaq accepted and eventually starred in an ad as a jockey riding a horse called Chunk of Love. Why? "They gave us a lot of stock."[17]

While 50 Cent and Shaq were loading up on Vitaminwater equity, Horowitz found himself looking for a different sort of energy boost. Following the sale of his core Loudcloud business to EDS in 2002, shares of his newly minted Opsware plunged to $0.35 apiece as investors struggled to understand the rationale behind the big switch. The Nasdaq exchange informed him the company would be delisted if shares didn't break the $1 mark within ninety days.[18]

That meant Horowitz needed to convince the markets, or at least one deep-pocketed investor, to start buying more Opsware stock. This time, Horowitz turned not to Ovitz but to another dealmaker who knew how to bring celebrity sizzle to Silicon Valley steak: Ron Conway, who counted Shaq and Sean Parker among his investing buddies. Horowitz explained that Opsware was actually in good shape, due to an agreement inked with EDS as part of the Loudcloud deal that promised Horowitz's company $20 million in annual revenue. Yet Opsware's share price indicated that investors inexplicably valued the company at just half its cash reserves—almost like saying a functioning car with $10,000 in the trunk was worth $5,000.

Conway recommended that Horowitz go see Herb Allen, the head of investment bank Allen & Company, and he arranged a meeting. Upon Horowitz's arrival at Allen's New York head-quarters, the latter started things off by noting how much he trusted Conway and took his referrals seriously. Horowitz then dug into the story of Opsware, explaining why it was undervalued. Allen nodded through the presentation and told Horowitz he'd see what he could do. Over the next several months, Allen and his company started buying up Opsware stock, and in less than a year the price increased by an order of magnitude.

Even as he leaned on advisors like Conway and Ovitz to help with large-scale issues, Horowitz looked to the entertainment world for inspiration to help him deal with day-to-day operations. In one case, he noted that Boston Celtics coach Tommy Heinsohn had lost control of the team after his tactic of throwing temper tantrums got old and players no longer understood why he wanted them to do a particular thing. So Horowitz resolved to make sure all his employees knew not only what he wanted them to do but why—thereby empowering them—a hallmark of good organizations.[19]

Horowitz also had to learn to tone down some of the tenden-cies learned at home from his firebrand dad. "With my father, everything was an argument to the death," he said. "My bar for 'inflammatory' was so high."[20] At one point, the younger Horowitz realized his penchant for profanity had created an environment of pervasive cursing in the office—and some level of debate among his employees as to whether or not that was acceptable. So he took a cue from the 1970s prison drama *Short Eyes*, which included a character whom the other inmates called "Cupcakes."[21]

"We will allow profanity," Horowitz told his employees, explaining that he didn't want Opsware to lose out on top hires by creating a reputation as a prudish place. "This does not mean that you can use profanity to intimidate, sexually harass people, or do other bad things. In this way, profanity is no different from other language. For example, consider the word 'cupcakes.' It's fine for me to say to Shannon, 'Those cupcakes you baked look delicious.' But it is not okay for me to say to Anthony, 'Hey, Cupcakes, you look mighty fine in them jeans.'"

While Shaq and 50 Cent fixated on Vitaminwater, a startup that had nothing to do with technology, a new online platform sprouted in Southern California—one that would begin to cure creators of what proved to be just a temporary tech allergy. Chris DeWolfe and Tom Anderson founded Myspace during the summer of 2003 in Los Angeles, though it would soon prove attractive to its northern neighbors as well.

The site piggybacked on the success of Friendster—the early-aughts social network funded by Silicon Valley giants like Benchmark (known for its investments in Dropbox, Twitter, and Uber)—but presented itself as a band-focused destination where fans could come to learn more about their favorite acts. That, along with a heavy dose of user-generated photos that ranged from innocent selfies to soft-core porn, helped Myspace accumulate 33 million users in two years. Among them: bands from Depeche Mode to Weezer, who used the service to push new albums.[22]

"A lot of entertainers were [beginning to use] startups basically for amplification of their message, to be able to connect with fans on a closer basis without any intermediaries," says Troy Carter, who was between stints managing Nelly and Lady Gaga at the time. "Myspace was the first wave of us really seeing it. Then, I think, founders at technology companies noticed the sort of fan base that a lot of these artists were bringing to their platforms and also created a lot of user stickiness as well. I think a lot of founders started to embrace it."[23]

DeWolfe and Anderson were savvy when it came to conceiving and executing their idea, but not so much when it came to securing their personal stakes. First, they created Myspace beneath the umbrella of Intermix, the company where they worked, instead of starting it independently. Second, when they raised $11.5 million in 2005 from Silicon Valley venture firm Redpoint in exchange for 25 percent and a $46 million valuation, they agreed to a bizarre provision guaranteeing that, in the event of an Intermix sale, Myspace would garner a fixed price of $125 million. It was a complex process with a simpler, yet underwhelming, result: when Rupert Murdoch's News Corp swooped in and bought Intermix for $580 million in June 2005, the founders shared a windfall of just $21.4 million, while Redpoint got $65 million.[24]

Even worse, DeWolfe and Anderson's idea would soon be eclipsed by Facebook (they reportedly turned down an offer to buy Mark Zuckerberg's company for $75 million in 2005). The social network sprung from a Harvard dorm room, founded by Zuck and several pals in 2004. That summer, Sean Parker—who'd bounced from his role as music industry villain to a new one as protégé of the aforementioned Conway (a Napster investor)—cold-emailed the company's founders to arrange a meeting. By the end of the year, he'd joined as president, serving as a bridge between

Facebook's fresh-faced founders and the Silicon Valley giants who would become the social network's biggest backers.

"Sean was pivotal in helping Facebook transform from a college project into a real company," Zuckerberg later explained. "Perhaps more importantly, Sean helped ensure that anyone interested in investing in Facebook would not only buy into a company, but also a mission and vision of making the world more open through sharing."[25]

As Facebook wormed its way from college campuses and high schools into the broader population in 2006, tech giants dangled increasingly large offers to buy the social network. Zuckerberg, contemplating ever larger bids, sought the counsel of Silicon Valley veteran Roger McNamee over one particularly tempting billion-dollar offer. The venture capitalist, who'd launched the firm Elevation Partners with Bono and several others in 2004, advised the young founder to hang on to his company; Zuckerberg followed his advice. McNamee became a mentor of sorts, eventually investing as an angel with Bono around 2007.[26]

Facebook, like Myspace before it, seemed to be part of a new group of tech companies that would prove useful to creators. Even so, Hollywood remained relatively lukewarm toward Silicon Valley and its latest exports. DFJ's Roizen remembers a meeting with a big-shot talent agent in the mid-2000s who was toying with the idea of turning her life story into a television show—but he decided not to, upon closer inspection.

"What was the takeaway comment?" says Roizen, with a rhetorical flourish. "It was, generally speaking, 'We don't want to do a show about Silicon Valley because the people are less attractive [than in L.A.], they don't seem to have as much sex, and they stare at computer screens all day. How can you even *make* a TV show out of that?'"[27]

Meanwhile, Vitaminwater surged in to the popular consciousness as its roster of celebrities appeared in a series of increasingly outrageous commercials. In one, Carrie Underwood, David Ortiz, Brian Urlacher, and Dwight Howard joined 50 Cent for cosmonaut training in Russia with the help of Glacéau's flagship beverage. In another, 50 appeared alongside NBA Hall of Famer Steve Nash in a mock infomercial praising the benefits of creating an energy drink. "I used to have to grind to get my vitamins—till I made my own flavor of Vitaminwater," says 50 in the spot. "Now I'm stanky rich!"

50 Cent would soon experience the distinction between rich and wealthy. In 2006, Glacéau clocked $355 million in annual revenue, forecasting a $700 million total the following year. Those sorts of numbers helped convince India's Tata Tea to buy a 30 percent stake in the company for $677 million. Then, in May 2007, Coca-Cola—looking for a way to slice into PepsiCo's lead in the noncarbonated beverage category—swooped in and bought Glacéau outright for $4.1 billion in cash.[28]

Tata Tea doubled the value of its investment in just a year, but 50 Cent did far better. In exchange for little more than his time, energy, and marketing savvy, the rapper walked away with about $100 million. The number has been reported as high as four times that sum and as little as one-third, but Oseary confirms the middle amount. He should know: former CAA agent Seth Rodsky gave him a chance to get in on Glacéau years earlier, but he declined, still smarting from the dot-com bust. "I was offered the deal when [50] did the deal," explains Oseary. "The guy who brought me that deal...I say yes to him on everything now."[29]

As for 50 Cent, the rapper became the scowling standard for leveraging star power. Soon he was expanding his portfolio from music, touring, and movies into a search for the next Vitaminwater—with his headphone line (SMS Audio), energy shots (5-Hour Energy competitor SK Energy) and, eventually, an investment in climate-controlled boxer briefs (Frigo). He even traveled to South Africa to meet with mining billionaire Patrice Motsepe with the goal of creating 50 Cent–branded platinum jewelry.

"People were talking about how much money I made" on Glacéau, 50 told me the following year. "But I was focused on the fact that $4.1 billion was made. I think I can do a bigger deal in the future."[30]

A chastened Oseary refocused his efforts on the music business, where he was well positioned to replenish his coffers managing Madonna. The Material Girl racked up $280 million in pretax earnings from 2007 to 2010, per the estimates of *Forbes*, and Oseary earned an eight-figure commission. When Rodsky brought him another opportunity, Vita Coco, he invested $1.2 million at a $28 million valuation and brought in famous friends from Matthew McConaughey to Madonna herself. By 2014, Vita Coco was worth $665 million.[31]

Even Oseary's Idealab investment was starting to look better as the 2000s wore on. Yahoo bought GoTo, rebranded as Overture, for $1.6 billion in 2003; Idealab got a $400 million cut, its best exit to date. As the decade drew to a close, the startup factory's early investors, including Steven Spielberg and Michael Douglas, had clocked healthy returns. Says Gross: "They've all made their money back many times over."[32]

Shaq, of course, cashed in on Vitaminwater as well. He wouldn't reveal precise numbers, aside from saying his haul rivaled that of the best years of his playing career. And even though Glacéau wasn't a tech startup, the success of 50 Cent, Shaq and others warmed the entertainment appetite toward taking equity over cash—a step that would help make creators more comfortable with the idea of plowing money into Silicon Valley upstarts.

Much like Gross, Horowitz gutted his way through the dot-com crash, keeping his company afloat through a combination of smarts, grit, and willingness to take advice from sources outside the Bay Area, like Ovitz. His shift from cloud computing company to software outfit worked. Within a few years, the market had recovered, leaving big tech companies free to pursue comparably large acquisitions. And that's exactly what Hewlett-Packard did, buying Opsware for $1.6 billion.

Horowitz suddenly found himself more than just a centimillionaire on paper: he and Andreessen had filled up their coffers and now had the time and energy to become venture capitalists themselves. They'd sold Opsware at just the right moment—in late 2008, the Great Recession struck, sending the markets tumbling once again to dot-com-bust lows, and not just tech stocks. Financial firms like Lehman Brothers and Bear Stearns went belly-up, and for a moment it seemed the entire world economy was on the verge of a complete meltdown. Investors once again went scurrying to the sidelines, seeking safety in bonds, cash, and gold—while fleeing stocks, including tech companies, even though the market contagion mostly traced back to the housing and banking sectors.

Like Gross, the two Opsware veterans were bullish on the long-term headwinds in the business world, and in 2009, as the public markets bottomed out, they launched Andreessen Horowitz. The duo had a vision for the venture firm and how it would be different from its Silicon Valley peers. First, since it was established by entrepreneurs and not paper pushers, Andreessen Horowitz aimed to be founder-centric. That meant investing in startups whose creators were still in charge, and giving more founder-friendly terms than the competition when possible.

Horowitz figured founders had two major disadvantages: they didn't necessarily have any management training, and they generally didn't have networks as broad as veteran corporate CEOs. His solution was to build a venture firm that could help entrepreneurs in those areas by emulating Hollywood—specifically, Ovitz's model for CAA.

Ovitz started his talent agency as a twenty-eight-year-old after leaving William Morris, then the top outfit in town—more a collection of loosely affiliated agents than a unified agency, something Ovitz was eager to change. To establish that culture, Ovitz and his colleagues at CAA deferred their salaries for several years, pouring their commissions back into the company—and a pot they'd share. Soon the agency was going head-to-head with William Morris in the battle for Hollywood's top talent.

"We decided to copy CAA's operating model nearly exactly," Horowitz later wrote. "Michael thought it was a great idea, but he was the only one. Everyone else offered some variation of the following: 'This is Silicon Valley, not Hollywood.'"[33]

CHAPTER 4

Dude, Where's My Startup?

I'm about to sit down with Ashton Kutcher for a very California breakfast of avocado and eggs at the home of his Beverly Hills neighbor Guy Oseary—it's part of an interview for my 2016 *Forbes* cover story on the duo—but all Kutcher wants to talk about is 50 Cent.

The rapper's Vitaminwater deal did more than just add nine figures to his own bank account—it served as an inspiration for all creators looking to monetize their fame to the maximum. When news of the agreement hit, Kutcher had just done a traditional endorsement deal for Nikon.

"I'm like, 'Whoa, hold on, wait a second,'" he tells me. "'I've got to figure out how to get in the equity game, because it just makes so much more sense.'... That deal in particular was a game changer."[1]

Before Kutcher started expanding his portfolio, he took a moment to console his pal Oseary over missing out on Vitamin-water.

"I remember coming to your house when that company got bought, and I sat with you," says Oseary.

"Yeah," says Kutcher. "I was like, 'Yo!'"

"I remember exactly what you said to me," explains Oseary, turning to Kutcher. "You remember what you said to me?"

Kutcher doesn't seem to recall, and now Oseary isn't so sure he wants him to. I prod him to tell me, but he hedges.

"That was really private," Oseary sighs. "I was just crying over the fact that..."

"...he had a deal in front of him and he didn't take it," says Kutcher, finishing Oseary's sentence.

"I had a deal," Oseary repeats somberly. "And I didn't take it."

As evidenced by the size and location of Oseary's home, he's certainly not hurting. But everybody hates missing out. Kutcher quickly moves the conversation along.

"Deals like that roll through the entertainment industry, right?" says the actor. "They're trying to take their company to the next level, they need to associate themselves with a brand that's bigger than their existing brand in order to get the brand lift, in order to start to mainstream whatever their product is. These deals come through, and you're always trying to decipher, 'Okay, is this just something that's hot right now, or do they have the real goods?'"

More than any other celebrity—and many full-time venture capitalists—Kutcher has been able to dig in and get a handle on those sorts of questions. He had plenty of built-in currency in Silicon Valley, where startup founders were hungry for social media demigods who could help them score hordes of new users. In the wake of 50 Cent's payday, Kutcher began traveling to San Francisco to meet with any venture capitalist who'd talk to him. He proved to be more than just a handsome face and started getting invited to invest in the tech world's most promising startups.

After teaming up with Ron Burkle to create their A-Grade fund, Kutcher and Oseary not only held their own—they quickly developed a reputation so strong that they had billionaires from former Google chief Eric Schmidt to Salesforce founder Marc Benioff entrusting them with millions.

"There are a lot of celebrity 'tourists' in our industry these days," billionaire Chris Sacca, an early Uber investor, told me. "Famous people lurking around trying to get a piece of the pie but without bringing any value to the table. For Ashton in particular it's been a daily commitment."[2]

Kutcher may have taken an unlikely route to Silicon Valley, but his path to Hollywood was equally unorthodox. He grew up in a working-class family in Cedar Rapids, Iowa, landing his first job around age ten: helping his father lay roof shingles as part of his home renovation business. Other early gigs included stints as a dishwasher, a mason, and a butcher.

He went off to college at the University of Iowa, where he hoped to major in biochemical engineering. To cover his room and board, he donated blood plasma for $60 per week and spent summers as a factory worker at General Mills. Kutcher's plans changed when he won a modeling competition, prompting him to drop out of college and move to New York, then Los Angeles. There, he caught his big break, snagging the role of Michael Kelso on *That '70s Show*.

Despite the program's success, few casual observers comprehended the smarts hidden beneath the dim-witted exterior of Kutcher's character, and he continued to land ditzy roles as his career expanded to film—perhaps most notably in *Dude, Where's My Car?*, the 2000 cult classic in which Kutcher plays a hunky stoner who can't remember where he parked (and, in his quest to find his automobile, ends up accidentally saving the universe). Even in his unscripted *Punk'd*, which debuted on MTV in 2003, Kutcher played up his goofball image by unfurling a series of practical jokes on famous friends.

On the side, though, Kutcher busied himself with clever pursuits. His own company, Katalyst, handled production on *Punk'd* and *Beauty and the Geek*. Kutcher knew he could make and own his content, but if he kept bankrolling Katalyst, he'd soon run out of money. So he turned to his digital chief, Sarah Ross, whom he'd poached from TechCrunch. Ross had been in charge of the news outlet's popular conference series that brought together some of Silicon Valley's most influential characters, and told Kutcher he should familiarize himself with them—perhaps they could help catalyze Katalyst.

"At the time, there weren't any celebrities coming to Tech-Crunch," he recalls. "She sat me down at a table and said, 'I'm going to organize ten meetings for you, and I want you to sit down with these people and just get to know them.... you have to build credibility within the community because they care. These people have worked for years to get to the place where they're at. You can't just come in over the top and be the guy and suddenly promote your thing.'"[3]

So Kutcher met with Silicon Valley mainstays like Michael Arrington, Ron Conway, and Marc Andreessen. He says he went into every encounter assuming he was "the dumbest guy in the room," making sure to spend 90 percent of his time listening and the rest asking every reasonable question that came to mind.

Kutcher realized that he'd stumbled into something even more valuable than finding backers for his production company. Building a network of savvy, well-connected investor and entrepreneur friends—and following them into deals—was how Silicon Valley types like Conway operated. He could do that, too. One of the first lessons Kutcher learned: sharing the hottest investment opportunities that came around not only allowed him to help his pals but also was a way of eventually expanding his own holdings.

"Every great investor that I've found was totally willing to do it because they were confident enough in what their value-add was to companies," says Kutcher, who now seems to deploy startup jargon even more liberally than the average Silicon Valley veteran. "You weren't going to steal deal flow from them. In fact, having you on board might add another level of expertise in a different domain that they don't have. That was how I started building the syndicate of other investors that were doing information sharing."

Though investors like Conway and Andreessen weren't strangers to fame, hobnobbing with celebrities from Shaq to MC Hammer during the first tech boom, they were intrigued by Kutcher's attitude—and his timing.

"There was definitely a period there in which very, very few people outside the Valley were taking any of this stuff seriously," Andreessen told me. "It really wasn't cool....A lot of people who got into it were like, 'Okay that's over.' He was one of the first of the new generation of guys to get in."[4]

Kutcher also had something that many entrepreneurs craved: a massively burgeoning social following. In 2009, he edged out Ellen DeGeneres to become the first person to reach 1 million Twitter followers. For startups whose growth depended on racking up large numbers of users as quickly as possible, adding Kutcher as an investor was a cheap way of gaining customers. Even if he tweeted about a company and only 1 percent of his followers signed up, that meant 10,000 new users—something that might cost $50,000 if one were advertising through traditional channels. For a founder, the only cost of Kutcher's help was selling more equity, kicking out other investors, or reducing their outlays in order to accommodate his cash.

At first, Kutcher's checks were quite small, but he chose wisely, dropping $25,000 into Foursquare. Then, in 2009, Andreessen Horowitz and buyout firm Silver Lake purchased a controlling stake in Skype for $2 billion from eBay, where it had been languishing as a third priority for years. Their idea: to turn Skype into a destination for video as well as voice calls. Andreessen phoned Kutcher, who signed on to invest $1 million in Skype. Kutcher says he subsequently spent a considerable amount of time "having conversations about how moving into video could lead to high-value video content on behalf of broadcasters." Before most of those ideas could be implemented, however, Microsoft bought the company for a reported $8.5 billion, increasing the value of Kutcher's investment by several times in just eighteen months.

"That was literally just Marc Andreessen calling me up and going, 'Hey, this is interesting,' and then explaining to me why the deal could be valuable," says Kutcher. "It was zero intelligence on my end.... The return on the Skype investment paid for all my other angel investments."[5]

Even as one of Hollywood's earliest movers in the latest Silicon Valley tech boom, Kutcher—and his fellow entertainers—caught on too late to invest in many of the platforms soon to dominate show business. But talent agency CAA almost managed to grab a piece of one of the biggest: YouTube.

A young PayPal programmer named Jawed Karim founded the streaming video giant with some friends in 2005, reportedly inspired by a desire to find footage of the infamous "Nipplegate" Super Bowl halftime performance by Janet Jackson and Justin Timberlake. The site was zooming toward unicorn status within a year.[6] By that point, Michael Yanover had left Macromedia for CAA, where his goal was to revive the love affair between tech and entertainment. "We were all excited about YouTube," he recalls. "Except no one's too excited about cats playing the piano or kids biting their baby brother's fingers, things like that."[7]

When Sequoia's Mark Kvamme mentioned to Yanover that the venture firm had just invested in YouTube, Yanover arranged an introduction to the startup's founders—and headed to San Francisco to try to strike a deal that could help both sides. His idea: to have CAA represent YouTube in exchange for a slice of equity. In theory, the agency could connect its stable of stars with the nascent platform, giving YouTube creative legitimacy it lacked thus far.

Yanover took YouTube's young founders out for lunch near their San Mateo office—an apartment above a fragrant pizza parlor— where they seemed more like Teenage Mutant Ninja Turtles than tech titans. "They ordered pizza at the restaurant, which I think was pretty funny," says Yanover. "You're smelling pizza all day long. I guess you got hungry for pizza."

After the meeting, Yanover kept negotiating, but the equity got more and more expensive with each passing week as YouTube skyrocketed to 20 million users watching more than 100 million videos per month. Finally, by October 2006, the company's founders decided they didn't need CAA at all—and sold to Google for $1.65 billion (a decade later, YouTube accounted for some $9 billion of Google's annual revenues, and the service is now likely worth orders of magnitude more than what its founders originally sold it for).[8]

The YouTube sale also meant creators had missed out on another opportunity to own the next big platform. That February, Yanover sat down with Kvamme again to discuss the YouTube phenomenon. It had been nearly a year since Sequoia had first invested, and though the site had exploded in popularity, YouTube was still mostly a maelstrom of user-generated pet videos and bootleg television clips.

"There wasn't any real professional content—no creators, no Hollywood people," says Yanover. "We just hypothesized, if we were going to create professional content on YouTube, what would it look like?"[9]

Kvamme and Yanover figured there might be a place for a platform backed by CAA and Sequoia that focused on short-form, relatively inexpensive videos. Comedy seemed to be the best fit— quick, catchy clips that could go viral with little marketing effort. Starting that March, they reached out to dozens of celebrities and managers, beginning with CAA's own clients. But most of the people they talked to had no interest in a tech venture that offered equity instead of cash. Finally, they found a potential fit: CAA client Will Ferrell, along with his production partners, Adam McKay and Chris Henchy.

Still, it wasn't an easy sell. Yanover and Kvamme met Ferrell and McKay in their trailer on the set of the 2007 ice-skating comedy *Blades of Glory*. McKay, whose résumé included a stretch as a writer at *Saturday Night Live*, loved the short clip format; Ferrell was intrigued, but skeptical at first.

"Well, how much budget will we get to do a video?" Ferrell asked.

"The budget is zero," Yanover replied.

"What do you mean the budget is zero?" said Ferrell.

"The budget is zero."

"Well, I don't get it," said McKay.

"You get a Handycam," Yanover replied. "You use that to make all your videos. There's no wardrobe. There's no hair. There's no makeup. There's no lighting."

"Shit, really?"

"Yeah, really."

"All right, okay, we get it."

It took several more meetings before Ferrell and McKay signed on, and Yanover repeatedly had to talk Sequoia out of backing away from the deal in the meantime. He finally sealed it at the Roosevelt Hotel, where Ferrell and McKay were holed up working on the script to *Step Brothers*. Yanover came armed with a suggestion:

they'd make something like HotorNot.com—a crude early Web 2.0 site where one could vote on the physical attractiveness of various women—except for comedy.

"It's 'Funny Or Not,'" Yanover explained.

"What about 'Funny Or Die'?" suggested Henchy, who was also on hand.

"Even better."

And that's how the site was born. On one of the first videos, McKay wanted to play a Van Morrison track in the background and assumed his new backers would be willing and able to get the clearances to make it happen.

"That costs money," Yanover told McKay upon watching the short. "You'd have to get a sync deal for that."

"Well, yeah, it would just be another thousand or two dollars."

"The budget is zero."

"We can't put in a music track?"

"No, the budget is zero. Like, zero, as in zero."

Still, Funny Or Die launched in April 2007 with ten shorts—and almost immediately made a splash. The star of the bunch was a viral hit called "The Landlord," where Will Ferrell meets the much-younger-than-expected person to whom he pays rent (a toddler named Pearl). The video, which now boasts more than 100 million views, racked up plays so fast that the startup had to scramble to buy more server space.

"Ferrell to this day has been compensated by equity, as has Adam McKay, and Chris Henchy," says Yanover. "CAA did not put up money. We were cofounders, so we got cofounder equity. The money was all Sequoia at that time."

By 2010, Funny Or Die was reportedly pulling in tens of millions of dollars in revenues—and not long after, corporate suitors placed its value in the low nine figures. Hollywood was warming up to Silicon Valley again.

Guy Oseary was starting to rekindle his relationship with the tech world, too, as broader market trends pulled the music industry back toward Silicon Valley. The debut of the iPod and subsequent launch of the iTunes Store opened up a new revenue source for artists and a fresh need for content for Apple. This time, record labels were more receptive than they'd been with Napster.

"Steve Jobs came out and said, 'I've already got all these iPods sold, and I'm only going to build this on the Mac first, which is only 3 percent of the customer base,'" recalls venture capitalist Josh Elman. "And he was like, 'We're Apple, we're going to do it this way and you guys all love the iPod.' Because then he was able to strike deals that other companies were having a harder time striking."[10]

After mostly sitting on the sidelines in the wake of the dot-com bust, Oseary avoided getting similarly hosed during the Great Recession, focusing mostly on managing Madonna during the downturn. When she wrapped up her Sticky & Sweet Tour in 2009, grossing over $400 million, he took some time to ponder if he wanted to give investing one more shot.

"My job was to identify great artists," says Oseary. "It's the same thing here. I had a feeling that I could be really good at identifying ideas and then helping them reach the marketplace."[11]

After regaining some of his investing mojo with his Vita Coco success, Oseary plunged back into web-based startups with Groupon, the service enabling people to get discounts when buying items as a group. He reached out to founder Andrew Mason, bringing him a few ideas and eventually becoming an advisor to—and an investor in—the company. Oseary's entertainment industry connections proved useful, as Groupon teamed with Live Nation to create concert ticket packages.

Oseary started looking around for other chances to unite tech and entertainment, with the goal of diversifying his portfolio to prevent himself from getting burned again. As he delved deeper into the startup world, he kept noticing one of his Hollywood peers doing the same thing: Kutcher. The actor was having a similar experience to Oseary.

"It was becoming clear that Guy was more than just dabbling in the space," says Kutcher. "I would be meeting with companies talking about what are we going to do, and they're like, 'Who's Guy? Who's Guy?' I was like, 'He's one of my good friends.' It just sort of kept coming up."[12]

So when Oseary called and floated the idea of teaming up, Kutcher said yes. Then they reached out to Oseary's friend Burkle. Impressed with the duo's smarts, their access, and their willingness to invest real money of their own—$1 million each—Burkle plowed in $8 million and let them use his back office for support. Oseary brought in a bright twentysomething digital expert named Abe Burns, who'd just started working for him at Maverick, to help power A-Grade (the first three letters represented the first names of Ashton, Guy, and Ron).

With the fund, the trio oriented their investments around three guiding principles: founders, mission, and relevance. Kutcher boils it down to questions. For founders: Who are they? What are they about? What do they believe in? What are they trying to build? How passionate are they? What kind of expertise do they have? Would they be fun to work with? "As soon as we invest, we start working for a company," he says. "If we wouldn't want to work for them, they just go off the list really quick."

Second, the A-Grade founders looked at what the startup was trying to do. Was it solving a real problem for people? Saving humanity a meaningful amount of time? Lastly, they tried to focus on companies they could actually help, passing on some startups that met the other two criteria if they didn't feel their expertise was relevant. Kutcher mentions a drone software startup called Airware that they turned down even though they loved the idea.

"'For us to apply our skill set to what you're doing doesn't really add value for you,'" Kutcher remembers telling the company's founder. "'Your cap space could be used more wisely with other investors.' I just want the kid to succeed because I think he's really bright and he was solving a real-world problem, we just didn't know how we could help."

A-Grade's founders knew Silicon Valley differed from Hollywood in a fundamental way: there was more of a collaborative culture. Unlike the movie business, where only one studio could get a hot film, or the music business, where record labels fought to sign top talent, early-stage tech investors often helped each other out. And based on their track record picking companies like Groupon, Vita Coco, Foursquare, and Skype, A-Grade's founders had little trouble lining up billionaire investors. Among the earliest: Andreessen.

"They're very serious, they're very focused, they dig in and help....we routinely hear from our companies that they're extremely productive," Andreessen told me while I was writing my cover story on Kutcher and Oseary. "They often have very good ideas on what the company should do. Then they now have a really deep understanding of how the entertainment business and the technology business intersect."[13]

And yet Andreessen often found that many observers were mystified by the duo. "I've had this conversation every four or five months with somebody else in the entertainment business," he explains. "It will start with...'How is it that those guys are able to do so much and be able to get all these good deals?' It's almost like disbelief."

Andreessen's response? "Basically, I always start with, 'You don't understand. They're really serious about it.' Then I'll get this look. I'll be like, 'No, no, I'm serious. They're being really serious.'"

As the great thaw in relations between Hollywood and Silicon Valley continued, celebrity investors started popping up like wildflowers after the spring retreat of an alpine glacier. And perhaps one of the best fits to unite the two sides, at least in terms of nomenclature, was Wu-Tang Clan cofounder Robert "RZA" Diggs, a man of many monikers who often went by the name Bobby Digital.

He'd grown up in hip-hop, a genre founded on a sort of technology: the turntable, which enabled early DJs to extend the most danceable parts, or breaks, of popular songs. Whether it was "b-boys" or "b-girls" showing their skills during these interludes or emcees laying verses, this advancement paved the way for the foundation of the genre that's now America's most consumed form of music. More recently, digital samplers have further streamlined the process, both in live shows and in the studio. As RZA points out, producers like him no longer have to use a razor blade to cut apart analog tape and paste it back together. He sees technology and music as eternally intertwined.

"I was Bobby Digital, so I always felt that the digital world was something that we needed to be involved with, or I needed to be involved with in some capacity," he says. "Fortunately, sometimes I don't fit my own money into things. I bring a value with my personality."[14]

RZA—who owns a piece of startups from tech-first instrument maker Roli to wedding planning and registry company Zola—started dabbling in the space around the same time as Kutcher, though with considerably less fanfare. His introduction came in the form of a project known as WuChess.

On the other side of the deal was Brian Zisk, a free-spirited entrepreneur partial to Hawaiian shirts who splits his time between Maui and San Francisco. He got his start by founding an internet streaming radio company around the same time Napster popped up but managed to sell before it became a legal headache. With his windfall, Zisk eventually started the SF MusicTech Fund and, later, a series of conferences with the same name. One of his investments was ChessPark, a site he cofounded that enabled users to play against a computer, other people, or even celebrities in the chess world.

RZA had grown up poor on Staten Island, but two of the things that opened his eyes to the broader world were martial arts and chess. He learned chess at age eleven from a girl he claims also took his virginity; throughout his adolescence, he says he engaged in more of the latter sort of one-on-one play, in part because his family couldn't afford a chess set.[15] His hobbies inspired the name of the Wu-Tang Clan and its songs, from kung-fu-inspired "Da Mystery of Chessboxin'" (1993) to the group's much-discussed lone-copy album *The Wu: Once Upon a Time in Shaolin* (2014).[16] So when RZA heard about ChessPark, he was eager to collaborate with Zisk's company.

"RZA was like, 'Okay, yeah, I wanna do tech,'" Zisk recalls. "Well, okay great. 'What do you have to add?' He was like, 'We should do this project together.' Which would entail a lot of work and a lot of money on our side. And I was like, 'I've seen this movie, let's not do it.'"[17]

But the idea they spawned was enticing: WuChess, a web portal that used the framework of ChessPark to create a Wu-Tang-themed site. Rooks and knights could be made to look like different members of the group. And Wu-Tang's millions of fans could play chess against each other, or even versus RZA, who received a sizable chunk of the outfit in exchange for his association.

WuChess launched in June 2008 with 5,000 fans preregistered and mere hundreds paying the annual $48 membership fee up front. With support from organizations like the Hiphop Chess Federation, which aimed to empower youth through the connection between hip-hop and martial arts—and the allure of playing against actual

Wu-Tang members—WuChess claimed its ranks would soon soar. But early reports criticized the site for spotty levels of competition, due largely to its relatively small subscriber base.[18]

To complicate matters further, RZA didn't show up on the site to play chess, and subscribers started asking questions. Days went by, and still no RZA. Zisk suggested that the hip-hop star delegate the task to an associate who could serve as a proxy RZA. That didn't elicit a response, either. Was RZA too busy with other projects, or could it be that he feared losing a public chess match?

"That's what we came to the conclusion of," says Zisk. "From our side, we couldn't figure out any reason why he wasn't going on except, I mean, that's Occam's razor, that's the most obvious thing, so it's probably true. But is it? I don't actually know."[19]

The site eventually faded away, and Zisk got burned; RZA simply lost equity he hadn't paid for. When asked what had transpired, Bobby Digital offered a slightly different explanation. "Something sloppy happened from my side of the table," he says. "I think somebody in my camp did some ghetto shit…I just remember somebody on my camp doing something really stupid, and it really was embarrassing."[20]

Zisk and his colleagues eventually sold ChessPark to Chess.com for a modest sum. "It was one of those things where everyone goes, 'Woohoo, exit!'" says Zisk. "But it doesn't really do anything." Ultimately, he learned a lesson that would prove valuable to entrepreneurs and venture capitalists looking to do business with celebrities: "Make damn sure it's in the contract that if they don't do what they're supposed to that they don't get compensated."[21]

At the same time, RZA also got a taste of the issues that can spring up on the entertainer side while investing in startups. "In these two worlds, as they cross-pollinate," he says, "the people gotta be able to cross-pollinate as well."[22]

A-Grade's investments started out relatively small, with check sizes in the $50,000–$100,000 zone. As the fund grew more successful, the founders placed bigger and bigger bets. Most required a fair amount of due diligence from A-Grade. Others were love at first sight, at least for Oseary.

"When Ashton showed me Airbnb, I did everything you're not supposed to do," he recalls. "Which is say, 'Okay, I'll just take every dollar I have in the world, and put it into this company.'"[23]

It was the same feeling Oseary had when he first saw Muse perform years earlier. The band had flown all the way from London to Los Angeles to audition for a spot on Oseary's roster at Maverick Records. He stopped them after one song, knowing immediately that he was going to sign the group—which went on to win multiple Grammys and sell more than 20 million albums worldwide.

When it came to Airbnb, Kutcher was a bit more wary than his colleague, even though he was the one who brought the deal to the table. *Wait a second, people are going to let strangers come and stay in their house?* he remembers thinking. *And give them just a key to their house?...People they don't know? That sounds super sketchy.*

"When you start to dig into the way that they build trust on the network, it starts to make more sense," he says. "Then when you start to dig into the use case and the velocity of growth, costs to acquisition and the lifetime value, then you go, 'Well, that doesn't sound nearly as sketchy as you would assume it to be.' If it doesn't sound crazy, it's probably not groundbreaking."[24]

Oseary remembers calling his business manager, who'd been with him since he was a seventeen-year-old newbie in the industry, and figuring out the maximum he could responsibly invest. Soon he was on a plane with Kutcher; they tried to convince Airbnb cofounder Brian Chesky—a Rhode Island School of Design grad well on his way to becoming a billionaire—to let them be the lead investor in the company's next round. The company instead went with Sequoia and Greylock for its Series A and Andreessen Horowitz for its Series B. Still, Chesky loved Kutcher and Oseary's enthusiasm and invited them to invest $2.5 million in 2011.

Once again, Kutcher had demonstrated another benefit of fame. If just about any other angel investor or venture capitalist had shown up and tried to get in on Airbnb during that round, the startup would have refused to let them in. But there was something about the combination of star power and track record that paved his path into one of Silicon Valley's biggest success stories.

Soon Kutcher was putting his mouth where his money was, all around the world. He traveled with Chesky to Asia in an attempt to help promote the launch of the service in Japan. He blogged about his favorite Los Angeles haunts on the company's website. He and Oseary sat with the company's marketing teams to review strategy. And, perhaps most importantly, Oseary played an instrumental role in helping Airbnb maintain its signature whimsy as it expanded abroad.

The appeal of Chesky's startup revolved around a quirky, homey ethos that convinced homeowners to entrust their dwellings to strangers—and weary travelers to feel welcomed in empty apartments. That vibe extended to Airbnb's offices, which often featured Ping-Pong matches and lunchtime yoga. "Pablo Picasso once said, 'It took me four years to paint like Raphael, but a lifetime to paint like a child,'" Chesky explained. "I think you must always live and think like a child. Or have that childlike curiosity and wonder."[25]

Unsurprisingly, Chesky listened closely when Oseary warned Airbnb would soon be under attack by an army of mercenaries poised to pounce on the fanciful startup like so many orcs on a hamlet of hobbits. The force in question was the Samwers, a trio of brothers who commanded hordes of twentysomething Germans from an un-air-conditioned factory in Berlin to copy American startups, devour their European business, and sell to larger corporations before moving on to the next target. They successfully deployed the strategy against Facebook, Twitter, Yelp, and Groupon, selling clones for billions and offering no apologies. The Samwers' motto: "BMW didn't invent the car." And Airbnb wasn't the first way to rent rooms.[26]

"I invited them to a Madonna show years earlier in Berlin, so I'd already known them," says Oseary of the Samwers. "I'd read about them and I wanted to meet them. Everywhere I travel, I always look up people that I read about and I want to meet and invite them to the concerts and hang with them."[27]

So when the Samwers cloned Airbnb and proposed a merger, it wasn't exactly a friendly offer. Chesky agonized over the situation, fretting that he'd either get stuck stunting his company's European growth or accelerating it at the expense of Airbnb's vaunted culture. Oseary then pointed him toward another German contact: entrepreneur Oliver Jung, who was a bit more willing to see things from the Airbnb perspective, especially after his first visit to the company's San Francisco office.

"It felt to me like only thirty people were there and everyone was relaxed," said Jung. "Someone brought a dog out, and it was its birthday. Everyone celebrated the birthday of the dog."[28]

Chesky made Jung feel right at home, offering him a job as head of international expansion along with a chance to invest in Airbnb, telling him this would be the best deal of his life. And it was: Jung opened offices from Milan to Moscow, taking along Chesky's "office in a box" kit that included touches like a portable Ping-Pong table and a copy of the Dr. Seuss book *Oh, the Places You'll Go!*

Airbnb eventually outlasted the Samwers' clone, in part because, as one of Jung's new hires said, "there was a soul in the business."[29]

That chapter might have ended differently if it hadn't been for Oseary's introduction. "A lot of things that we do for people are not obvious," says Oseary. "They're just our relationships and the quality of the people that we're lucky to be around, and we bring that to whatever we do."[30]

Oseary and Kutcher raised $30 million for A-Grade by 2012 from an impressive roster including media mogul David Geffen and Dallas Mavericks owner Mark Cuban. Why? "They both have a great feel for what works with consumers," Cuban told me of Kutcher and Oseary.[31] Added Geffen: "Tech startups are hit-and-miss, and I trusted these guys to have more hits."[32]

Geffen was right to trust them. A-Grade got in early on Uber, Warby Parker, Spotify, and many more. By 2016, A-Grade's $2.5 million investment in Airbnb alone had ballooned to $90 million, bringing the value of its fund to $250 million, nearly an 8.5x return. As Kutcher points out, it's possible that many of A-Grade's investors put in their cash mostly to get in on existing portfolio companies, as opposed to a blind faith in Kutcher and Oseary's abilities to score future home runs.

"When those people were putting money in, they were actually investing into assets that they already know," Kutcher tells me as we wrap our interview in Oseary's Beverly Hills home. "They could see that there was upside in that existing portfolio, and that there was access in that portfolio that wasn't available...whether they were betting on us or betting on the portfolio, there was already upside to be realized. We knew that."[33]

That sort of self-awareness was just part of the package.

"Ashton would be successful in many things, not just being an actor...he could have been a fantastic executive at General Electric, or he would have been a superstar at Facebook, had he chosen that," says Yanover. "I just think these are talented people, not just because they're artists, but they understand business."[34]

As big as Airbnb was for Kutcher and Oseary, the investments they made in Uber would prove to be just as compelling—and, soon, a host of Hollywood passengers would hop along for the ride.

CHAPTER 5

From Gaga to Google

W hen Apple decided to roll out its now defunct social networking service Ping back in 2010, Steve Jobs turned to an
unlikely duo for some informal consulting: Lady Gaga and her then
manager, Troy Carter. He invited them to the company's Cupertino
headquarters to check out the product and provide feedback.

It was an unlikely pairing: Carter, a thirtysomething executive
with the slight frame of a teenager, eternally decked in stylishly
blocky spectacles that added a decade or two to his appearance;
Jobs, who famously favored blue jeans and black turtlenecks; and
Gaga, known for showing up to important events encased in outer-
wear ranging from a giant translucent egg to a dress made of meat.
On this particular day, though, Jobs's design sensibilities were the
main attraction.

"You see that table right there?" the Apple chief asked, after
ushering Gaga and Carter into a conference room. He pointed to
an array of a half dozen objects, including the iPhone, iMac, and
iPod. "That's our entire company. Every single product that we
make is sitting on that table. Don't think about things in terms of

scale. Think about simplicity. Think about really getting a product right, or a few products right."

Jobs's advice stuck with Carter.

"This was a very valuable lesson," he tells me over the phone one winter afternoon. "You don't always have to have a million products to be successful. Focus was important."[1]

Carter heeded Jobs's words in his own career, paying particular attention to his investments in Uber, Lyft, Spotify, and a few others. Gaga did, too: she turned herself into one of the world's biggest stars despite releasing a total of just four solo studio albums in her career at press time, thanks partly to the monumental impact of each one as well as her ability to amplify her reach with the help of the platforms invented toward the beginning of her career.

Though Kutcher was the first person to reach 1 million followers on Twitter, Gaga and Justin Bieber each quickly accumulated north of 100 million followers across all platforms, opening important doors for themselves and their tech-savvy managers.

"The beauty of social media and this era of technology was [how] we were able to disintermediate aggregators and distributors and gatekeepers," says Carter. "What we found out was a lot of the technology companies became gatekeepers themselves....Our philosophy was, 'How do you build a platform to be able to reach these audiences yourselves?'"

For Carter, sitting with Jobs was a key moment on a remarkable journey that began in southwest Philadelphia and blossomed into a fruitful career as a venture capitalist—and a role as one of the few young black venture capitalists in a world dominated by old white men—all following a failed career as a rapper in his early days. "I was broke," he says. "I didn't even have a car, let alone any money to invest."

Carter started his hip-hop run as a teenager, forming a trio with a pair of friends. ("We called ourselves 2 Too Many because we only used to have enough money for one of us," Carter explained.) They decided to hang outside a Philadelphia recording studio frequented by DJ Jazzy Jeff and Will Smith every week in hopes of meeting their hometown idols—and one day, they did. After playing their demo, they signed a $35,000 record deal through Smith's production company, releasing their album via Jive Records. Carter went straight to a car dealership and bought a stick-shift Audi, burning through his advance—and his clutch—within weeks. To make matters worse, 2 Too Many's debut, *Chillin' Like a Smut Villain*, bombed.

"We found out...that we sucked," said Carter, who simultaneously discovered something more important. "More than anything else, more than even the music, [Jeff and Will] respected our hustle."[2]

On top of jobs at McDonald's and Burger King, Carter caught on as a personal assistant—first for DJ Jazzy Jeff, then for Jeff and Will Smith's manager (now business partner), James Lassiter. He ran the latter's phone calls, looping in contacts and staying on the line to take notes. Lassiter, who lived eight blocks from Carter's childhood home, amazed his young charge with the way he could hold his own with the heads of studios and record labels, and gave Carter a blueprint for how executives carried themselves in the entertainment world.

Carter started promoting concerts on the side, luring hip-hop acts from the Wu-Tang Clan to Notorious B.I.G. for shows. One night in the mid-1990s, he booked Biggie for a gig at the Philadelphia Civic Center, only to have the rapper cancel the night of the show. This led to an argument with Biggie's manager, which turned into a shouting match with Sean "Diddy" Combs, the twentysomething chief of Bad Boy Records. Carter managed to convince the impresario to return Biggie's performance fee—and to give him a job as an intern, where he learned even more about show business.

Diddy "was the guy who literally could party until three in the morning and still be the first guy in the office," says Carter. "That really resonated with me. Just to be able to have that sort of maniacal work ethic, but also be able to deal with the guys in the streets...and all the corporate partners as well."[3]

After his stint at Bad Boy, Carter moved to Los Angeles to work for Lassiter. He didn't have a car, so he started using the company's cab service for transportation—both for work events and to visit a woman he'd gotten involved with. When Lassiter found out, he fired Carter on the spot, and the youngster moved back to Philadelphia, he says, "with my tail between my legs....I thought I knew everything."[4]

Carter dusted himself off and in 2001 teamed up to start a management company with J. Erving (the son of NBA legend Julius "Dr. J" Erving), taking on clients including hip-hop songstress Eve and actor Idris Elba. Three years later, Sanctuary Group—a bigger management company whose leadership included Mathew Knowles (father of Beyoncé)—gobbled up Carter's outfit. The cultures of the two companies clashed, and by 2007, Carter was out of a job. Soon he and his wife were nearly out of their home, too. Then Carter got a call from an old friend who wanted him to meet a potential client signed to Interscope Records: Stefani Germanotta, soon to be better known as Lady Gaga.

"She walked in with these big sunglasses on, no pants, fishnet stockings, and played hit after hit," Carter recalls. "What I loved was it looked like she landed from another planet, but she owned it."[5]

He agreed to manage her, launching a new company called Atom Factory to house his operations in the Culver City section of Los Angeles. When Gaga's first single, "Just Dance," didn't immediately light up mainstream radio stations upon its April 2008 release, he put her on a Diddyesque schedule, sometimes playing as many as four shows a day. To further boost her reach, Gaga started using Twitter, Facebook, and YouTube for promotion.

Most record labels were still suspicious of tech-based platforms during their post-Napster hangover, but Carter saw social media as a cheap way to reach large audiences. Following the May launch of Gaga's "Just Dance" music video on YouTube, the song crept up the charts, taking the top spot after twenty-two weeks, eventually clocking more than a quarter-billion views. He even brought Gaga to Twitter's headquarters.

"She talked a lot about how she's fairly shy and this actually gave her a voice," says Elman, who worked at Twitter and remembers a parade of celebrities showing up to learn about the increasingly important platform. "Kanye came through the office and sang a little bit and just talked about how this is the first time he's had a chance to talk to his community in a direct way, and actually have a voice, and didn't have to wait for the interview or find the right show. He could just say what was on his mind."[6]

Gaga's debut album, *The Fame*, went on to sell some 15 million units worldwide, and Carter saw an opportunity to leverage her growing social following for more than just promotion. He helped her fund the video for her song "Telephone," featuring Beyoncé, by teaming up with Interscope to place a lengthy list of brands in the footage. In one sequence, Gaga feeds diner patrons a batch of poison-laced sandwiches topped with Miracle Whip (a paid integration confirmed by the company); in another, she uses a cell phone from Virgin Mobile (her tour sponsor) and headphones by Beats (her own Heartbeats line).[7]

Gaga earned $62 million in 2010 and another $90 million in 2011, by my estimates, and Carter's bank accounts suddenly swelled with his eight-figure managerial cut. Finally flush, he still worried about what would happen if the cash stopped flowing—always a possibility, given the whims of entertainment and entertainers alike. So when Guy Oseary pointed him toward a chance to invest in a video messaging startup called Tinychat, Carter leapt in, quickly reorienting Atom Factory's mission to include startup investment in addition to artist management. An outlay into eyewear startup Warby Parker soon followed.

"Few people understand the way that information travels and trends start better than Troy,"[8] noted the company's chief, Neil Blumenthal. Or, as Elman puts it: "Troy was very early at making relationships with these companies and really trying to understand how to have his artists use them to grow their own influencing communities."[9]

Perhaps more than anyone, Ron Conway helped Carter get his bearings in Silicon Valley. The manager spent the better part of a day sitting in the angel investor's San Francisco apartment, taking notes on a legal pad about how to build his investment strategy. Conway's strategy of cultivating a circle of savvy friends and following each other into intriguing deals made sense to Carter, especially as his Northern California circle grew.

"The network from being a talent manager fit quite naturally into some of the needs that young founders were looking for...in terms of business development, marketing, branding support," says Carter. "Just having that experience of working with talent over the years was transferable to the work that I've done with founders."[10]

In 2012, when arguably the world's most famous pop star was seventeen years old, I wrote the *Forbes* cover story on him with the unlikely title of "Justin Bieber, Venture Capitalist." Yet when we sat down for the interview in a Hollywood recording studio, it was the singer, not the reporter, who opened with a question.

"Did you see the Taylor Swift *Punk'd*?" he asked, referencing an episode in which he goads the superstar into joining him for a songwriting session in Malibu, convincing her to set off fireworks that appear to set a boat alight in the midst of a marine wedding. "She was like, 'I hate you!'"[11]

Pranking celebrities was one of several ways in which Bieber was attempting to mimic Kutcher. With the help of manager Scooter Braun, the party promoter turned megamanager who'd discovered Bieber on YouTube in 2008 and guided his rapid ascent, he'd accumulated stakes in an array of tech companies. Bieber settled into a chair behind a keyboard as I began to ask him questions—most importantly: Why had he, a teenager from an obscure hamlet of 30,000 in central Canada, suddenly begun to invest in startups?

"The tech aspect is just fun for me," he said, tapping out a fresh beat on a nearby drum machine. "I'm always finding new apps that I love on my iPhone and my iPad."

Boom. Boom-boom chuk. Boom. Boom-boom chuk.

"But I'm not going to invest in something I don't like. I have to believe in the product."

Beeeep boop boop boop beeeep boop boop boop.

"Each week I'm learning something about my business and what I need to know for my career," he continued, still clearly focused on the composition assaulting our eardrums. "I'm turning eighteen, you gotta take responsibility."

Thunk. Thadunk dunk dadunk dunk-dunk.

"And I can tell Scooter what the young people like."

Braun admitted the same. "He showed me Instagram before I knew what it was," the manager told me of his teenage charge.[12]

Bieber was able to relate to youngsters in a way that Braun, twelve and a half years his senior, could not. But the latter knew his own demographic quite well—back in 2004, he attempted to place an angel investment in a nascent social networking site then known as Facebook.com. He emailed Mark Zuckerberg, whose contact information was listed on the site, only to be rebuffed; the Facebook founder wasn't looking for any capital at the time. Had Braun been invited to plop even a five-figure sum into the startup at that point, he'd have become a billionaire years ago.

Braun found a worthwhile consolation prize: guiding Bieber to the top of the pop-culture heap throughout the late aughts. By 2012, Bieber was a social media demigod with 43 million Facebook fans, a greater total at the time than that year's presidential candidates—Mitt Romney and Barack Obama—combined. He also had 21 million Twitter followers, more than anyone on earth besides Lady Gaga, and some credited him for helping build the microblogging site. Elman recalls his colleagues pinning a poster of Bieber on the office wall.

"To be honest, that was about the fact that he was very popular on Twitter and his fans were very rabid, not like, 'Oh, he's the reason we're growing,'" says Elman. "Those were more cool things that it was nice to be an employee and see, but most of what we were building had nothing to do with celebrity."[13]

Braun disagreed, and he was ready to capitalize. In Bieber, he'd found not only a generational pop star who would earn hundreds of millions of dollars before he was old enough to rent a car without paying extra, but a human password that would allow both of them to enter exclusive deals in Hollywood and Silicon Valley. And Braun took full advantage of the chance to build an empire of his own, starting in 2009. The idea: to leverage the newfound power a star like Bieber possessed through direct communication with his fans on social media.

"For the first time ever, artists themselves are their own network," said Braun. "I grew up in a time when an artist didn't get radio play, you didn't hear about him, and he would fall out of existence. So [Bieber] and Lady Gaga, they could talk to millions and millions of their fans every single day...we're never going to lose Twitter or Facebook."[14]

By the time I interviewed Braun and Bieber, the duo had amassed stakes in a dozen or so companies. The duo usually joined more experienced investors—to get into social curation app Stamped, they teamed with Google Ventures and Bain Capital—or entertainment world peers: to invest in Tinychat, they joined Oseary, Kutcher, and Carter in a $1.5 million round. They also tried to focus on properties with a philanthropic hook. Ellen DeGeneres (who's had Bieber on her show many times) pointed them toward Sojo Studios. The social gaming outfit had created a FarmVille-type app called WeTopia in which players earned virtual points that could be translated into real charity donations.

In most of these cases, Braun and Bieber were following the playbook written by Oseary and Kutcher: invest a mid-five-figure or low-six-figure sum in a publicity-hungry startup, leveraging fame for a chance to get in on a private company usually available only to high-flying Silicon Valley investors. It was a good deal for them, but perhaps even better for the entrepreneurs who couldn't yet draw attention from the likes of Sequoia and Greylock. For such giants with billions to throw around, writing checks smaller than seven figures isn't worth the trouble.

The traffic on the Hollywood–Silicon Valley highway grew heavier in the early 2010s, and the difference between investment styles grew sharper. While some startups remained insistent that all investors have skin in the game, others lured celebrities with the promise of free stock—known as "advisory shares" or "sweat equity," with the latter suggesting a higher degree of involvement than the former. One startup known for giving away small stakes: Viddy, an "Instagram-for-video" app that brought on Bieber, Will Smith, and Jay-Z as minority owners and soon had racked up 50 million users.[15]

The company's founders recognized that stars brought with them a relatively cheap way to generate impressions. One Facebook post by Bieber might not reach all 43 million of his followers, but if even 1 percent saw him post about Viddy and 5 percent of them downloaded the app, that's more than 20,000 new users. As the cost of user acquisition approached $10 per customer and brand mentions on Kim Kardashian's Instagram soared to $300,000, a single Bieber post could be worth several hundred thousand dollars on the open market—easily worth giving away a tiny bit of equity. And Bieber was one of many stars willing to make that trade.

"I don't know where Twitter or Facebook or any of these things will be in ten years," he told me. "There could be a new thing that's going to be better, you never know. I'm always—and [Scooter's] always—trying to find the next thing."[16]

For Braun, still smarting from missing out on an early Facebook outlay, and annoyed that Bieber wasn't getting anything out of Instagram aside from a massive amount of engagement, Viddy seemed quite attractive—for the right price.

"If we're coming in and saying he's going to be a silent investor and no one's going to know, then we don't ask for any special treatment," Braun said. "But if we're coming in and putting his name to it, and his brand and likeness and his social media power, then we will try and figure out a proper compensation for that."[17]

Despite Viddy's early promise, a change in Facebook's algorithm gutted its traffic; Instagram itself became a destination for watching videos as well as browsing photos. Viddy sold itself to a company called Fullscreen for a mere $20 million in 2014—far from the nine- and ten-figure dreams held by its early shareholders—before closing down at the end of that year.[18]

Braun, Bieber, and their peers were learning that the companies offering free equity weren't always the best ones. Tinychat served as another example: despite the Bieber plugs, the startup never became the next big messaging app. In cases where equity in such companies didn't come for free, the result was fairly catastrophic for shareholders who'd actually paid for their stakes.

"The impression at first was, 'Wow, what a great opportunity to invest in an early-stage technology company,'" says Carter. "It was a good learning experience, but not so great an investment."[19]

To the techies who'd helped create platforms like Facebook and Twitter, it seemed entertainers had gained quite a bit from the advent of social media, even if they didn't own stakes in the budding industry's key players.

"The stars who really rose up during that era really were able to create a lot of value for themselves by building an audience in a direct channel to them in a way that they controlled," says Elman. "A bunch of these early tech products grew and got very large just because they were great technology."[20]

Many creative celebrities had other ideas. Aside from Bono and his early Facebook investment, stars felt they were generally missing out on getting a piece of the platforms where their work was consumed and shared. In 2011, Gaga decided she wanted to change that, with Carter's help.

"We went through a stage, especially when Facebook and Twitter really started to gain traction, where it was this sort of direct way to be able to reach fans and communities," says Carter. "This was something that we had never seen at scale before as an industry. Then, what we realized after making that time investment on these platforms [was] that, [at] any given moment, these companies can change the algorithm and start charging you for the ability to reach fans that you brought to the platform."[21]

Gaga's solution was called Backplane. Named for the board connecting the circuits of a computer, the startup began by creating the underpinning of her million-strong fan site, LittleMonsters.com, with the goal of using that template to build social networks for other brands. Joe Lonsdale, who'd previously cofounded data giant Palantir with Facebook investor Peter Thiel, came on to run the company. Silicon Valley titans including Google Ventures, Sequoia, Menlo Ventures, Greylock, and Conway's SV Angel piled in for a $12.1 million Series A, valuing the company at $40 million. (Due to a nondisclosure agreement, Carter couldn't comment on his or Gaga's financial involvement, but it seems they received equity as founders of Backplane.)

As Carter's community grew, so did his investment opportunities, allowing him to diversify his portfolio. Facebook was one of the first investors in Zimride, and Carter's connection to the social networking giant allowed him a chance to get in early—before it turned into Lyft. Then he met Shervin Pishevar, an Iranian American investor who invited him to invest in another ride-sharing app: Uber, cofounded by Los Angeles native Travis Kalanick, of Scour.net infamy. Kalanick had crafted his new company to be a sleek limousine-on-demand app, a lineage that would later differentiate it from its crunchy competitor Lyft. Uber had other connections to the entertainment business: namely, its name, which Kalanick had purchased from Universal Music Group.[22]

Pishevar's journey to the bleeding edge of the transportation industry traced back to his own father, who drove cabs in the United States after fleeing Iran with his family. "I basically grew up in a taxi," says the younger Pishevar, who came to America as a child, speaking little English. His education got a boost when he was accepted into a program for gifted and talented students; in high school, he won a science fair for a project that fought malaria-infected red blood cells.[23] After graduating from Berkeley, he started a handful of dot-com boom companies, including one that sold to Vistaprint for $118 million. He landed a job at Menlo Ventures after the first bust and guided the firm to lucrative investments in Warby Parker and Tumblr, among others.[24]

By September 2011, Uber was generating $9 million in monthly fares from its 9,000 San Francisco users and needed to raise double-digit millions to expand to other cities. Pishevar's firm and Andreessen Horowitz were both eager to lead the round, with Kalanick initially preferring the latter, due to its reputation for entrepreneur-friendly terms. When it seemed the deal had been done, Pishevar congratulated Kalanick on the funding and said he'd happily remain on standby in case it fell through. Shortly thereafter, Andreessen Horowitz reportedly requested a larger pool of shares to be set aside for future hires, lowering the proposed valuation from $300 million to $220 million in the process.[25]

Kalanick, in Ireland for a tech conference, called Pishevar, in Tunisia for a speaking engagement. "He asked, 'Hey, is that still on, what you said?'" Pishevar recalls. "I said, 'Absolutely,' and I got on the next flight to meet him.... I'm very thankful that I picked up that phone call. My mantra has always been: Get on the plane."[26]

The pair spent an evening wandering the cobblestone streets of Dublin, and Kalanick told Pishevar for the first time that he wanted to not only take on the taxi business but challenge the notion of car ownership altogether. Pishevar wrote up a term sheet that valued Uber at $290 million later that night and texted it to Kalanick.

"I nearly had a panic attack waiting for his response, fearing he was shopping it to someone else to get a better deal, so I upped the offer," says Pishevar. "But he didn't negotiate. He said, 'No, two hundred ninety [million] is fine. We'll do it at that.' Once I received that text, we closed the deal, and with the support of my partners at Menlo, we were off to the races."

Pishevar had a plan. As he'd grown closer to Hollywood operators like Carter, he'd come to the increasingly popular realization that the entertainment industry's renewed interest in Silicon Valley startups could be converted into a very cost-effective way of acquiring new users during Uber's expansion. With Carter's help, he put together what later became known as a "party round," bringing in dozens of stars and handlers with the goal of increasing visibility.

"During that time, most people in L.A. had not heard of Uber, because it was only the black car service in San Francisco at that time," says Carter. "Me being able to introduce [Pishevar] to some of the managers and artists and talent...pretty much helped fill out the L.A. round for Uber during that time."[27]

Notably, the chance to invest in Uber gave creators who felt they'd missed out on owning a piece of the startups directly connected to their business a chance to leverage their fame in exchange for a piece of another valuable, if unrelated, property. Uber announced its Los Angeles presence in 2012 with a bash at a renovated garage venue called SmogShoppe, featuring celebrity investors including Kutcher, Ed Norton, and Olivia Munn. Norton took one of the first rides in the city, a fact that Uber made sure to publicize in a blog post.

They all wrote checks, mostly in the range of five to six figures, joining other stars from Britney Spears to Jared Leto (who has invested in dozens of startups, including zero-commission brokerage outfit Robinhood and meditation app Headspace). There was no free equity, but the creators got in at the same valuation as Uber's regular investors in the previous round, meaning they'd made significant paper gains the moment they signed on. By 2016, their stakes were worth twenty times what they'd initially paid.[28]

Kutcher and Oseary had actually invested in Uber previously, after Kutcher persuaded Oseary and Burkle to plow some of A-Grade's money in a fund operated by Chris Sacca. A onetime close friend of Kalanick's, Sacca lived in Los Angeles and favored embroidered dress shirts that made him look more like a cowboy heading to a square dance than a high-flying venture capitalist (he has since retired from investing). Sacca got into Uber when the company was valued at less than $10 million, and A-Grade got a slice by extension. Like Sacca, Kutcher recognized that Uber wasn't just taking on grungy yellow cabs but the very notion of purchasing automobiles.

"I remember the first time we heard about Uber, I was like, 'Everybody wants to ride around in Lincoln Town Cars? What?'" he says. "Then you start to dig into the power of the network effect and the immediacy, and that you're not actually taking on the limousine companies. You're not even actually taking on the taxi companies... once it gets that foothold, the potential of it is, 'Why own a car?'"[29]

Sacca was also helpful in recruiting celebrity investors to Uber, including ones who couldn't write seven-figure checks, like actress Sophia Bush. Best known at the time for starring in the TV series *One Tree Hill*, she signed on for a low five-figure sum. "Quite low," says Bush, who'd made her first startup investment in online beauty-booking service StyleSeat a year earlier alongside Kutcher, Sacca, and Uber's cofounders. "But they were closing a round and it was essentially like, 'This is what we have left, and this is how many people want in on it,' and, you know, 'What would you like to take?' And I would have liked to have bought more shares than I was able to, but I basically essentially said, 'I'll take what's left. Let's go. This feels like it's going to be a really big deal.'"[30]

Creators may have missed out on owning a sizable chunk of Facebook and YouTube. Still, with the help of Carter and Pishevar, stars from Bush to Jay-Z—a much more diverse cast than Silicon Valley's traditional investor class—had leveraged their fame to get their cut of the next multibillion-dollar company. "I say all the time that Shervin made more people wealthy in Hollywood than any film or any album," says Oseary.[31] Adds Bush, who would go on to become a startup-investing regular: "Not going to lie, there was a part of me that wishes that of the checks I've written, I wish 80 percent of them I had just written to Uber, but it's okay."[32]

About a year after his inspirational visit to Apple, Carter approached Google about bringing Gaga to the company's offices for a meeting ahead of the tech giant's planned launch of music streaming service Google Play. Carter wanted to get a sense of what they were building and whether there were any collaborations to be had.

Larry Page, one of Google's billionaire cofounders, met with

Carter and Gaga, as did Marissa Mayer, who left the company to head up Yahoo! in 2012. The latter showed them two shades of green that Google had A/B tested for one of its products, finding that people were much more likely to click on a certain shade than the other. Page extolled the virtues of such research and asked Gaga if she did the same.

"Did Picasso A/B test his paintings?" she replied.[33]

Carter saw both sides.

"I do believe in pure art and letting art live and be expressive," reflects Carter. "At the same time, when you have access to information and data of what's going to work and what's not going to work... it just shows the difference between pure gut and just going with what you feel is right, which works really well for an artist like Gaga, and going with data, that works really well for a company like Google."

Despite the philosophical differences, Carter was able to broker a few deals between Gaga and Google, including a commercial for the company's Chrome web browser and an investment from its venture arm, Google Ventures, in Backplane. Yet for Gaga, creating a platform of her own proved much more difficult than endorsing established giants: the company never really caught on, eventually suffering the same fate as Viddy.

"Technology companies fail," says Carter, with a seeming shrug that carries through the phone line, toward the tail end of our interview. "I don't think it's specific to these particular companies....look at Apple, [which] failed at Ping and trying to do social....I think it's execution."

Another way of looking at it: no major artist is bigger than a major platform. As YouTube helped boost Google to a valuation in the hundreds of billions and Facebook's Instagram acquisition ensured it would stay in the stratosphere, content creators gained new ways of distributing their work. But most of them had little to show in the way of equity for their efforts. Yes, Funny Or Die created some wealth for Will Ferrell and a few others, but it was always something of a niche property.

"Do I think one artist is ever going to have a platform of just their content with a billion users like Facebook?" asks Carter rhetorically. "It's...next to impossible to build."

But a handful of startups not connected to the entertainment business—like Uber—were beginning to enrich a slew of superstar creators. Those individuals would soon get their chance to own a piece of media platforms as well, thanks partly to the efforts of yet another A-List Angel.

CHAPTER 6

Nasdaq Dough

N as is the sort of investor who makes house calls. In 2012, the legendary rapper met the founders of a startup called Rap Genius at their headquarters: an apartment in a converted warehouse on the Brooklyn waterfront, a couple miles south of the Queensbridge housing project where he spent his youth. After a few minutes clicking around the lyrics annotation site, Nas was hooked. "This is gonna be bigger than Twitter," he declared, and invested in the company shortly thereafter.[1]

Founded in 2009 by three Yale grads—Ilan Zechory, a Google project manager (and trained hypnotherapist); Tom Lehman, who'd been working as a hedge fund computer programmer; and Mahbod Moghadam, a Stanford law alum—the site sprung into existence as Rap Exegesis after an argument over the meaning of a song by Cam'ron. The founders cobbled together a site to provide crowdsourced annotations, changing its name to the more manageable Rap Genius after a few months.

Shortly after Nas invested, he became the site's first Verified Artist, meaning he'd actually go onto Rap Genius and annotate his own songs, sometimes in video form. Like Twitter and Facebook's blue check marks, this program brought a level of legitimacy to the site, cementing it as a place where creators could connect directly with their fans. Nas also gave a cultural stamp of approval to a trio whose demographics didn't exactly match those of the genre upon which Rap Genius initially focused. "It's not always [just] money you bring to the table," he tells me.[2]

For Nas, the company is just one part of a growing investment portfolio. Starting in the early 2010s, with the help of a young, forward-thinking manager named Anthony Saleh, the Queens-born rapper became hip-hop's answer to Ashton Kutcher. He accumulated stakes in companies including Dropbox, Lyft, and Ring, either as an angel or through QueensBridge Venture Partners, which he and Saleh later founded.

As Nas himself has noted, he was lucky to make it out of his firm's namesake—America's largest public housing complex—in one piece, let alone become a multiplatinum recording artist and a successful venture capitalist. He grew up in a maze of "streets or corners with zombies, ghouls and gangstas / Cops, drug dealers with pools of blood anger," as he rapped on his 2001 song "Destroy and Rebuild." With that sort of verbal dexterity, Nas secured himself a spot in every serious who's-the-best-emcee-ever debate. But he could never measure up to the three kings of hip-hop wealth: Jay-Z, Diddy, and Dr. Dre, who all founded major companies of their own to capitalize on their fame.

That started to change when Nas invested in Rap Genius, which has since dropped the "Rap" from its name and expanded into annotating all corners of the web, albeit with a continued focus on music. "We think they have a real shot at building the internet Talmud, which we think will be a really big deal," Ben Horowitz told me in 2012, shortly after writing his first check to the company.[3]

Indeed, Nas's success as an investor likely wouldn't have been possible without assistance from Horowitz and his fellow A-List Angels—many of whom invested in Genius—or his deep roots as a creator.

Though Nas has been fighting the odds his whole career, he wasn't the most improbable sprout to burst through the Queensbridge concrete, at least musically speaking. His father, Olu Dara, gained a measure of renown playing the cornet, a trumpetlike instrument; Dara also worked as a singer and guitarist, appearing in a range of blues, funk, and jazz bands over the years, even releasing two solo albums.

Immersed in music from his earliest days, Nas picked up an interest in technology as a middle schooler, when the Commodore 64 machine first captured his imagination. "I learned programming from my computer teacher, Mr. Woods at P.S. 76, who trained us that this is the future, and if you don't do this, nothing else will matter," says Nas. At the same time, he was starting to hone his voice as a rapper with the help of another sort of technology: the genre's trademark turntables.[4]

Nas, an eighth-grade dropout, feels he became a businessman the moment he signed his first record deal back in the early 1990s. His first eight albums went platinum, including his debut, *Illmatic*, which many hip-hop historians still consider an all-time best. As time went on, Nas prophetically flicked at his future tech riches on songs like 2001's "Got Ur Self a Gun," in which he rapped: "This is Nasdaq dough, in my Nascar with this Nas flow." A protracted verbal dustup with rival Jay-Z juiced both rappers' careers in the early 2000s, as did their equally well-publicized reconciliation. When Jay-Z took the helm of Def Jam Recordings, he signed Nas and helped guide him to his third No. 1 album, *Hip Hop Is Dead,* in 2006.

But for much of his career, his financial feats never seemed to catch up to his lyrical triumphs. *Hip Hop Is Dead* was the last of Nas's efforts to go platinum, and as sales slowed, the artist encountered trouble in his personal and professional life. He split with his wife—"Milkshake" singer Kelis—and as alimony and child support payments weighed on his accounts, the IRS tagged Nas with a $2.6 million lien in 2009.[5]

In the midst of this turmoil, he linked up with Saleh, a future *Forbes* 30 Under 30 honoree who became his manager. The youngster stabilized Nas's finances, steering him into multimillion-dollar endorsement deals with Hennessy and Sprite. And, with the help of Saleh's shrewd moves, Nas had the cash flow to start investing in nascent tech companies.

"My whole thesis around investing was that I was really frustrated with the lack of innovation in music," says Saleh. "We set out to surround ourselves with smarter people, and one of the guys who was really helpful in that was Troy Carter."[6]

Saleh caught on at Carter's Atom Factory, serving as EVP and general manager. They spent much of their time searching for promising startups and uniting the best ones with entertainers like Nas. And in 2011, the rapper made another career-changing contact: Ben Horowitz.

"Nas is clearly one of the best...and clearly that's what Ben is, and I thought there's a lot more that connects these dots than one ever realizes," says Steve Stoute, a former music executive who'd started his own marketing agency, Translation, and introduced the pair at a salon-style dinner. "I think Nas didn't even realize at that moment in time that this guy was one of the leaders in Silicon Valley, because it was almost like, 'Why would a guy who leads Silicon Valley know the lyrics for 'It Ain't Hard to Tell'?"[7]

As the two continued to talk that evening, Nas bonded with Horowitz over their shared interests, particularly music and barbeque. "I was blown away about his education on hip-hop," says Nas of

Horowitz. "We would go back and forth on that. It just grew, our friendship grew. Next thing you know, I'm tapping into this [startup] world at the same time, and what better mentor than Ben?"[8]

At the same time, investing opportunities were opening up even more, with some help from the U.S. government. Barack Obama signed the Jumpstart Our Business Startups Act, better known as JOBS, in 2012. The law relaxed some of the country's more byzantine securities regulations with the goal of stimulating investment in early-stage businesses across a series of provisions, called titles.

Some, like Title I, which enabled companies to stay private longer or go public cheaper, went into effect immediately. Others kicked in later: Title II arrived in 2013 and removed previous restrictions on general solicitation. The tweak allowed fundraisers to market themselves to accredited investors—individuals earning more than $200,000 per year or with a net worth in excess of $1 million— making it easier for startups to attract attention. In other words, an exclusive space for wealthy insiders became slightly less exclusive and not quite as insidery. As veteran angel investor David S. Rose puts it: "Until the JOBS Act of 2012, the only way you could raise money for a private company was to not tell anybody about it."[9]

That opened the door for a new wave of backers. Some came in through platforms like SeedInvest, which sprouted up to serve accredited investors as a marketplace for pre-vetted deals. But many of the best ones still arrived via insider connections available to A-List Angels like Nas. Among the most intriguing: the chance to invest in Rap Genius, which felt like a natural evolution to the rapper.

"We were moving forward, and it's always been about that with hip-hop," says Nas. "I felt like I was always there just waiting, waiting for this turn."[10]

Y Combinator is to burgeoning companies what Nas's brain is to rap lyrics: a place where the germ of an idea, or perhaps something close to fully formed, gets sculpted into a polished entity before being fully released into the world.

The startup accelerator brings a handful of lucky entrepreneurs to Silicon Valley twice a year. Once ensconced, they spend three months honing their mission, as well as their pitch to investors, culminating in Demo Day. That's when venture firms and angels show up, looking to invest in an array of startups alongside Y Combinator itself, which typically pours $150,000 into each company.

"I never miss it, no matter what I do, no matter what's going on in the year," says Guy Oseary. "What's going to be the next Airbnb or the next Dropbox, what do they have up their sleeves?...I never get jaded about it."[11]

All in all, the accelerator has invested in some 2,000 such outfits—including the aforementioned Dropbox and Airbnb—which together boast a value north of $100 billion today. Graduating from Y Combinator is the startup equivalent of an Ivy League degree: though it doesn't guarantee anything, it serves as a valuable stamp of approval. And in the venture capital world, that sort of vetting brings some efficiency to a labor-intensive market, as the average angel turns down forty deals before taking the plunge on one.[12]

In 2011, the Rap Genius triumvirate joined Y Combinator to help supercharge the site, with web traffic ramping up to 1 million monthly views. After graduating from the incubator, the founders caught the interest—and checks—of several A-List Angels, starting with A-Grade. "I will always have a very special place in my heart for Guy as well as Ashton," says Zechory. "They were the first real angel investors...people feel much, much better and safer if someone else has made that commitment."[13]

Among those who invested subsequently: Troy Carter. Saleh remembers sitting in his office at Atom Factory when the Genius founders came in to pitch their company to Carter, who immediately brought them to Saleh. "That guy right there manages Nas," Carter explained. "He can change everything."[14] Nas couldn't believe what they'd created in such a short period of time, finding new meaning in his own music because of the annotations. ("People have their own ideas and they break it down for me, what I'm saying, in an even better way than *I* even thought," Nas told me when I interviewed him about the site in 2012.)[15]

The rapper and his manager each invested a six-figure sum, with Nas receiving some sweat equity as well.[16] The startup raised just under $2 million in its seed round, and with Nas leading the way, Rap Genius recruited scores of hip-hop acts to record video annotations for the site, including RZA, A$AP Rocky, and 50 Cent. Zechory remembers talking to the latter's late manager, Chris Lighty, who told him having Nas on the site gave 50 the confidence to join up. In 2012, fellow hip-hop star Pharrell Williams invested through a venture fund, convincing its general partners to plow cash into a company they probably wouldn't have considered on their own.

That same year, Andreessen Horowitz poured in $15 million, envisioning Rap Genius's annotation feature as something that could be used beyond hip-hop lyrics (Marc Andreessen had wanted to include a similar feature in his original Netscape prototype). "There was a snowball effect that came from Nas's goodwill," says Zechory. "The people in and around the music industry have been great."[17]

Rap Genius leaned on that goodwill while accumulating enemies from both the tech and entertainment worlds, often in avoidable ways. The trio tried to cultivate an image as startup bad boys, throwing decadent parties at their Brooklyn headquarters while adopting an outlandish swagger when interviewed on industry panels or by major publications. They eschewed the startup world's understated jeans-and-hoodies uniform in favor of flashy high-tops, flamboyant blazers, and oversized sunglasses (often while indoors). In 2013, during a party at Horowitz's home, Moghadam posted a picture of attendees including Mark Zuckerberg, who asked him to take it down. He did, but shortly thereafter told a reporter about the incident and offered some choice words for the Facebook founder: "Suck my dick." (A subsequent comment directed at Warren Buffett lost Rap Genius a meeting with Jay-Z.)

The startup also managed to antagonize music publishers, the entities that represent the underlying composition of songs. Rap Genius was unlike Napster inasmuch as it didn't showcase recorded music illegally, but despite the founders' insistence that their content was crowdsourced, not stolen, many music executives saw any lyrics site as the publishing equivalent of Napster. In 2013, the National Music Publishers' Association placed Rap Genius atop its "Undesirable Lyric Website List" amid a flurry of takedown notices.[18]

The founders turned to their investors for help. Carter proved particularly useful, helping them sort through some of the more confusing copyright questions while making introductions between Rap Genius and publishing executives. The site eventually struck a licensing agreement with major music publishers that put an end to the legal wrangling, no doubt boosted by creative allies like Nas and Pharrell. Its army of Verified Artists, which had come to see Rap Genius as a valuable promotional tool, helped the startup present itself as different from Napster—and avoid a similar fate.

There were some issues, though, that the Rap Genius founders had to handle on their own. On Christmas Day of 2013, they awoke to find that Google had penalized the site for questionable search engine optimization practices, bumping the startup's lyrics down to the sixth page of Google results—even when users typed in "Rap Genius"—a potentially deadly blow to their business, not unlike the Facebook algorithm change that doomed Viddy. Among the indiscretions: a "Rap Genius blog affiliate program" that Moghadam had been touting, leading to the sort of inorganic links that Google's formula attempts to discount.

The founders immediately went to work trying to address every single controversy-causing link. Their engineering team put together a list of 177,781 inbound links to Rap Genius. Of those, they identified 3,333 URLs that might be problematic, manually examining each one and whittling the list down to a few hundred of the worst offenders to be eliminated (a full explanation of the technical remedies undertaken by Rap Genius can be found in a blog post by the company's founders and engineering team).[19]

Within a few days, things were back to normal. "It was Christmas Day, so we could have been too stressed out and hitting each other or whatever and yelling," says Lehman. "But instead we banded together, everyone did their part and we solved it, and we triumphed over what could have been a pretty bad episode."[20]

Several months later, however, when Moghadam posted insensitive annotations to a manifesto left by a gunman who went on a killing spree at the University of Santa Barbara, it seemed he'd stretched his cofounders' patience to the maximum. He resigned shortly thereafter.

"Mahbod is my friend. He's a brilliant, creative, complicated person with a ton of love in his heart," wrote Lehman on the site. "Without Mahbod Rap Genius would not exist, and I am grateful for all he has done to help Rap Genius succeed. But I cannot let him compromise the Rap Genius mission."[21]

Within five years of its founding, Rap Genius had exploded into the mainstream, enduring both a high-profile split with a cofounder and a Google scandal that might have ended another startup. The company was becoming the most popular hip-hop site on the web even as it expanded into other areas, annotating everything from news stories to the Bible.

A swath of investors recognized the breadth of Rap Genius's potential enough to write ever larger checks, starting with Nas in the seed stage and moving on to Ben Horowitz for the Series A. And their grasp of the startup's essence came as constant comfort to its founders. "These guys really understood as they played with the site that this is a really powerful resource," says Zechory. "That was really important to us to find, and I think [for] any company to find investors who truly get what you're doing."[22]

Perhaps reassured by the number of savvy investors already involved, billionaire Dan Gilbert—owner of the Cleveland Cavaliers and Quicken Loans—led the company's $40 million Series B in the summer of 2014. "The possibilities are endless," wrote Gilbert on the site, which subsequently dropped "Rap" from its name in a nod to its expanded mission. "Collaborative annotation is the future of text on the internet."[23]

As Genius went through its growing pains, Nas was busy building his venture capital profile. In 2012, he doubled down on his strategy of leveraging his fame to invest in startups by teaming with Saleh to start QueensBridge Venture Partners, a venture firm that would focus on early-stage investing.

"You're diligencing an idea and people, that's it—so what you really need to understand is, is it a great idea?" says Saleh. "We realized we had a knack for it. And we were like, 'The only way to scale this is to go get more capital.' . . . We didn't have the capability to just invest millions and millions and millions of dollars at a rapid pace, out of our own pocket."[24]

For Nas, starting his own venture firm was also another way to be a trendsetter—as opposed to mimicking Jay-Z or Diddy's strategy of launching clothing lines or landing sneaker deals. "When I woke up to start being an investor, it was because I didn't see anyone else doing it, it felt fresh," he says. "I wanted to do something brand-new."[25]

Helped by a growing team, Nas and Saleh built QueensBridge with the access afforded by the former's celebrity and the latter's ability to source deals, raising $10 million for their first fund. Saleh wouldn't reveal who any of their investors were, aside from himself and Nas, citing nondisclosure agreements common to the venture world, but describes them as "regular rich people."[26]

In 2013, QueensBridge added stakes in startups including brokerage app Robinhood and cryptocurrency platform Coinbase.[27] The following year, QueensBridge piled into Lyft and Dropbox, which counted other creators, including members of U2 and Pearl Jam— and Guy Oseary—among its investors.[28] Andreessen Horowitz invested in all four.

"Ben teaches us when we invest with him," says Saleh. "It's not like, 'Hey, put money in this,' it's like, 'Hey you should *think* about this.' [He] talks to us about how he evaluates people, or how he evaluates opportunities, just super-high-level stuff."[29]

Nas had hip-hop in his bones and understood he could help companies like Genius take off. Unlike Kutcher, he didn't really dig into the fundamentals of every business he invested in, relying instead on trusted partners like Saleh and mentors like Horowitz— and gut instinct. His common-sense approach also proved valuable as he built the portfolio at QueensBridge, particularly when Saleh wanted to pass when offered a chance to make an early investment in mattress startup Casper (another A-Grade portfolio company).

"Nas was like, 'I kinda think it's cool that a mattress shows up in a box...if you live in New York City, could you imagine if it came in a box? It's so much easier,'" Saleh recalls. "I was like, 'You know what, that's a good point. All right, cool.' And I called the guy back to invest."

Robinhood, Casper, Coinbase, Lyft, and Dropbox are all now billion-dollar companies—either listed on the Nasdaq or headed that way. And Nas's success in the startup world soon attracted many of his peers in hip-hop, fittingly including his erstwhile archrival. As Uber expanded beyond limos, Jay-Z reached an agreement to invest $2 million—and then personally wired founder Travis

Kalanick an additional $5 million in hopes of increasing his stake. But even for Kalanick, celebrity investment had its limits. He knew Jay-Z's influence would be just as valuable without the additional sum, and didn't want to sell any more of his company than he had to, so he returned the rapper's fresh $5 million outlay.[30]

The list of rapper-investors kept growing, with Snoop Dogg adding investments in Reddit and Robinhood in 2014, and launching his own marijuana startup venture fund, Casa Verde Capital, the following year. Long after the peak of his hip-hop career, Will Smith joined Nas to invest in sock startup Stance. They also teamed on recommendation engine Fancy—think Pinterest meets Amazon— where offerings include everything from a hammock designed for cats ($62) to an underwater jet ski ($13,500).

Rappers hailing from places beyond the tech hubs of California got in on the startup action, too. Atlanta native T.I. added stakes in a range of companies including Moolah, an app that feeds advertisements to customers through their mobile phones in exchange for rebates and cash rewards.[31] Houston's Chamillionaire, best known for his 2005 smash "Ridin' (Dirty)," invested in Maker Studios before Disney bought it for half a billion dollars.[32]

Indeed, successful hip-hop acts found themselves in something of a sweet spot for angel investing: rich enough to have the expendable income needed for startups, but not too wealthy to be bothered with small companies. Billionaires like Bill Gates might not want to spend time worrying about a $10,000 investment in an early-stage startup.[33] But millionaires like, well, Chamillionaire just might. And hip-hop stars often had life experiences that instilled a natural affinity for startups.

"These companies...they don't need another MBA, they have a ton of those," says Saleh. "They need culture, they need perspective, they need a consumer's eye."[34]

Before he started investing, Nas was already a lyrical legend. His outlays earned him additional respect from his fellow hip-hop impresarios—including those who pioneered new ways of monetizing success in the rap world starting in the 1990s. "Puff tells me, 'Young man, you're the one that we watch,'" says Nas, who insists he doesn't need the additional attention. "I'm already known for doing music. I don't really care for any extra recognition."[35]

The best writers are known, in clichéd terms, for making their words come to life—and in the late winter of 2018, Nicki Minaj's did precisely that in a Los Angeles warehouse, where a furry red couch shaped like a pair of lips lurked beneath two lavender eyes and a plush gold crown. Minaj inspired the ten-by-ten-foot installation with her line "In this very moment, I'm king," from her song "Moment 4 Life."

The physical manifestation came together thanks to artist Peggy Noland and a partnership between Genius and Dropbox called Lyrics to Life, which drew crowds to an exhibition of several expressions like the Minaj diorama. The exercise also offered a preview of the latest pivot by Genius, one that involved doubling down on its musical roots and focusing more on video series like Verified (in which artists dig into their lyrics) and Deconstructed (where producers explore their biggest hits).

"The change in Rap Genius to Genius, it wasn't like, 'All right, we did some stuff in music and now we want to expand.' It was our way of adapting the product to what was going on in the community with how people were using it," says Zechory, noting his site's popularity for annotating more than music lyrics. "As of basically 2015, we thought, 'Okay, we are really, really doing something very, very interesting and important in music,' and that's what we set out to do. We built the site and that's where the community energy is so powerful, and that's where there's an opportunity to really change something culturally."[36]

The strategy showed promising signs. In December 2017, Genius totaled 100 million unique views—more than twice the December 2016 total—en route to $10 million in annual revenue, doubling the following year.[37] It's not a massive amount for a company that's raised more than $75 million. But in the context of Silicon Valley, where venture firms routinely wait years before seeing their startups shift from audience-acquisition mode to moneymaking, it's certainly an encouraging step.[38]

Even at its increased size, Genius continued to lean on its early investors. For example, when planning the first-ever IQ/BBQ—a small festival at the company's Brooklyn headquarters featuring music trivia quizzes and a concert—Zechory picked Oseary's brain about the live music business and received a handful of useful introductions as well. Soon he was talking to Oseary's friends at Live Nation, exploring partnerships involving real-time lyrics analysis at shows.[39]

And the legitimacy conferred upon the site by Nas remains, even when he's not actively touting Genius. Zechory remembers rapper 2 Chainz upping his game in one particular Genius video. "[His] mind was blown about how deep people were going into his lyrics, and then he spoke in a certain way to that audience," says Zechory. "He was like, 'Okay, I'm really gonna talk about my craft here. This isn't a shallow interview, because these people respect it.'"

The shift in strategy wasn't the one its estranged cofounder Moghadam would have followed. "If I had stayed with Genius, it could have become a universal annotation tool," he told me in 2018 for a *Forbes* story on the company. "Instead, it is a rap music website."[40] His cofounders look back with a degree of fondness on their early days while acknowledging youthful mistakes. "When it's just three of you in an apartment you can get in your own world, and there are consequences," says Zechory. "It's [not] about you, or your personality, or the funny joke you have, or whatever, like, funny blazer you can wear."[41]

In any case, Nas seems to be doing well for himself. He has never released the exact amount he invested, and Genius is coy about its current valuation. It's certainly possible the company will never find a big exit. But for now, there's no question the rapper's outlay is now worth orders of magnitude more than what he first put in. Says Nas: "The tables have turned in my favor."[42]

On the second floor of the WeWork building in Manhattan's trendy SoHo district, you'll find the headquarters of another hip-hop-oriented media outlet, Mass Appeal—and a veritable shrine to the intersection of entertainment and venture capital. Hanging on the wall of the lobby are several vinyl records, covers facing outward, among them the soundtrack for HBO's *Silicon Valley* and several Nas albums.

That's no coincidence—Nas has owned a chunk of Mass Appeal ever since investing a six-figure sum in 2013. Since then, he's employed a similar strategy to the one he used with Genius, helping transform a dying magazine into a multimedia company and creative agency.

"The capital that he brought is incredible," says Peter Bittenbender, Mass Appeal's CEO, seated next to Nas in a second-floor conference room. "But everything else he's done is a hundred times more valuable than the actual check."[43]

Indeed, Nas persuaded pals Kanye and Diddy to appear in Mass Appeal documentary *Fresh Dressed* and linked the agency side with onetime Def Jam chief Lyor Cohen, now at YouTube, to arrange a Google campaign centered around hip-hop's forty-fourth anniversary.

"I knew there was more to this magazine," adds the rapper in his raspy baritone, between bites of a lobster roll. "I felt like the torch was being passed to us."[44]

These days, Nas and Saleh are focused on their next step. At the end of 2016, with QueensBridge's funds deployed into an impressive array of startups, Saleh teamed up with a handful of operators—including DreamWorks cofounder Jeffrey Katzenberg—to launch WndrCo, a company that backs and develops consumer-focused companies (tellingly, the firm is based in both Los Angeles and San Francisco). Saleh serves as "the deal guy," and Nas frequently co-invests, usually in the sort of early-stage companies that have proven to be his sweet spot.

Even though he has spent the better part of a decade collecting startup stakes, Nas is still in a relatively early stage of his venture capital career. Companies can take fifteen years to get bought out or become profitable; only recently did Nas start to see his six-figure investments turn into seven- and eight-figure windfalls.[45] That happened with a handful of his portfolio companies while this book was being written: Pluto TV went to Viacom for a $340 million, while Amazon bought door-to-door pharmacy PillPack and virtual doorbell outfit Ring for about $1 billion apiece.[46] Thanks mostly to his exits, Nas earned $35 million in 2018—a career high at age forty-four—and followed it up with another $19 million in 2019.

The other startups that have yet to go public or be acquired will continue their trajectories even if Nas never plays another show in his life. To be sure, many—even most—of them probably won't work out. But as any Silicon Valley veteran knows, one winner can more than make up for a dozen losers. Best of all, the value of his stakes in these companies isn't tied to the success of his musical career, a wonderful bit of security in an industry notoriously devoid of it. Nas's main regret is that hip-hop's earliest pioneers, from Melle Mel to Grandmaster Flash, never got a chance to have the same sort of nest egg.

"They broke down the door so that I could be here that when the tables did turn, that someone would be here to take over," he says. "Jay-Z and Puffy [knew] the old way of doing things was dead in the nineties. People were starting their own record companies to ensure that they wouldn't die poor, to ensure that they would not get screwed over."[47]

Nas helped usher in the next step in hip-hop's ongoing commercial evolution. And, while he and his peers weren't able to get in early on YouTube or Facebook, a handful of A-List Angels did manage to invest in the next big platform.

CHAPTER 7

Spotify Spotter

For an ascendant musician turned venture capitalist, D. A. Wallach certainly has the proper trappings. He's got the requisite house in the same hills where generations of Hollywood stars have lived; parked in front is a Tesla, a fitting nod to Silicon Valley.

Wallach greets me inside his airy abode decked out in all black—save for his shock of curly red hair—and takes a seat, cross-legged, on a cabernet-colored velvet couch. Though he's in his mid-thirties, Wallach has already parlayed a critically acclaimed music career into a full-time role as a venture capitalist, securing stakes in companies from Spotify to SpaceX. At times, he's played yenta between startups and some of the entertainment industry's biggest names.

Wallach's role as connector had an inauspicious beginning. In 2007, while still a senior at Harvard—where he first met school-mate Mark Zuckerberg—he brokered an introduction between the Facebook founder and Interscope Records' then chief Jimmy Iovine, who'd just signed Wallach's band, Chester French. Iovine was looking for a way to expand into the tech world and decided to fly to the Bay Area to take meetings.

"Jimmy is forty-five minutes late to this meeting," Wallach recalls. "And he says, 'Oh, I'm sorry I'm late. Our jet got in . . . and then we swung by Apple to see Steve.' Like, my big buddy, Steve [Jobs], and not sort of realizing that Zuck was very quickly going to be a bigger deal [than Iovine]."[1]

Wallach had imagined himself orchestrating the first of many significant pacts between the music industry and the emerging social media world. He felt that a connection between a founder like Zuckerberg and a label chief like Iovine could start to harness the power of Facebook for the benefit of musicians; perhaps features like the company's "Like" button could help artists develop a direct line to their fans. But Iovine didn't make much of a first impression on Zuckerberg.

"Jimmy, you've used Facebook, I assume," Wallach began.

"No, I can't use Facebook," Iovine replied. "People are going to be messaging me left and right and I'm going to be overwhelmed with stuff."

Man, I set up this big meeting, this is me throwing everything I have, Wallach thought to himself. *This is the sum total of my powers that I can introduce these two. And Jimmy doesn't know what Facebook is, basically.*

After about five minutes, Zuckerberg concluded there wasn't anything to be gained from sitting there any longer. The young billionaire had allocated an hour for the meeting, and Iovine had burned through most of that before he even entered the conference room.

"Sorry, I have a hard stop at three thirty," Zuckerberg declared. "I'm not sure what we could actually do together, but I appreciate you coming here. Nice to meet you, and I've got to go."

Though the meeting proved unproductive for all involved, Wallach and Iovine would both find a way to get in on two of the next big platforms for musicians, Spotify and Apple Music. And, thanks in part to Wallach, several A-List Angels—along with a host of other creators—grabbed their piece of the streaming revolution as well.

One day in 2006, Iovine went for a seaside stroll in California with longtime pal Dr. Dre. They started discussing a shoe deal the superproducer had been offered, not dissimilar from the ones Jay-Z and 50 Cent had inked several years earlier. "Fuck sneakers," said Iovine. "Let's sell speakers!"[2]

And that's more or less what they did. Iovine and Dre initially teamed up with Monster Cable Products' Noel Lee to design, engineer, manufacture, and distribute headphones, giving him a mid-single-digit stake in their company, Beats by Dr. Dre. Smaller stakes went to the Black Eyed Peas' Will.i.am and NBA star LeBron James; Iovine and Dre held the largest. Universal also received a piece of the company, encouraging its biggest stars to place the headphones in music videos—especially acts on the Iovine-helmed Interscope, one of Universal's top labels. By the end of the 2000s, Beats were popping up on famous heads from Lady Gaga to members of the U.S. Olympic basketball team.

Around the same time Dre and Iovine took their walk, two men who'd just started a music streaming company were yelling gibberish at each other in an apartment in Stockholm, hoping to stumble upon a nonsensical name that hadn't yet been used anywhere else on the internet. Daniel Ek misheard his cofounder, Martin Lorentzon, thinking he'd said "Spotify," and found zero Google hits for the name. The Swedish serial entrepreneurs—Ek in his twenties, Lorentzon in his late thirties at the time—hired engineers to design an interface and spent two years trying to convince European labels to license their catalogs. The service still reeked of Napster to many, and it wasn't until Spotify's founders proffered million-dollar advances that the labels relented.

"We bet our personal fortunes, and sometimes we bet the entire company," said Ek. "We led with our conviction rather than rationale, because rationale said it was impossible."[3]

Record sales had declined precipitously in the post-Napster universe following their 2000 peak of 785 million U.S. album sales. Though the advent of Apple's iTunes store in 2003 offered a bit of relief, the service also trained consumers to buy music by the $0.99 single, rather than album to album. Total sales dropped 45 percent from the beginning of the new millennium through 2008. By the time Spotify came along, the major labels had gotten desperate enough to mull ideas once considered unacceptable.

Spotify's success in Sweden, where it reversed a decade of industry-wide declines by 2011—accounting for half of the country's recorded music revenue from a combination of free and premium subscriptions—caused the majors to give Ek a long listen. Some may have regretted not striking a deal with Napster to create a Spotifyesque service a decade earlier. The majors didn't seem deterred by the involvement of old foe Sean Parker, who reportedly paid $15 million for 5 percent of Spotify in 2010.

In any case, the major label executives knew they held a great deal of leverage, given that there could be no Spotify without access to the virtually unlimited buffet of music their catalogs offered. And, like the creators who'd watched companies such as Facebook and YouTube grow, they wanted a piece of the platforms themselves. They decided to bargain accordingly, eventually amassing about 10–20 percent of Spotify. The labels' blessing cleared the way for Ek to raise $100 million at a valuation of around $1 billion ahead of Spotify's U.S. launch in 2011.

"He solved the puzzle and gave people an incredible platform, with all the music you can eat and with the most incredible interface, and changed the game," says Oseary. "Of our many investments, we haven't made many in our core community. [With Spotify] we saw something in our world and jumped in on it. And understood the potential: if the record companies supported it, we could see where it could go. And they did, and the rest is history."[4]

Wallach wasn't able to link Facebook and Interscope, but he'd soon find a way to help foster another intersection of technology and creativity, something he'd almost been designed to do. He grew up in Wisconsin loving computers and music, uniting the two in high school as an audio engineer ("which is, essentially, basically, primarily computer programming," he argues).[5] Wallach didn't think much about business until college, when he started to contemplate how he might begin to monetize his music with Chester French (Zuckerberg was an early fan).[6]

"We were part of the first generation of artists that built its audience mainly through social media, not mainly by driving around in a van," says Wallach. "I didn't choose for these technological things to happen in my early career, but they did. And my early trajectory was driven by my choice to embrace those things, and really think from the beginning about, 'What does it look like to build a band in a social media world? What does it look like to make recordings in a digital recording world?'"[7]

In 2007, Wallach moved to Los Angeles, where his music career took a promising turn. Pharrell Williams heard Chester French and signed the band to his Interscope label, releasing its first album, *Love the Future*, which peaked at No. 77 on the *Billboard* charts in 2009. Through a mutual friend, Wallach met fellow midwesterner Kutcher, who'd snagged a piece of Popchips—the snacking love child of rice cakes and potato chips—shortly thereafter. The next thing Wallach knew, he was negotiating with the company's executives as they rolled out an influencer marketing campaign.[8]

"They were raising money and they go, 'Do you want to invest in us?'" Wallach recalls. "So I put five thousand dollars into Popchips...I'd never done this before. Five thousand dollars was a pretty big purchase for me. And it wasn't tech; it was a potato chip company."[9]

For Wallach, the investment represented a way to establish a foothold in the venture capital world, even if it wasn't the ideal company for him. (Today, is his outlay worth $1 or $20,000? "No idea," he says).[10] If he'd waited a little longer, Wallach could have made a much better first investment. The year after tucking into Popchips, he was still living in his mother's house in Milwaukee when he received a call from Shervin Pishevar, then working at Menlo Ventures in Silicon Valley.

"I remember him calling me about Uber: 'Hey, do you want to put a little fifty grand in?'" says Wallach. "I'm sitting there in my boxers at my computer with Shervin on the phone, and I'm like, *Fuck, I don't want to sound like I don't have any money, but I can't make a $50,000 investment. I barely have $50,000.* So...I may have overweighted my skeptical theories of the company."[11]

Wallach's self-imposed pessimism faded as Uber's valuation climbed from $300 million into the billions while he toured the world with Chester French—sometimes drawing decent crowds, but playing audiences as small as just a few people in one unfortunate tour stop in Bristol, England. Wallach itched for a way to delve deeper into startups—and found one in Spotify, which he first discovered in 2010, pestering early investor Shakil Khan for an introduction to Daniel Ek and Sean Parker. The young musician was impressed by the combination of the two ("Daniel was just so rational and so level-headed and kind of unemotional....Sean had created the whole space, and he was a maniac and he was one of the best salesmen I'd ever met, and brilliant").

Wallach desperately wanted to invest, but he still didn't have enough cash to buy a meaningful stake. So he struck a deal: he would come on as Spotify's artist-in-residence, serving as an ambassador to musicians. That meant working to create things like a dashboard that could tell acts where their streams were coming from, which could help prevent costly occurrences like Chester French's Bristol debacle. In exchange, Wallach would be "significantly paid in equity," grabbing a slice of a company already worth nearly $1 billion.

Even more importantly, Wallach became an evangelist for Spotify in a way that Pishevar had for Uber, especially after he set about raising a party round of his own in 2012. Three years earlier, Chester French had released a song with Diddy called "Cîroc Star," an ode to Las Vegas partying that featured the hip-hop mogul and his Diageo-backed vodka, so Wallach called him up and extracted an investment.

Diddy was one of many creators Wallach brought along, but Spotify wasn't necessarily an easy sell—particularly to artists who'd gotten hosed in the Napster era. Still, a handful saw a rare chance to own a piece of the platform that represented the future of their industry. Wallach helped the company ink deals with rocker Jack White, rapper Eminem, Blink-182 drummer Travis Barker, teenager Justin Bieber, and manager Scooter Braun, raising about $15 million in total. Braun was one of several prominent artist managers to grab a piece of the platform, and the involvement of his ilk didn't sit well with everyone.

"I think they are actually distractions," said venture capitalist Fred Davis, a founding partner at investment group Code Advisors. "Are they misusing their platform as a representative to an artist to sweet-talk their way into investment deals they should not be a part of, or are they good investors? Good investors provide value."[12]

For Spotify, however, the support of managers and artists alike proved to be of immense value as the company continued to expand. Even though the labels licensed their catalogs to the streaming service, such deals generally have a defined term—meaning that the labels had lots of leverage when it came time to re-up. With high-profile managers and their clients holding stakes in Spotify, though, Ek and his pals had valuable supporters.

"It's good to have a bunch of musicians investing in Spotify," says Brian Zisk, cofounder of the SF Music Tech Fund and conference.

"It's *really* good to have when you're theoretically gonna come under attack from an industry, to have the bread-and-butter folks of the industry involved."[13]

While Spotify fought to establish itself in the U.S. market, Iovine and Dre busied themselves looking for new sectors to conquer beyond headphones, where Beats now controlled two-thirds of the premium side of the market. They'd gotten there by establishing headphones as a fashion accessory. As Best Buy's chief, Brian Dunn, explained: "The consideration set [is], 'Do I buy the Beats or the Air Jordans?'"[14]

Dre had found a way to compete with sneaker brands without even entering the shoe business as he'd planned before his seaside chat with Iovine. The pair received plenty of help from other famous stakeholders, including Will.i.am, LeBron James, and Diddy, all of whom displayed the Beats brand prominently in their highly scrutinized daily lives. And, after gobbling up music service MOG in 2012, Dre and Iovine employed a similar formula for streaming. Beats hired Nine Inch Nails front man Trent Reznor to head up the creation of its answer to Spotify, Beats Music, which debuted in early 2014; Ellen DeGeneres starred in an early commercial for the service.

Apple, meanwhile, was still mourning the loss of Steve Jobs, who passed away in 2011. Yet his death opened the door to a new plan for distributing music. According to Troy Carter, Jobs said in 2010 that the populace would never fully adopt streaming, and that people wanted to own their music. His successor, Tim Cook, had a different philosophy—as revealed by his decision to buy Beats for $3 billion in the spring of 2014.[15]

In addition to bringing the world's most popular premium headphones into Apple's fold along with Iovine and Dre, who joined the tech giant's staff, the acquisition brought Beats Music itself into Apple's core. The following year, the company launched Apple Music to battle Spotify, abandoning the digital download–first mentality that built the once-vaunted iTunes and its online store in favor of the streaming model launched by a team of creators headed by Dre and Reznor.

The deal underscored the gargantuan size of Apple, a company worth many hundreds of times what it paid for Beats, but it also showed the entertainment world once again the value of ownership. At the time of the deal, two veteran music producers—Dre and Iovine—took home centimillion-dollar checks; Will.i.am and LeBron James pocketed double-digit millions for their troubles. Thanks almost entirely to the Apple buyout, Dre clocked $620 million in pretax pay in 2014, by my estimates for *Forbes*, the highest single-year total tallied by an entertainer in recorded history to that point. These individuals had gone from rich to wealthy.

With Dre wrapped up in Apple Music and Diddy ensconced in Spotify, Jay-Z remained the last of hip-hop's three top moguls (who also happened to be the three wealthiest musicians in America) without a significant financial interest in a streaming service. Jay-Z quietly went to work securing a platform of his own; one of his lieutenants pointed him toward Aspiro, a publicly traded Scandinavian company home to two tiny streaming services, Tidal and WiMP. In late 2014, an employee in Aspiro's Oslo office got a call from someone acting on behalf of a wealthy U.S. investor interested in buying the struggling company (and thought it might be Donald Trump).[16]

As the year came to a close, Jay-Z emerged as the mysterious bidder—and bought the publicly traded Aspiro for $56 million, about 60 percent more than its open market value. At the time, most of Spotify's musician-investors hadn't been revealed (Diddy, for one, didn't get outed as a stakeholder until the publication of my book *3 Kings*). Apple Music had musicians like Dre in the fold, but it wasn't an artist-owned company by any stretch. Jay-Z decided to distinguish his streaming service from all rivals by positioning Tidal as a company owned by and built for artists.

Other musicians had tried to create their own distribution systems in the past, with little success. In 2001, Prince launched something called the NPG Music Club. For $100 per month, the service would distribute new music directly to fans, provide early access to concert tickets, and offer a fan-hosted radio program. Prince lowered the price to $25 for a lifetime subscription before shuttering it altogether in 2006.[17] Eight years later, Garth Brooks tried launching GhostTunes, a digital music store; he shut it down in 2017 after striking a multimillion-dollar deal with Amazon to bring his music to a streaming platform for the first time. "It's no secret to anyone that I'm very involved in my business," Brooks subsequently told me. "I know enough just to be dangerous... [but] my job is the fun."[18]

Jay-Z aimed to differentiate his plan in typically bold fashion, holding a press conference featuring his roster of artists as they officially signed on as musician-owners. The lineup was impressive on paper if a bit awkward on stage: the masked DJ known as Deadmau5 whiffed on a high-five as he greeted Madonna, while country star Jason Aldean and rocker Jack White looked about as comfortable as in-laws meeting for the first time. Jay-Z, Kanye West, and J. Cole struck identical hands-in-pockets poses, and Beyoncé smiled uneasily next to the silent, chrome-helmeted duo Daft Punk. Coldplay front man Chris Martin and superproducer Calvin Harris joined via videoconference, making the event feel as much like a standard corporate sales meeting that happened to take place on Halloween as a gathering of musical superheroes.

Things got stranger as the Tidal investors all came up to sign some sort of document. Madonna suggestively slung her leg over a table as she added her signature, while Kanye West made a vague analogy to oil exploration and Alicia Keys quoted Nietzsche

("Without music, life would be a mistake"). Surreal as the event may have been, Jay-Z lured each artist with a very tangible offer—a low-single-digit percentage stake—in exchange for promises of exclusive content.[19] It seemed he figured that was the best way to compete with Spotify and Apple Music, while granting artists an opportunity to own the next big streaming platform outright. "Right now, they're writing the story for us," Jay-Z said of the music industry's established power players. "We need to write the story for ourselves."[20]

He also took a different path than Spotify, which had to hand over a significant chunk of itself to the labels to get the licenses needed to stream an unlimited amount of music. In Tidal's case, the process happened over a matter of months, not years—perhaps in part because the labels didn't want to ruffle the feathers of some of their biggest stars. Indeed, Jay-Z's roster included multiple acts from every major label and several indies.

But getting traction proved tricky. Even after a stream of exclusive releases from Jay-Z, Beyoncé, and Kanye, Tidal kept losing money—double-digit millions annually, according to numerous reports, with a few million subscribers by the end of 2016. That was a fraction of Spotify's and Apple Music's totals, and even that ballpark number seemed like it could be overstated (according to a pair of Norwegian business journalists who wrote an exposé on Tidal a year later, the real number of active users was probably closer to 1 million at the time; the larger numbers probably included inactive and closed accounts).[21]

In January of 2017, though, Sprint pounced on Tidal, investing $200 million for one-third of the company, and giving Jay-Z a corporate partner to cover the bills. The deal also gave him a tenfold on-paper profit, though only time will tell how wise his gambit was. Regardless, Jay-Z's moves with Tidal represented a fascinating turn of events in which a creator had become wealthy enough to be on the other end of the content-for-ownership trade, doling out pieces to musicians who were merely rich. Interestingly, for a hip-hop star who'd once invoked Chris Rock's famous bit by rapping "Fuck rich, let's get wealthy," Jay-Z's strategy mirrored the comedian's formula for spreading generational prosperity: Walmart's owners pass down wealth by building new Walmarts, not by frivolously spending their cash.

"The equity ownership...that's really important philosophically, not just from a dollars and cents perspective," Jay-Z said. "All artists who come in—and this is an open platform, an open invitation— will participate in the equity upside. And that is important, too, because of that participation in the process, by having a board seat, by actually being an owner in this. It's a different type of involvement."[22]

While Shawn Carter busied himself doing battle with Spotify, another crucial Carter in the music business—Troy—would find a home at Daniel Ek's streaming company as global head of creative services. But first, he had to be convinced of Spotify's merit by Wallach.

The two first bonded in 2008 at a twenty-second birthday party for Solange Knowles (Beyoncé's sister), where Chester French had played a set. Carter was so impressed with Wallach that he brought his band along on Lady Gaga's Fame Ball Tour the following year. Afterward, Wallach took Carter on a hike in Los Angeles. The latter was still managing Gaga at the time (they parted ways in 2013) and felt ambivalent about Spotify.

"Troy and I had a two-hour hike deeply debating," says Wallach. "At the end of it, Troy tentatively was down with what Spotify was trying to do."[23]

Carter's skepticism revolved around Spotify's ability to get licenses around the world, much of which came down to the whims of the major label chiefs. Once he realized they were on board, he was, too—so much so that he invested in the company. The more he got to know Ek, the more he realized he agreed with the Spotify founder's vision of where the music business needed to go. Soon Carter was fielding calls from other managers who were skeptical about bringing their artists onto the platform; his conversion made him a potent evangelist. In 2016, Carter joined Spotify full-time.

"It's just one of the rare times that musicians have been able to capture value from one of the companies that captures value from them," Carter says of the streaming service. "I think it was a great opportunity for the artists."[24]

The bonanza wasn't limited to musicians. Diddy introduced Wallach to Burkle, which led to an investment with his A-Grade cofounders. Kutcher quickly inserted himself into Spotify's inner circle, befriending Ek and peppering him with ideas. A devoted Spotify user and avid jogger, Kutcher pointed out that there wasn't a way to listen to music with his smartwatch.

"I'm calling Daniel going, 'Dude, hack me together an application for my Moto 360 so I can listen to my Spotify offline, on my watch, with my Bluetooth [headphones],'" he recalls. "So we were trying to work out something there."[25]

Wallach had emerged as another useful conduit between the worlds of content and technology, helping Spotify do what Napster couldn't: win over scores of musicians, particularly the high-profile sort who could torpedo the service with vocal complaints or lawsuits (of course, plenty of musicians remain skeptical of Spotify's model to this day, but not enough to sink the service).

At the same time, Wallach served as another example that one needn't be a billionaire venture capitalist or a megastar celebrity (or her manager) to grab a piece of the action. Along the way, he began to develop an investing methodology of his own, through a series of steps. First, he would dig deep into every company he considered, trying to come to a complete understanding of the markets in which they operated, avoiding those he couldn't comprehend. Of the ones that piqued his interest, he'd spend time with management, talk to competitors, look at their financial models and sometimes build his own.

"You learn what different types of investment instruments mean in terms of the rights they give you as an investor and the liquidation preferences, and what will happen in different scenarios," he says. "They're the difference between you getting paid back your money or not, or getting a return or not, or getting diluted to hell. If you don't know any of that stuff, you can be screwed very easily. There are a lot of snake oil salesmen."[26]

Over time, he devoted more and more of his time to investing and less to music. Chester French released its last album in 2012 and it failed to chart; Wallach's well-reviewed solo project, *Time Machine*, suffered the same fate in 2015. "He was just a multi-talented individual who was also a musician," says Zisk. "He seems to have done better as an investor than as a musician."[27]

Wallach's pal Burkle seemed to agree. The billionaire had been winding down his A-Grade investing activities with Oseary and Kutcher and was looking for other ways to pour money into the startup world—so he gave Wallach a call. In 2015, the duo started a fund of their own, dubbed Inevitable Ventures. There, Wallach has since gravitated toward businesses much more esoteric than Spotify. Among them: Glympse Bio, an MIT spinoff that uses advanced sensors for early disease detection, and 8i, which creates holograms of humans for use in augmented and virtual reality.

At the same time, Wallach has been thinking about the model for the modern creator-owner in the context of his light reading, like Thomas Piketty's *Capital in the Twenty-First Century*. "His fundamental point is that the reason you get inequality in capitalism is because the returns on capital are much greater than returns on labor, and the growth over time in the returns on capital are much greater," says Wallach. "In other words, having wealth has become a greater asset over time than it used to be. And relatively, labor has become a less valuable asset. I'm still in the process of going from being primarily a laborer to being a capitalist."[28]

As Wallach and I wrap up our interview in his living room, he lets me in on another reason he gravitated toward investing with Burkle rather than the sorts of creators he helped bring into Spotify. Wallach enjoyed helping artists pile up equity, to be sure. But he found a poignant element at the intersection of creativity and capital, something he likens to a fictional fan going backstage to find Krusty the Clown (of *Simpsons* fame) chain-smoking cigarettes.

"All these artists I really admired as artists were just being dragged into this gutter of money conversations," says Wallach. "These people are my creative idols and they kind of existed in this untouchable, platonic realm of pure art...even though they're artists, they live in the economy, too, and they have to survive. And they have to think about money just like everyone else does in the world. And it was so sad to me to see them preoccupied with this stuff."

As Wallach looked on, the desirability of startups as an investment roared back from post-recession lows amid the ensuing bull market. With governments around the world keeping interest rates low to boost what seemed at first to be a fragile recovery, stocks soared toward new heights, leading scores of wealthy investors—including individuals and government entities from Russia, China, Saudi Arabia, and elsewhere—to seek value by plowing cash into venture funds.

These outlays weren't limited to the usual Bay Area suspects. SoftBank, the giant Japanese venture firm, raised $45 billion from Saudi Arabia for its Vision Fund; the kingdom has aggressively pursued other avenues toward startup investing, though most Silicon

Valley outfits won't reveal their backers publicly. Some don't even accept investments from American public pension funds, probably because the required disclosures might reveal more about their investors than they'd like.[29]

In any case, the influx of capital helped push the demand for targets of venture dollars past the supply of worthy companies. "Relatively speaking, it put the entrepreneur in a greater position of power than the investor," says Wallach. "With the exception of marquee firms like Sequoia and Andreessen Horowitz, the power dynamic went from 'We're a little startup; we're so lucky to get Ashton Kutcher tweeting about us' to 'Jared Leto, *you're* lucky if we let you put money into this thing,' as if it's risk-free, which is insane."[30]

As such, the best startups became even stingier with free or discounted equity. But on account of the groundwork laid by early A-List Angels, savvy creators continued to find good startups—and in some cases launch their own.

CHAPTER 8

New Ownership

In early 2013, twenty-eight-year-old singer-songwriter Jack Conte
decided to finally put together a music video he'd had in mind his
entire life. He'd grown up in the Bay Area as a *Star Wars* fanatic,
watching the films seventy-two times in a single summer; now, in
adulthood, he set about re-creating the cockpit of Han Solo's *Millennium Falcon* to form the backdrop of the video for his thumpy
electronic track "Pedals."[1]

Conte started by storyboarding the video from start to finish,
recruiting two inventors—a teenaged American prodigy and a
middle-aged tinkerer from the UK—to bring along their creations
(a spidery black android and a disembodied animatronic human
head) as his costars. Next came the *Falcon*. Conte bought 1,000
washers on eBay and 150 wall plates from Home Depot. Over
the course of fifty straight sixteen-hour workdays, he spray-painted
each panel and glued every wire nut himself. By the time he and
his robotic compatriots recorded their video, he'd spent $10,000,
draining his savings and maxing out two credit cards.

The numbers didn't add up for Conte. After clocking over

2 million views on YouTube, the video earned him less than $1,000 in advertising revenue. In other words, there were more ways than ever to distribute content, but the means of monetization remained meager. Conte's experience inspired him to found Patreon, a platform where musicians, authors, podcasters, and all sorts of other creatives could release projects to an audience of patrons who'd pledge to pay an artist-specified amount of money per month, or per creation. Patreon would take a mere 5 percent cut, plus a processing fee, generally delighting creators accustomed to splitting microscopic advertising revenue totals with YouTube, as Conte had with "Pedals."

"That was the video that launched Patreon," says Conte, bald-headed and bushy-bearded at his company's San Francisco headquarters, where his *Millennium Falcon* re-creation resides to this day. "I thought it'd be cool to have that set in the office as a reminder of where we came from. Just the hard work—the weird discrepancy between all the work that we put into this video—and the dollars that I was paid for it. It's a great symbol for why Patreon exists."

Conte started training to be a creator much earlier than he did for his role of tech company CEO. He began playing piano at age six and never stopped, ending up in an ill-fated pop band after college before forming a duo called Pomplamoose with his now wife, Nataly Dawn, in 2008. Together they covered popular songs from Beyoncé's "Single Ladies" to Edith Piaf's "La Vie en Rose." Their quirky, do-it-yourself videos racked up hundreds of millions of YouTube views, but not many dollars, at least not before Patreon.

To create the company, Conte teamed up with his Stanford roommate—a programmer and entrepreneur named Sam Yam—sketching out the idea on fourteen sheets of printer paper following the launch of "Pedals." Within two weeks of Patreon's 2013 debut, Conte's monthly music video income had ballooned from $200 to $5,000 as scores of users signed up to pay him and other creators, chiming in with ideas for new features and functionality. By 2018, Patreon was passing along some $300 million annually from 2 million monthly active patrons to a community of 100,000 creators, with plans to distribute $500 million in 2019 via 3 million patrons.

Individuals backed the creators, but Conte turned to Silicon Valley to provide the funding for Patreon itself, eventually raising more than $100 million. Conte is one of a handful of entertainers to raise a nine-figure sum for a company of his own, and among a rare bunch who managed to build a platform capable of lifting the earning potential of his fellow creators. At the same time, the company's journey is one of a few that offers valuable lessons regarding the perils presented by growth—and the unexpected dilemmas that come along with raising vast amounts of cash.

As Conte launched Patreon, a number of other industry veterans were beginning to see the value in creator-owned enterprises, among them a serial entrepreneur named Adam Lilling. A former record executive who'd launched Southern California startup accelerator Launchpad LA in the early 2010s, Lilling started spending time speaking with top managers and attorneys in the entertainment business, offering to educate them on the startup world for free. His reward: a Rolodex full of names that would help him launch Plus Capital, a firm dedicated to pairing stars with startups, in 2013.

"There are people who effect more change in one day than [some] do in a lifetime, but they need to be married up with operators and entrepreneurs," he says. "In Hollywood, there's a force field around celebrity. And the only people that could [navigate] it are the con men and crazy people and the hairstylist's best friend's cousin."[2]

And people like Lilling, whose model offered a simple alternative. He'd link celebrities with startup founders looking for a way to boost their companies' profiles, arranging equity deals and taking a cut for Plus along the way; the outfit would only get paid if the star did. Celebrities had long hired agents for landing gigs or writing books; why not have, in essence, an agent for securing startup stakes? Perhaps in part because of those analogous layers of show business—and the legitimacy gained by working on a deal with Ellen DeGeneres—Lilling found it relatively easy to recruit others in the entertainment world.

In the early days of his company, Lilling focused on fixing the endorsement-for-equity model. Skeptics of the setup rightly claimed that stars often negotiated the largest stake they could get in exchange for the smallest amount of effort they could contribute; just because celebrities had a stake in a company didn't mean they'd actually promote it. Lilling advocated deals that included a commitment—his stars usually promised a minimum amount of promotion on social media.

"It's the same way you do a traditional endorsement," says Amanda Groves, a partner at Plus Capital. "You don't give them half a million dollars to do nothing, you do it because they're going to post four times or whatever it is."[3]

As time went on, though, stars grew increasingly hesitant to flood their social streams with product placement, even if they owned a piece of the company in question. Another option remained for well-known creators: starting their own companies, but not necessarily in the ways they did in the 1990s, when enterprises seemed to be inextricably linked to the celebrities themselves, in cases like Martha Stewart Living and Diddy's Sean John.

The companies in this new generation were a bit more independent of the entertainers behind them. Lilling took advantage of the new trend by opening an arm of his business called Plus Foundry, built to help celebrities create their own companies. For example, Plus partnered with singer Hayley Williams of Paramore to start cruelty-free hair dye brand Good Dye Young; it became a

Sephora mainstay within a year and a half of its 2016 launch. Says Lilling: "If a celebrity has a cofounder, then it's magic."[4]

It wasn't always the most famous names that made the biggest impact. Just as Williams and Conte were part of music's vast middle class before starting their businesses, Jessica Alba had been plodding along the B-movie circuit in search of something better. She was getting plenty of work, to be sure, but mostly in cheesy rom-coms and mid-budget thrillers that weren't exactly thrilling. In 2010 alone, Alba appeared in five movies, but only one received a positive audience score on film review aggregator Rotten Tomatoes (her worst, *An Invisible Sign*, didn't earn a single positive review from critics, according to the site).

Alba's career trajectory changed thanks to a pile of onesies. Before giving birth to her first child in 2008, she broke out in hives after trying to wash the garments, which she'd received as baby shower gifts. Alba became determined to find detergents that wouldn't have the same effect on her child, but couldn't. As she researched household staples, she learned many common products were packed with potentially harmful chemicals. Inspired, she became an expert, even traveling to Washington in 2011 to advocate for new legislation to replace the Toxic Substances Control Act of 1976, which permitted some 80,000 untested chemicals to remain in household goods.

"People have to get sick or die from a certain ingredient or chemical before it's pulled from the marketplace," Alba said in 2015 (through a spokesperson, she declined to be interviewed for this book). "I felt like my needs weren't being met as a modern person."[5]

Alba's solution: founding the Honest Company, which would sell everyday products featuring eco-friendly ingredients free of harmful chemicals. Alba's husband, the entrepreneur and film producer Cash Warren, introduced her to LegalZoom cofounder Brian Lee, who came on as CEO and teamed up with two other cofounders, helping to seed the startup with $6 million. In 2012, the company's first year selling products, Honest reached $10 million in revenue.

Alba would soon have to compete with existing giants in her space, as did Conte in his. For Patreon, those included crowdfunding pioneers such as Indiegogo, GoFundMe, and Kickstarter, all of which first appeared shortly before Patreon.[6] (Kickstarter, the best known of the bunch, counted Kutcher among its investors, albeit in a roundabout sort of way: he insisted on plowing a slug of A-Grade cash into billionaire Chris Sacca's Lowercase Capital, which had gotten in on Kickstarter shortly after its launch in 2009).

But Kickstarter was a service for crowdfunding specific projects. Patreon aimed to support individuals from musicians to illustrators to YouTube stars in an ongoing manner, becoming a home for everything from podcasts to web comics to writing to animation, with a healthy dose of racy images as well. Conte served as the startup's creative soul, while Yam focused on linking Patreon with its first investors—mostly from the cast of usual Silicon Valley suspects. Though they would go on to raise nine figures for Patreon, Conte initially didn't want to top $700,000; one of his backers convinced him to push that number to $2 million. "That allowed us to hire a few more people," says Conte. "And make a few more mistakes."[7]

Conte took the DIY approach he employed for his music videos and applied it to Patreon. The company's first office was the two-bedroom apartment where he lived; during the day, his early employees came by and worked in the living room. Still, for Conte, adding big backers was complicated. He insisted that Patreon keep its cut of artist income at 5 percent (plus a processing fee) even as potential investors pushed for an upward modification. "There were people who said things like, 'Hey, look, if you're not gonna adjust the rate, if you're not gonna go up to 15 percent or 20 percent, then we're not gonna work with you,'" Conte recalls. "And we didn't work with those people."

Some of his investors seemed like modern versions of the very Renaissance-age patrons of the arts whose support Conte aimed to re-create, in aggregate, through crowdfunding. For instance, Danny Rimer of Index Ventures—an early investor in Patreon and Dropbox, among others—was a former trustee of the San Francisco Museum of Modern Art. Conte remembers walking into his home and finding it packed with sculptures and photography from around the world.

Index led Patreon's $15.3 million Series A in 2014, and Conte soon secured a proper office. The firm was joined by Bay Area investors including Ron Conway's SV Angel as well as the venture arms of Hollywood talent agencies CAA and UTA. While all investors ideally bring more than just cash to the relationship, the latter two names came with a very different sort of Rolodex than the typical venture capital outlet.

"They're constantly looking for ways to help their creators and artists make money," says Conte. "They realized that it's a new day and age, and ad revenue isn't gonna cut it. They have relationships with thousands of amazing creative people, which is important to us. It felt like a good fit. Over the years, we've maintained relationships, looked for ways we can partner, help them with their creators in their roster, and their needs....we're a tech company now, I guess."

Of course, Conte had a Rolodex of his own, and put it to good use recruiting musicians like Amanda Palmer, known for her work as half of cabaret duo the Dresden Dolls. With her solo releases, she'd become one of the earliest examples of how an artist could fully fund projects on Kickstarter—raising $1.2 million for an album—but for her, that was essentially a loss leader en route to her next crowdfunding home, Patreon.

Palmer released her first song on Conte's platform in 2015, an acoustic lament called "Bigger on the Inside," also available for free on YouTube. She set donation levels at $1, $3, $5, $10, $100, and $1,000, with escalating perks. The top two levels included personal communication, so she capped them at thirty and five people, respectively—and they sold out almost instantly. All in all, she raised about $25,000 for the song, and that was just a starting point: by 2016, she was earning over $150,000 per year from 8,500-plus patrons on the site,[8] doubling her audience within three years.

"But it isn't about making money, it's about creating a sustainable environment in which I can grow in a noncommercial way," she says. "I haven't had to sell my soul to corporations. I haven't ever had to compromise the work. That's been the biggest win."[9]

As Patreon grew, Conte found himself grappling with some familiar issues faced by founders across all industries: hiring new employees and firing old ones that don't work out, keeping users happy, and expanding his company without destroying what made it sing to begin with. While he was learning to be an executive, Conte's experience as an artist came in handy.

"That's definitely a skill," he says. "With a creator turned executive, you're gonna get somebody who deeply understands the customer. At least for me, I feel a personal obligation toward creators, people using Patreon, many of them are my friends and peers. I care about them immensely."[10]

As Alba's Honest Company grew, she decided to expand into a category every young family needs: diapers. To go bottom-to-bottom with giants like Procter & Gamble, though, she needed more cash—and turned to Silicon Valley.

Alba found an ally in Lightspeed, which had previously funded Kim Kardashian's subscription fashion service ShoeDazzle alongside

Andreessen Horowitz. Though ShoeDazzle at one point sported a valuation as high as a quarter-billion dollars, it ended up merging with a competitor in a deal that reportedly valued it at just $30 million or so. Part of the reason ShoeDazzle may not have reached its superstar potential: Kardashian seemed to be a celebrity attached to the company, as opposed to being a celebrity who built the company, like Alba.

"Jessica was in the office every day...this was her company," says Lightspeed's Jeremy Liew. "It was her idea, which makes a really big difference...she built the community around something."[11]

Long before becoming Lightspeed's first consumer specialist in 2006, Liew had gotten his start at Citysearch selling websites in the mid-1990s, eventually moving along to Andreesen's Netscape ("after the rock stars left the building," he says). Liew witnessed Silicon Valley moving away from consumer-oriented businesses after the first dot-com crash; when he started out at Lightspeed, ecommerce seemed fairly lonely. Yet a lot had changed in the intervening decade. The cost of starting companies had fallen drastically—by 90 percent or so, according to Liew—and soon-to-be behemoths such as Facebook were beginning to hit their stride, providing channels for famous creators to drive customers to their startups.

"Historically, ecommerce company startups really only get an opportunity to grow when there's a new scalable, repeatable customer acquisition channel," says Liew, referring to social networks where stars like Alba gain immense followings. "There's usually a short window of maybe three to five years...and then over time, it gets priced efficiently."

Liew was eventually joined at Lightspeed by Nicole Quinn, a former retail analyst at Morgan Stanley. They loved what they saw in Alba and the Honest Company, and Lightspeed teamed with two other firms in 2012 to lead a $27 million Series A. By 2015, the company had raised over $100 million and was doing $150 million in revenue, sporting a valuation approaching $1 billion—while making Alba herself a centimillionaire on paper.[12]

Two years later, Quinn and Liew teamed up with a pair of Lightspeed colleagues to appear on Apple TV's first original show, a startup competition called *Planet of the Apps*, headlined by a panel of four A-list judges. Alba brought her Honest Company expertise, while entrepreneur Gary Vaynerchuk lent his experience growing his family's liquor store into a $60 million ecommerce site for wine. Will.i.am of the Black Eyed Peas arrived with insights gleaned as a stakeholder in startups like Beats; actress Gwyneth Paltrow shared tips inspired by building her startup, Goop, from a weekly newsletter to a lifestyle company curating everything from health food to skin cream to pseudoscientific wellness advice.

Contestants on the ten-episode series were given sixty seconds to pitch the merits of the app they'd created. Winners got to pick one of the four judges as a mentor before moving on to bring their ideas to Lightspeed for a chance at funding and a prime spot in the Apple store. The show lasted only one season but spawned a number of valuable business relationships between the judges and contestants, like Lauren Farleigh, founder of virtual mall app Dote. That's especially valuable in the context of Silicon Valley, where the dearth of female founders can result in limited options when it comes to finding mentors who've faced similar challenges.

"They still have meetings, phone calls, and Lauren loves to get the perspective of Gwyneth," says Quinn. "Not just because she's a celebrity, but because she's a founder."[13]

Paltrow got plenty out of the experience, too: after befriending Liew, Quinn, and their colleagues on *Planet of the Apps*, she landed Lightspeed as a lead investor in Goop's $50 million Series C. "It's great to be Gwyneth Paltrow when you're raising money, because people take the meeting, but then you get a lot more rejections than you would if they didn't want to take a selfie," Paltrow said.

"It becomes easier when you have a thriving business and your unit economics looks good."[14]

Quinn attributes the company's initial success to Paltrow's ability to make people feel that a Goop store must be just like her own house—and that they can approximate her way of living by purchasing a few items (the merit of those items, however, is another issue altogether). In any case, startups launched by stars often seem to resonate more with consumers than products pushed under typical endorsement deals, whether executed on television or Instagram.[15]

"No one believes that Tiger Woods did a comprehensive check to decide that Rolex was the best possible watch in the world for golfers, and that's why he's sponsored by Rolex," says Liew. "Gwyneth was developing Goop as an expression of her own interests and tastes in lifestyle for years…it's very clearly hers. The same thing is true with Jessica with the Honest Company."[16]

The way Liew sees it, there's a set of people who are founders and a set of people who are entertainers; in the Venn diagram between the two, there's a thin area of overlap. His experiences with Alba, for example, haven't been much different from his experiences with non-famous founders: they sit in a conference room and review slides. And, like most other entrepreneurs, she has learned by experience. "Unless you've been a founder before, you have to teach them how to be a founder," he says. "That's what circumstances demand."

Within several years of Patreon's start, meanwhile, some of its most promising creators were finding ways to earn tens of thousands of dollars per month on the platform. More patrons meant more money for creators, but also more headaches for Conte.

"When you have automation, the rate at which you have to scale is unreasonable, it's very weird," he says. "You have instant scale, and so, just to keep up with the inbound influx of tickets and customers and payments, you have to add employees at a rate that's unprecedented."[17]

As Patreon became mainstream, the company also started to appear on the radar of malicious types. In the fall of 2015, employees discovered hackers had gained access to scores of users' names, emails, and mailing addresses. The episode shook Conte's community and resulted in additional expenses for his company, including the hiring of a security firm to conduct an audit and implement "new tools and practices to ensure industry-leading security."[18]

In addition to security threats, Patreon faced challenges from well-funded competitors, including Kickstarter, which launched a new feature called Drip—allowing creators to receive ongoing funding in a manner similar to Patreon—in 2015. That same year, Conte's company acquired Subbable, a Patreonesque video subscription service launched by YouTube stars. Terms of the deal weren't disclosed, but Subbable added some 40,000 subscribers to Patreon's total of roughly a quarter million at the time.

To fund all these endeavors, Patreon turned to its Silicon Valley backers again and again. The company raised some $30 million in a 2016 Series B round and double that in a Series C the following year, putting its total north of $100 million and reportedly valuing the company in the neighborhood of $450 million.[19] Expansion yielded more tough decisions for Conte, and he admittedly didn't always make the right ones.

In the first week of December 2017, for instance, Patreon changed its fee structure. While holding its own piece of the pie steady at 5 percent, the company shifted additional transaction fees from a sliding 2–10 percent to a fixed 2.9 percent plus a flat $0.35 fee. The goal was to streamline the Patreon process and make payments more predictable, but the decision resulted in a community uproar, particularly for creators dependent on $1–$2 donations. Within a week, Conte reversed his decision and apologized to users, promising to come up with a better alternative.[20]

"I still think of Jack as my artist friend who decided to become a CEO," says Palmer. "I love that he is taking it for the team and steering this ship, but I also know that a successful business can be a different sort of reward than a successful artwork, and I understand that dilemma more than anyone. So I call him and hug him occasionally. And thank him for what he's made possible in all of our lives."[21]

Conte seems to have grown more comfortable with the business side of his role. Shortly after the Series C, for example, one team wanted to work on building a way to more efficiently sort through new creator signups to Patreon; the most promising ones would be flagged and linked with a team that could help them boost their content releases. Conte didn't feel this would really be helpful but challenged the team to prove him wrong—"disagree and commit," as he describes it.[22]

"Sure enough, they were able to sift through inbound signups and collaborate with the sales team and the creator team to help identify really awesome creators that were gonna launch on the platform, and then potentially help their launches be even better," says Conte. "They finished the quarter exceeding their goals...you just have to trust people around you who've done things like this before."

By 2018, some of Patreon's top creators were pulling in more than $100,000, not per year but per month. Among them: the snarky commentators of *Chapo Trap House*, news junkie Phil DeFranco, and online entertainment outfits Kinda Funny and Complexly. The following year, the company announced a $60 million Series D, with funding coming mostly from its usual cast of Silicon Valley investors. For the first time, the group also contained creators—including comedian Hannibal Buress and musician Serj Tankian, known best for fronting rock band System of a Down.

Conte doesn't claim to be anything close to perfect as an executive; in fact, he seems more willing than most to admit past mistakes and potential challenges coming down the line. What rankles him more than the notion of being wrong is the idea that any bad decision he makes is the result of investor pressure, as some suggested when he made the fee structure switch. Conte claims his investors actually hold *him* back from making controversial business-first decisions. He says that at one point he suggested bringing in brands to become patrons of individual creators, but a prominent venture capitalist told him to slow down. "Patreon's so cool right now," he said. "Don't ruin it."

According to Conte, his backers are not setting financial targets for Patreon; rather, the company's numerical goals are set by him and his team. He sees financial success—and the ability to control his company's destiny—as inextricable from Patreon's ability to help creators get paid, since a different sort of corporate structure could yield a less palatable platform for them.

"I don't want to sell Patreon to YouTube," he says. "I don't want to get into a position where the company has to exit because we're running out of cash, or whatever. So I care very deeply about Patreon being on a healthy trajectory toward independence. For me, that means an IPO down the road, or whatever it is, but a way for Patreon to stay an independent company."

Even while running the show at Patreon, Conte still finds time to create. He cranks out about 100 music videos per year, split evenly between Pomplamoose and Scary Pockets, the funk band he started in 2017. Once a month, he spends a weekend in Los Angeles to make music like a particularly catchy cover of Radiohead's "Creep"—Scary Pockets now has more than 400,000 YouTube subscribers as well.[23]

"That would not work without Nataly essentially being the CEO of Pomplamoose and my buddy Ryan basically running Scary Pockets," he says. "That allows me to basically be a creator with weekly releases, publishing content frequently, but still be at Patreon."[24]

Constant vigilance is crucial, as Conte learned in the wake of Patreon's hack and the blowback over its fee structure. Other entertainer-owners have gone through even more daunting controversies: legal action over the Honest Company's labeling led to class action settlements[25] as well as a reformulation of its laundry detergent and a voluntary recall of its baby wipes and powder; along the way, the outfit replaced cofounder Brian Lee as CEO and reportedly lost its unicorn status in 2018.[26] That same year, Goop settled a false advertising suit with the California Food, Drug, and Medical Device Task Force for $145,000[27] after the agency argued that the company had made deceptive claims about fifty-one of its products.[28]

Patreon, Goop, and the Honest Company are vastly different companies sporting healthy valuations, but they face the same dilemma as many well-funded startups shifting from youthful promise to awkward adolescence: too big for a centimillion-dollar buyout to serve as anything other than a letdown to investors, they must either become sustainably profitable as private companies or get big enough to go public.

In Silicon Valley, the founders of a company that raises $100 million and sells for $200 million could conceivably walk away with nothing if their investors have negotiated a favorable liquidation preference. The idea of raising too much money—and the expectations that go along with it—is a lesson many entrepreneurs learn only by doing. That's assuming they can even make it to the point of an exit.

"Whether you're an artist or whether you're building a company, nothing works, everything's on fire, you get hacked, it's just fucking so hard," says Conte. "I think a lot of people experience that, and maybe think, 'I guess I'm not doing this right, I guess I should just give up. The universe is giving me signs, maybe I'll just do something that's easier.'...You just have to muster it up and just keep going."[29]

The soundtrack coming from Patreon's speaker system as we wrap our interview—Journey's "Don't Stop Believin'" and Chumbawamba's "Tubthumping" ("I get knocked down, but I get up again")—underscores that notion. And, in the end, Conte's tribulations as chief of a tech platform haven't changed his fundamental belief in the merits of his mission, as he makes clear with a final analogy.

"The museum is there to serve the paintings, to be a frame for the paintings," he says. "I feel the same about Patreon and YouTube and all these other distribution platforms. In the end, distribution platforms come and go, new technologies come and go, but art is often hanging in there for thousands and thousands of years, the same art. And art in general will always be the focus of those things."

CHAPTER 9

Stocks for Jocks

Tony Gonzalez is a man who loves cheeseburgers. Smothered in cheddar and topped with bacon, these were the staples of his diet as he pounded protein, built muscle mass, and became a fourteen-time Pro Bowl tight end in the NFL.[1] So it may come as a surprise to learn that, shortly after his retirement, he plowed his money into the plant-based protein startup Beyond Meat—alongside Bill Gates, the Humane Society, and several Silicon Valley venture firms, as well as fellow athletes Shaquille O'Neal, DeAndre Hopkins, and Kyrie Irving.

"Beyond Meat, that's something I can be a spokesperson for because I've done what I've done, and what I do off the field," he tells me in a telephone interview. "So I bring that celebrity to the table, and I can be someone that you get some extra space [for in a round]."[2]

For Gonzalez, it was all part of a broad shift in appetites—both for food and investment prospects—that began toward the end of his playing days. Gonzalez started experimenting with the notion of eating less meat after reading a book called *The China Study*, which advocated adding more fruits, nuts, and grains to one's diet, in place of animals.[3]

At the same time, Gonzalez knew he would have to stop plowing his money into questionable side projects in order to make the money earned in his twenties and early thirties last the rest of his life. One such investment: his window washing company, Xtreme Clean 88, which was shattered by unqualified partners. A supplement outfit, All Pro Science, seemed more promising, especially when its products made it onto the shelves of Whole Foods. Gonzalez finally felt like he'd become a proper businessman.

"I had a briefcase—I was looking sweet!" he says. "I had an office and I'd go there and I was hiring and firing and reviewing supplements. I was writing up reviews and stuff. I threw myself into it full speed."[4]

But Gonzalez's business crumbled when Scilabs, the company that manufactured All Pro's goods, got hit with an injunction over allegedly adulterated products.[5] He says the episode ended up costing him over $1 million, and though that wasn't a life-altering loss for a man who made north of $70 million in his playing career, it caused him to ruminate more deeply on why athletes had such an appetite for risky outside investments.

"To play pro sports, I mean, the odds of us making it were so slim," says Gonzalez. "And we did it. So I think we just have that mentality, like we can be there. And that's why a lot of guys go broke...because we have the audacity to think that we can...defy the odds."

It wasn't until Gonzalez put in the same sort of punishing practice responsible for his NFL triumphs that he finally found success in the investing field. And he was one of many A-list athletes who charged through the doors Shaq and others had helped to open.

Cristiano Ronaldo boasts nearly half a billion followers across Instagram, Facebook, and Twitter—among them: fans of Manchester United in the UK, where he started his soccer career; loyalists to Spain's Real Madrid, his home during the prime of his run; and backers of his next team, the Italian squad Juventus—but his first online supporter was a bearded, baseball-obsessed Yale grad on the other side of the Atlantic.

"I physically created his Twitter account and his Facebook account," says Michael Blank, now the thirtysomething head of mobile at CAA. "I like to tell people I'm his number one fan."[6]

Back in 2010, Blank was working for a company that represented Ronaldo. Blank's task: to build up the soccer star's following ahead of the World Cup that year. That meant reclaiming social handles others had been squatting on, starting accounts for Ronaldo, and building a direct line to his fans. As Blank pushed forward, he decided to move over to a position at CAA where he could help other athletes and entertainers monetize these new channels, joining Funny Or Die dealmaker Michael Yanover in business development.

Apple's App Store was in its infancy at the time, and its sports offerings didn't yet measure up to the elaborate console games headlined by stars from Ken Griffey Jr. (*Slugfest*) to Mike Tyson (*Punch-Out!!*) years earlier. CAA had a chance to attach some of its clients to apps and really make them pop. And Blank, a lifelong baseball fan, dove in headfirst with star catcher Buster Posey. Players who attached their names to such apps in the early 2010s did so in exchange for backend payouts rather than the up-front fees for games of old. To create what would soon be known as *Buster Bash*, CAA teamed up with a developer known only by his first name, Jeff ("and that's it, period, full stop," says Blank). Jeff operated out of a coworking space in Santa Monica.

Much like Funny Or Die, they had effectively no budget. When they wanted to add a comic strip–style intro to the game—opening up a toy chest, taking out a baseball glove, going to a backyard—the only artist they could afford was one in South Africa who insisted on working off of stick figure mock-ups, which Blank ended up having to draw himself. When he wasn't busy working as an amateur artist, Blank would drive to Santa Monica with bags of junk food to keep Jeff fueled up.

The game went live in 2012, around Major League Baseball's All-Star break. Posey was in the midst of his best season as a pro for the San Francisco Giants. His technologically inclined home-town crowd picked up *Buster Bash* quickly—and the star catcher found a way to generate plenty of free publicity. "We launched the game and then, over the next five days, he had four home runs or something," says Blank. Every time Posey launched another one, he adds, "all the newspapers started using the term 'Buster Bash.'"[7]

Posey wasn't the only one of CAA's athletes to find success off the field. After the Scilabs fiasco, Gonzalez decided to play it safe, sticking to the annual single-digit-percentage returns offered through stocks and bonds—until his agent at CAA reached out to him about a company called FitStar. Just as the rise of the VHS player brought about the wildly popular workout videos of the 1990s, FitStar aimed to revolutionize the industry two decades later by creating adaptive fitness apps that could be used on any screen.

At the time, its founding team, led by AOL alum Mike Maser, had little more than an idea and a PowerPoint presentation. The group couldn't afford to pay for a proper endorsement deal, but offered a profit share to lure Gonzalez. Though he was playing his last year in the NFL, it was a well-publicized victory lap that resulted in even more press than he might have otherwise received; he also seemed set for a broadcasting role that would keep his face familiar even after retirement.

The arrangement with FitStar appealed to Gonzalez at first because he wouldn't have to put in any of his own money. He joined the company's board of directors; soon, he was giving feedback on products and even recording training videos on the platform. As he grew increasingly impressed with Maser, Gonzalez had a change of heart when it came to the proceeds of his profit share.

"I became closer to Mike, and I saw how he ran the company and how well he was doing. I was like, 'Well, Mike, you don't have to pay me anything,'" says Gonzalez. "'I'd like to put that all back into the company.'"[8]

Gonzalez chose wisely. In 2015, Fitbit—the San Francisco–based wearable fitness giant—bought FitStar for double-digit millions, with much of the total coming in the form of Fitbit stock. CAA cashed in again, and Gonzalez did quite well, too. Though he won't reveal his precise number, he confirms it's more than he made in the first five years of his playing career, signaling a healthy seven-figure haul.

"Like anything else, you suck at it—at least I did—when you first start doing it," he says of picking startups. "It takes a little while to figure it out, but once you figure it out, you try to stick to that formula."

With less than a minute left in the 1981 National Football Conference championship game, the odds weren't looking good for Joe Montana's San Francisco 49ers. They trailed the fearsome Dallas Cowboys by six points as the quarterback rolled to his right, chased by a squadron of defenders, including the six-foot, nine-inch Ed "Too Tall" Jones. But Montana kept his cool, losing Jones with a pump fake before lofting a spiral into the gray sky toward the deepest part of the end zone—where the football landed in the outstretched hands of tight end Dwight Clark to put the Niners ahead for good.

Thanks to that singular play, now known to football fans simply as "The Catch," San Francisco went on to win the Super Bowl,

Montana's first step toward a perfect four-for-four record in the NFL's biggest game. He won three Super Bowl MVPs and didn't throw a single interception in 122 pass attempts along the way. And yet Montana counts his subsequent 1986 return from injury as perhaps his most worthy achievement under pressure on the field. Just fifty-six days after surgery to repair a ruptured disc in his back, he faced off against linemen twice his size and threw for 270 yards and three touchdowns, leading the 49ers to a 43–17 victory over the Cardinals.[9]

"I just didn't know how I was going to hold up," says Montana, who continued to play through 1994. "I had lost a lot of weight so I was 187 pounds, which was really, really thin for me."[10]

Several years after announcing his retirement, Montana entered the venture capital world. The Hall of Famer now divides his career decision-making into two arenas: the football field and the investing field. He says his best clutch performance in the latter realm came at an event with startup guru Ron Conway, an old friend from the San Francisco philanthropic circuit, several years ago.

"Go in another room…don't leave, I'll be right in," Conway told Montana before disappearing. He returned a few minutes later with what could have been construed as a tip, a challenge, or a direct order: "You're going to write the biggest check you've ever written personally."

"Oh, no," Montana remembers saying—before taking the plunge. "It was the biggest pressure moment and it was the biggest check I've ever written. I won't tell you the check [size], but it was big. It was Pinterest."

Montana secured his piece of the digital inspiration board around the same time as its spring 2011 Series A, which valued the company at $40 million. By the end of the year, A-Grade and Andreessen Horowitz had piled in, pushing Pinterest's valuation into nine-figure territory (the company subsequently reached deca-corn status and had its IPO in April 2019).

For Montana, Pinterest represented one of the best investment opportunities in a career filled with them.

Back in Montana's playing days, his fellow 49ers would trade stock picks and real estate ideas. Some enterprising athletes took advantage of their proximity to Silicon Valley power brokers, especially after retirement. Two of Montana's former San Francisco teammates—defensive back Ronnie Lott and offensive lineman Harris Barton—started a fund of funds (essentially a mutual fund for the ultrawealthy, with a portfolio consisting of funds operated by other exclusive firms). Launched in 1999, Champion Ventures initially raised $40 million to plow directly into the investment pools of firms like Sequoia and Greylock. Montana joined Barton and Lott in 2003; the company changed its name to HRJ in a nod to the football trio's first names.

When Montana checked out of HRJ in 2005 to spend more time with his sons Nate and Nick, who were launching their own quarterback careers in high school and college, Joe's partners didn't do quite as well without him as the 49ers (his replacement, Steve Young, led the team to a Super Bowl win in 1995). Though Barton and Lott had $2.4 billion under management by 2008—with a list of clients ranging from baseball legend Barry Bonds to the Houston Firefighters' Relief and Retirement Fund—the firm had taken a risky, unorthodox approach. Most funds of funds raise money from investors before placing it with firms, but HRJ made its allocations before collecting cash. When the credit markets dried up during the financial crisis, HRJ couldn't cover its commitments, and appeared to be plummeting toward insolvency until a Swiss firm bought its assets in 2009.[11]

Montana's sons, meanwhile, didn't end up following their father to NFL stardom. As Nate investigated other career options, Joe started taking him to Y Combinator events with Conway. There, they'd meet startup founders, and both Montanas would take notes on Conway's approach with entrepreneurs. Nate eventually caught on as an early employee at social media monitoring startup Niche; in 2015, Twitter bought the company for double-digit millions.

Around the same time, Conway suggested Joe start a fund of his own. A friend of a friend introduced him to Michael Ma, then a twentysomething Yale grad who in 2011 had sold TalkBin, his local business review startup, to Google. They added a third founder, Mike Miller, a Y Combinator alum whose data startup Cloudant was purchased by IBM in 2014 (Nate Montana joined after spending a little over a year at Twitter).

"Joe appreciated how honest I was," says Ma. "I remember a lot of that initial conversation being like, even, 'Hey, maybe it isn't good to do this.' He can make a lot of money just managing very little money by himself. [But] we're trying something slightly different."[12]

Montana, Ma, and Miller started their early-stage fund with something of a trial run in 2015, working together without pay to see if they liked the dynamic. They quickly realized they'd found a winning combination: Ma and Miller brought their entrepreneurial savvy and Y Combinator connections, while Montana contributed a feel for business with an unmatched Rolodex. So they launched their own firm, Liquid 2 Ventures, a wry nod to the decidedly illiquid nature of their investments.[13]

Throughout his career, Montana would get invited into promising investments by prominent Bay Area acquaintances. Sequoia billionaire Doug Leone, for example, was one of several Silicon Valley bigwigs who coached Montana's kids in Little League ("Those are the kind of relationships that you had to have," says the quarterback. "Better investors than coaches, for sure, but they were entertaining to watch.") In one instance, billionaire investor John Doerr of Kleiner Perkins walked into Montana's office, interrupting him in the middle of a meeting to tell him about a hot startup investment. "You guys want in?" he asked. "I have an event coming up right here—show up and you're in."[14]

The Liquid 2 founders realized that they had plenty of company in the seed world—some 200 funds launched in 2016 alone—but with Montana, they had the advantage of someone who could add value far beyond the money he invested. No matter how crowded a startup's round happened to be, it always seemed there was room for an NFL Hall of Famer.

Founders loved how easily he could make introductions for them. In one case, a portfolio company called TrueFacet, an online jewelry marketplace, needed a link to someone at American Express; Montana, who had just given a talk at the company's office, made it happen. In another, sports-focused social media startup GameOn wanted an intro to Snoop Dogg—no problem: Montana knew him from football camps their sons attended—and the rapper became an investor.

"Whenever I talk to founders," says Ma, "I'm always like, 'Look, you never know when you might need the additional brand [boost] that sort of celebrity or sports figure can bring.'"[15]

In just a few years, Montana's Liquid 2 has already scored some touchdowns of its own. One portfolio company called Geometric Intelligence got acquired by Uber in 2016; two others, software developer tool GitLab and food delivery startup Rappi, are now unicorns. By 2017, Liquid 2 was among America's ten most active seed funds, Ma figures.

As for Montana, when all the numbers are tallied, does he think venture capital is more lucrative than pro sports? "Well, if I was playing today, maybe not," he says. "Back when I was playing, absolutely."[16]

In autumn of 2013, entrepreneur Jamie Siminoff found himself in a rather unusual situation: pitching his virtual doorbell company to Ashton Kutcher inside a converted shipping container that served as the actor's office on the Burbank set of *Two and a Half Men*.

A-Grade's Abe Burns had arranged the meeting with Siminoff, joining him in the metal box with Kutcher and a surprise guest. "Dude, this is Mila," said Kutcher, introducing his famous wife. Siminoff, desperate for investment and already nervous, could barely muster a response. Yet Kutcher seemed intrigued, inquiring about different features Siminoff could build in the future and asking why he hadn't created them already. In the end, though, he decided to pass.

"I think he was close on this," says Siminoff, a trim forty-something who bears a passing resemblance to Bradley Cooper, over lunch in Santa Monica. "He was fascinated by it, and at the same time, the hardware stuff scared him. We were still very early and had a lot ahead of us."[17]

A lifelong tinkerer, Siminoff had started out in his New Jersey childhood basement by actually trying to build a better mousetrap— in particular, a more humane one. He attempted to make boxes with netted doors and contraptions with four walls that lock into place simultaneously, all to no avail.[18] During college at Babson, he decided the term "entrepreneur" encompassed what he wanted to do. He tried his hand at businesses from telecom to email security but never found a niche.[19]

By 2012, Siminoff had committed to being a full-time inventor, hunkering down in his Southern California garage to plow through his running list of things that didn't exist yet but should. One minor issue: Siminoff couldn't hear his own doorbell. So he rigged up "a contraption with a bunch of crap and strapped [it] to the front door"—he'd receive an alert via smartphone with a live video feed of his stoop whenever someone rang. He called it the Doorbot.[20]

Soon he'd abandoned the garage in favor of a proper office and started hiring people to help him bring the Doorbot to market. One day while Siminoff was settling into his cramped new digs, a colleague informed him that someone was waiting for him outside in a two-door Bentley. It turned out to be Anthony Saleh, Nas's manager, whom he'd met at a conference a few weeks earlier. Siminoff invited Saleh inside, showing him the product and the team behind Doorbot. Saleh didn't need much convincing: "Love it. Love the energy. Let's do it."

Nas also committed "a pretty big check" at around the same time, according to Siminoff, who couldn't have been more elated—and not just because he'd secured a famous backer. "I grew up listening to his music," says Siminoff of Nas. "But I needed money. So as cool as it was, I would have been just as happy if anyone was investing."

Siminoff soon caught the attention of several other well-known angels. A friend of a friend heard that a fresh batch of entrepreneurs was needed on *Shark Tank*, the reality show in which contestants compete for a check from legendary "sharks" including billionaire Mark Cuban, FUBU founder Daymond John, real estate maven Barbara Corcoran, and notoriously cranky software entrepreneur Kevin "Mr. Wonderful" O'Leary. Just as *The Voice* isn't necessarily indicative of the record-making process, *Shark Tank* doesn't exactly represent a typical startup experience.

"*Shark Tank* has as much to do with angel investing as Indiana Jones has to do with archaeology," says veteran angel investor David S. Rose. "It is written much larger in the popular consciousness and in the press than it is in the real world."[21] Yet the program offers the sort of exposure that can jump-start an incredible run—and took angel investing mainstream. "What *Shark Tank* did, I think, is opened up this dialogue," says Troy Carter, who served as a guest shark in 2015. "You look at that panel and you look at some of the people who come in and pitch, you feel like you can do it and be part of that."[22]

Siminoff cold-emailed one of the show's producers, who invited him to apply; he was accepted shortly thereafter. In mid-2013, he went to work building a set for his upcoming taping, spending $15,000 to build a miniature house in his backyard, convinced that Cuban would be the one to offer him a life-altering investment. Siminoff instead got his only offer from Mr. Wonderful, who dangled a $700,000 loan in exchange for 10 percent of sales until it was paid off, plus 5 percent of the company's equity and a 7 percent royalty on future sales. Siminoff turned down the deal; sure, there was cash on the table, but it would've had to get paid back eventually. "It was bullshit," he says. "It wasn't a real offer. I mean, it was crazy."[23]

Siminoff sat back and waited for the episode to air. And waited. As his company's resources dwindled, he began to worry the segment would never air, removing his last best hope at massive exposure. Finally, in November 2013, he got his fifteen minutes of fame—twelve, to be more precise—on national television. Almost immediately, he felt the impact on his company. His chipmaker offered him better terms; previously unreachable engineers who worked for his video supplier suddenly couldn't wait to help.

Shark Tank gave Siminoff credibility when he went to pitch his product at Best Buy, helping him stand out in a crowded holiday gift field. The first month after the appearance, Doorbot did $1 million in revenue, selling out of the product within a year. Even after Siminoff changed the name to Ring—a moniker that suggested an all-encompassing approach to home security—the halo effect remained; he figures *Shark Tank* has been responsible for $5–$10 million in sales for his company over the years.

"That show, more than anything else, in a mainstream way, has shown people how business is spoken about," says Siminoff. "How you can raise money, how you can have a dream and actually work it into something…that's inspiring to people that are not surrounded by those stories of success."

One person who happened to be inspired was Shaquille O'Neal. Despite the fact that he'd trained as a reserve law enforcement officer, Shaq still wanted to know who was at his door, and had gotten a Ring of his own. So when Siminoff told a friend at WME that he was in the market for a gripping commercial and word got back to Shaq, the latter's team reached out to the Ring founder in hopes of meeting up at the Consumer Electronics Show in Las Vegas. The tech confab, better known as CES, attracts some 200,000 attendees every winter. "We always go," Shaq explains. "Word gets around that Shaq will help with a startup."[24]

Siminoff assumed the superstar would want to talk in a private room—until he saw Shaq ambling over to Ring's booth. "He was as excited to meet me and the team as I was to meet him," says Siminoff. They started talking about filming a commercial; Shaq was so impressed with Ring that, like Gonzalez with FitStar, he decided to invest his fee back into the company, and then some.[25] He ultimately poured a "substantial amount" into Ring, according to Siminoff, who says Shaq wanted to throw down even more, but there wasn't enough room in the round.[26]

Shaq brought his impeccable comedic timing to a series of commercials he recorded with Siminoff, in one instance playing a game of Hide and Go Shaq in an unsuccessful mock effort to evade the Ring's reach. The big man's contacts proved even more valuable to the startup than his fame as Siminoff sought local subsidies to deploy Ring as a crime-stopping tool (the company touted one pilot program in Los Angeles that slashed burglaries by "as much as 55%," though that number was questioned in a report by the *MIT Technology Review*).[27]

In any case, police departments gravitated toward the technology, especially once Shaq alerted them to it—and he boasted an enviable contact list from his days in law enforcement. So if Siminoff happened to be talking to Shaq about an initiative in the Miami area, for example, his biggest investor would hand him the phone moments later—and the city's chief of police would be on the line.[28]

"We made more impact...with Shaq working with police, and actually having him introduce us to chiefs and help us, than all of the marketing combined," says Siminoff, now a regular speaker with Shaq at security conferences. "It's a unicorn of a Rolodex...he didn't get it because he was famous. He got it because he was respected by doing this over the course of his life of supporting the police."

Siminoff didn't need a video doorbell to see that Ring had developed an even more high-profile admirer: Amazon, which started investing in Ring after turning its attention to Alexa and the connected home in late 2013. Ring worked with Amazon on a number of products, bringing the two companies ever closer. Though Siminoff wasn't really looking to sell, he changed his mind when Amazon offered more than $1 billion for Ring.

The deal closed in 2018, guaranteeing Siminoff would never have to spend another second tinkering in his garage unless he wanted to. Though details of the payouts for Shaq and Nas were never released (neither star would comment on the total, nor would Siminoff), the celebrities clocked an estimated eight-figure haul from the Ring deal. Amazon's purchase served as further evidence that athletes' startup investment successes could give them earning power on par with their on-field peak. "Especially the Ring one," says Shaq.[29]

To Siminoff, it makes a great deal of sense that sports stars have been able to find a home in the startup world. Like Gonzalez, he points out that athletes face long odds to excel on the professional stage, just as top entrepreneurs need to overcome similarly sized hordes of competitors to reach the heights of their field. And, in the end, his Amazon jackpot served as a potent rebuttal to skeptics of celebrity investing, or Hollywood-style branding in general.

"A couple years ago, there were big leaders in Silicon Valley saying, 'A real company never markets...a real company only relies on its product,' and I think it was just wrong," says Siminoff. "It's kind of going away now because there's so much success."[30]

In addition to bringing their star power to an array of startups, Shaq and Tony Gonzalez—the latter traces his heritage to Argentina by way of Portugal—also helped shift the demographics of Silicon Valley's traditionally old white male investor base.[31]

So have a growing number of other athletes. LeBron James has turned small stakes into eight-figure holdings in Beats headphones and Blaze Pizza. Alex Rodriguez landed as a guest judge on *Shark Tank* while racking up pieces of messaging juggernaut Snapchat and Chinese ride-hailing app Didi Chuxing. Tennis superstar Serena Williams built a portfolio with dozens of startups, including cryptocurrency unicorn Coinbase, and cashed in on SurveyMonkey's IPO in 2018. "I want to be a part of it," she explained to *Forbes* the following year, after launching her own fund, Serena Ventures. "I want to be in the infrastructure."[32]

As for Gonzalez, the rewards continue to roll in. Following his score with FitStar, he regained his willingness to put hard cash into startups, but only for companies that seem to be slam dunks and boast a heady list of fellow backers. Gonzalez joined NBA legends Kobe Bryant and Chris Paul as an investor in sports medicine outfit Fusionetics and, critically, made his Beyond Meat outlay.

He appears to have gotten into the plant-based protein company at a valuation of about $500 million and saw his initial investment more than double within a year; the company went public in mid-2019, with a market capitalization of $1.5 billion, before tripling by the end of the year. So, in just a few years, Gonzalez's investment grew by several times—all while he worked toward a goal that aligns with his personal values.

"The way I look at it, I'm getting involved with stuff that I know is helping to make the world a better place, as corny as it sounds," says Gonzalez. "I'm not going to invest in shit that I'm not into."[33]

Even as Gonzalez's portfolio took off, however, other highfliers along the Silicon Valley–Hollywood route were heading for a crash—and not just financially.

CHAPTER 10

Icarus, Inc.

B ack in the late 1980s, when Heidi Roizen was the CEO of software manufacturer T/Maker—before she joined Apple, then Softbank, then venture firm Draper Fisher Jurvetson—she found herself observing an awkward encounter in Las Vegas.

Long before Shaq ever set foot at CES, Sin City's tech conferences came to be infamous for their "booth babes," which Roizen describes to me over the phone as "really attractive women wearing really skimpy costumes whose job was nothing more than to stand in a booth and make men want to come talk to them when they don't really have any purpose at a technology trade show." At one particular event, Macworld, Roizen's company had sent a delegation of employees to staff its booth. All of them happened to be women, which piqued the interest of one particular male attendee.

"Yeah, I wanted to come see your demo, 'cause I hear this is the booth with all the booth babes," the man said to one of Roizen's colleagues, whom she describes as "a rather militant feminist [who] happened to be extremely attractive." The result? "She bit his

155

head off," Roizen recalls. "The perception was we had hired these women to be in the booth, but the truth was, these were our actual employees, these were not hired 'booth babes.'"[1]

Unfortunately, attitudes didn't change all that much in the decades that followed, and female representation in the tech world actually declined. Women now hold about a quarter of all computing jobs in the United States, down from more than a third in 1991. For black women, the number is only 3 percent; for Latinas, it's just 1 percent. Less than 10 percent of partners at top venture firms are female, so perhaps it's not so surprising that companies led by women receive a mere 2 percent of venture capital funding.[2]

To be sure, the new millennium has seen a number of high-powered women in tech: Sheryl Sandberg joined Facebook in 2008 as chief operating officer and became a billionaire while the social network's sales increased by a multiple of nearly 100 on her watch; as chief of YouTube, Susan Wojcicki grew the video giant's revenues by billions. And yet both have endured more than their share of adversity due to their gender.[3]

"I've had my abilities and my commitment to my job questioned," noted Wojcicki, in an open letter published by *Fortune*. "I've been left out of key industry events and social gatherings. I've had meetings with external leaders where they primarily addressed the more junior male colleagues. I've had my comments frequently interrupted and my ideas ignored until they were rephrased by men. No matter how often this all happened, it still hurt."

For some women, including Roizen, everything from underrepresentation to subtle forms of undermining to outright sexual harassment long seemed like a part of the Silicon Valley reality that wasn't likely to change. There were also gray areas she and her cohort navigated earlier in their careers, places where the tech world felt a lot like Hollywood.

"A lot of your personal life, and therefore your personal relations, happen at work, because you're just working 24/7 and those are the people that you're working with—probably not that different from costars having affairs," she says, noting that she no longer has to deal with the same unwanted advances she did early in her career due to her position and reputation. "My cohorts who are twenty years younger, I think it's a different world."[4]

On Valentine's Day in 2013, the on-and-off relationship between Hollywood and Silicon Valley appeared to be in full swing, if the launch party for BlackJet—billed as the "Uber for private jets"—was any indication. The company's backers ranged from Ashton Kutcher and Jay-Z to San Francisco billionaire Marc Benioff and Uber cofounder Garrett Camp (the latter also came on as cofounder of the jet-sharing app).[5]

BlackJet took over San Francisco's Union Square for the day in celebration of new routes to the Bay Area and Las Vegas, drawing a crowd of revelers who queued up on a red carpet as the festivities began. It seemed little had changed since the days of the booth babes: the startup's scantily clad "Sky Angels" posed for photos with anyone willing to wear a BlackJet hat, while some guests were given leis (the company had no Hawaii routes). The first 1,000 guests received a free membership to BlackJet; everyone else, presumably, would have to shell out $2,500 in annual dues for the convenience of using a smartphone to buy a $1,500 pair of seats on a plane, shared with perhaps a dozen fellow passengers, from San Francisco to Las Vegas—and more for longer routes—on demand.[6]

"A charter flight where you book a whole airplane is currently done in a very analog way," said BlackJet CEO Dean Rotchin. "Now you can instantly book just like you can order a cab through Uber."[7]

Perhaps the most notable guest, however, was Shervin Pishevar, who'd just been named BlackJet's chairman. Just as he had with Uber, the venture capitalist played a key role in amassing a cast of backers from both Hollywood and Silicon Valley. Besides Kutcher, Nas's QueensBridge Venture Partners invested. So did a host of familiar faces, including Ron Conway's SV Angel and Will Smith's Overbrook Entertainment.

According to Crunchbase, the group included more than thirty investors in all, a rather large number for a round of $2.1 million. Pishevar himself invested $100,000.[8] Yet many of the usual suspects seemed divided over the idea of a company bringing ridesharing to the skies. "The market wasn't as big as the market Uber was going after, and the unit economics didn't make sense to me," says Troy Carter. "Lack of frequency and limited customer base."[9]

Another wrinkle: the Union Square party was more of a re-branding exercise than a startup launch. SEC documents filed in 2012 reveal that the company was actually incorporated as Green Jets Inc in Delaware—back in 2008. The outfit declined to disclose revenues at the time but was clearly counting on an influx of famous backers to raise its profile with the jet set, banking on an accompanying spike in sales.[10]

The San Francisco–Las Vegas route was among the cheapest of a steep bunch, yet there was an economic argument to be made for the wealthy traveler for whom time is money. A cross-country BlackJet flight would cost $3,500 each way, about the same price as a first-class ticket from JFK to LAX; a private charter would cost many times that sum. Still, that wasn't enough to win over all the skeptics in BlackJet's own industry.

"So many people who have tried to create models to share seats have failed because it's very hard to get people wealthy enough to hire a private jet to share a flight," said Ken Starnes, chief of jet chartering service PrivateJet.com, at the time of BlackJet's launch. "Their egos are as big as office buildings."[11]

The same might have been said of its investors who ignored the likes of Starnes and Carter. Yet plenty seemed willing to leap into an increasingly overheated market.

"A million dollars isn't cool. You know what's cool?" asked Justin Timberlake, in his role as venture capitalist Sean Parker, in the 2010 film *The Social Network*. "A billion dollars."

He was speaking to the actors playing Facebook cofounders Mark Zuckerberg and Eduardo Saverin; the three men dominated the scene, set over a meal at an Asian restaurant, while largely ignoring the mostly silent fourth character in the scene, Brenda Song, playing Saverin's girlfriend. *The Social Network* drew its fair share of praise from movie reviewers, but some seized upon its minimization and objectification of women. Aaron Sorkin, who wrote the film, claimed it merely reflected the misogyny of Silicon Valley.[12]

Indeed, life and art were becoming indistinguishable in the newly combined worlds of venture capital and entertainment. The 2011 final season of *Entourage* included a plotline where Adrian Grenier's main character, based on Mark Wahlberg, invests in a tequila company; that same year, Wahlberg poured money into alkaline water brand Aquahydrate. Many of the actors playing the main characters in *Silicon Valley*, a comedy about startup founders, started investing in real startups as well.

Timberlake himself dove into startups, with mixed results. He participated in a $35 million buyout of News Corp's Myspace, where he became the public face of the company's effort to reconstitute itself as a music destination (before the site changed hands yet again). In 2012, he joined a handful of other stars as celebrity ambassadors at ecommerce outfit BeachMint, peddling furniture through an online-only product line called HomeMint. Timberlake explained in a press release that the move was inspired by his "love of architecture and interior design."[13] Few people bought that—or the company's wares—and by 2013, BeachMint had flopped, folding into an odd merger with *Lucky* magazine the following year. Myspace, meanwhile, ended up as a footnote in the 2016 sale of its parent company to Time Inc.[14]

Eventually, Timberlake found a winner in Bai Brands, purveyor of antioxidant infusion drinks, with the help of Rohan Oza, hoping to bottle the same sort of magic he'd found with 50 Cent on Vitaminwater.[15] Timberlake invested in 2016, and later that year, Dr Pepper announced plans to buy the company for $1.7 billion.[16]

What exactly Timberlake did for Bai before the buyout remained nebulous; his subsequent appointment to the ambiguous post of "chief flavor officer" didn't clarify things. Timberlake did give the brand a very public boost in the wake of the deal, appearing in a Super Bowl ad alongside Christopher Walken and tweeting it out to his 65 million Twitter followers. In the spot, the pair sits in front of a crackling fire in a wood-paneled living room as Walken recites the lyrics to "Bye Bye Bye," one of the most popular songs from Timberlake's days in the boy band 'NSync.

Though it proved to be a lucrative investment, Bai may have left a sour taste in Timberlake's mouth. The singer was later named in a class action suit accusing the beverage company of falsely advertising its drinks, billed as containing only natural ingredients. Despite his chief flavor officer title, Timberlake's legal team reportedly claimed he did not know what Bai's flavors were made from—and that nobody could prove he ever did.[17] (Timberlake was eventually dismissed from the suit.)[18]

At the same time, other big names were contending with the complications that came with owning a piece of a high-profile company.

Shervin Pishevar raised $153 million in 2013 and launched his own fund, Sherpa Capital. By the time BlackJet struck his fancy, he had expanded from ridesharing to vacuum tubes—namely, the hyperloop system Elon Musk unveiled, at Pishevar's insistence, onstage at a conference that same year.[19]

"We're looking at the end of one civilization and the beginning of another, and this transportation infrastructure we're building is the beginning of that new lattice," Pishevar explained two years later, shortly after his Hyperloop firm came out of stealth mode. "There's no turning back."

BlackJet's acceleration, however, was far from supersonic. In fact, within a year of its gaudy San Francisco launch, the company was in free fall. Unable to score additional funding, Pishevar stepped down, and BlackJet laid off most of its employees in September 2013. A former employee claimed the planes flew mostly empty, causing the company to lose $200,000 per week. As Carter had predicted, the unit economics hadn't worked out: it simply proved impossible to guarantee a cross-country seat for $3,500 when operating each plane cost $20,000 per trip regardless of how many passengers were on it.[20]

"We should have just incubated it from scratch," says Pishevar, lamenting his aerial escapade. "It just wasn't the right team, and it was too early with a totally different cost model than Uber."[21]

Yet another intriguing detail can be found in BlackJet's 2012 filing. The company's minimum investment for new backers was $0, meaning that its celebrity stakeholders may not have paid anything for their equity.[22] In that case, all they would have lost was time. Though BlackJet suffered from a suspect business plan, perhaps it could have generated enough wealthy users to survive if its famous investors had pushed harder to promote it—and they might have had the incentive with a little more skin in the game.

Meanwhile, Pishevar continued his own high-flying lifestyle, popping up in photos with Snoop Dogg and other celebrities, becoming a star in his own right. *Forbes* placed his net worth at $500 million and, in 2014, *Valleywag* reported that the recently divorced mogul had started dating Tyra Banks, the supermodel turned startup investor. (In 2013, she joined Ashton Kutcher as an investor in social shopping site The Hunt.)

There was turbulence on the way, though. In late 2017, Bloomberg published a story citing several women who claimed Pishevar used his status to pursue unwanted sexual encounters and relationships (he denies the accusations).[23] Some efforts by Silicon Valley pals to defend him fell flat, including that of an anonymous source who insisted Pishevar couldn't have groped anybody at one particular Uber Christmas party because he was holding a drink in one hand and the leash of a live pony he'd brought to the festivities in the other.[24]

Pishevar subsequently took a leave of absence from both Hyperloop and Sherpa Capital;[25] at the same time, he maintained that he'd been the victim of an elaborate smear campaign.[26] (Sherpa later rebranded itself as Acme Capital). Similar scandals were simultaneously unseating other powerful figures in Hollywood, Silicon Valley, and beyond.

Throughout the fall of 2017, the #MeToo movement grew into a national revolution, sparking necessary changes to the toxic upper ranks of a vast range of industries. Harvey Weinstein, the King Kong of film producers, was taken down by a pair of reports published in the *New York Times* and *The New Yorker* alleging rampant sexual harassment and assault; even as he denied the accusations, he got fired from his own company and at press time was awaiting trial on a bevy of charges, including rape.[27]

In the year that followed, dozens of the planet's most influential men were toppled from powerful perches across the entertainment world due to sexual misconduct, including hip-hop mogul Russell Simmons, CBS chief Leslie Moonves, Hollywood filmmaker Brett Ratner, news anchor Matt Lauer, and many more—over 200 powerful men, by the *New York Times*'s count, half of whom were replaced by women.[28]

"Men who demean, degrade or disrespect women have been able to operate with such impunity—not just in Hollywood, but in tech, venture capital, and other spaces where their influence and investment can make or break a career," Melinda Gates, the co-chair of the Bill & Melinda Gates Foundation, told *The New Yorker*. "The asymmetry of power is ripe for abuse."[29]

Of course, women in Silicon Valley had been sounding the alarm years before the #MeToo movement went mainstream. Heidi Roizen wrote a blog post in 2014 titled "It's Different for Girls," describing the culture that had long dominated her world—and one particular instance where, in her days as a CEO, her biggest customer unzipped his pants at a dinner party and shoved her hand below his belt. "You didn't have anyone to complain to," she says. "Especially when you're a CEO."[30]

Perhaps the most explosive missive was penned in 2017 by Susan Fowler, who had joined Uber as a site reliability engineer two years earlier. On the first day with her new team, Fowler's manager informed her via company chat that he was in an open relationship and was "trying to stay out of trouble at work" but couldn't help doing so "because he was looking for women to have sex with." In another instance, the company ordered leather jackets for every-one in the engineering group—according to Fowler, the half dozen women on the team received an email explaining they wouldn't be receiving jackets because "there were not enough women in the organization to justify placing an order." She reported both inci-dents to human resources, to no avail. When she took subsequent problems up the chain of command, Fowler wrote, she was met with threats of retaliation.[31]

The experience prompted Fowler to take a job at another company. She recounted her experiences in a February blog post titled "Reflecting on One Very, Very Strange Year at Uber." A cascade of criticism of Uber's toxic culture followed, prompting chief executive Travis Kalanick to take an indefinite leave of absence in mid-June. One week later, an investigation commissioned by Uber and led by former U.S. attorney general Eric Holder called for reviewing Kalanick's role. His investors—including Menlo Ventures, Pishevar's old firm—demanded his resignation, and he stepped down as CEO. By the end of 2017, Fowler had earned a place among the "Silence Breakers" who appeared on the cover of *Time*'s Person of the Year issue for her role in pulling back the curtain at Uber.

The episode was a major step in the quest to make Silicon Valley a more hospitable place for all. It also served as an unpleasant reminder of lingering prejudices—no doubt for female Uber investors like Sophia Bush. At the same time, it underscored the significance of their involvement both in the ridesharing company and in the clubby venture capital community more broadly.

"A lot of people get in at the beginning, and then they have other friends that they got in with, and then they all make money, and then they reinvest their money, and the circles stay closed," says Bush. "It is really important to have people choosing to be conscious and saying, 'Who else is coming in here? Who else is going to be allowed to take up space here?'"[32]

To a Silicon Valley veteran like Heidi Roizen, recent progress is just a start—but it's a reason for cautious optimism, as she suggests toward the end of our interview.

"The discussion we're having around harassment here has a different tone because a lot of it is around equal pay, recognition in the workplace, a non-hostile environment," she says. "There is definitely some abuse of power."[33]

Indeed, Roizen's own firm is no stranger to this sort of controversy. DFJ's founding partner, Steve Jurvetson, left the company after reports of extramarital affairs with women he'd met at business conferences.[34] In a statement, Jurvetson alluded to an "ill-advised relationship" but denied any allegations of "sexual predation and workplace harassment," blaming his departure instead on "interpersonal dynamics with my partners."[35] DFJ recently rebranded itself as Threshold Ventures.

To Roizen—who stayed at the firm in the aftermath of the crisis—Silicon Valley still breeds situations that blur the line between business and personal lives. She points to a hypothetical situation: two people are having a consensual sexual relationship, and one of them is wealthy and powerful. The latter person brings the other along on private jet rides and to events frequented by billionaires and celebrities. "Is that abuse of power if…when you're no longer having sex with them, you deny them all that access?" asks Roizen. "There are a lot of men who would say, 'No, that's not abuse of power, that's dating in this day and age.'"[36]

As for the broader culture in Silicon Valley, Roizen is somewhat pessimistic about the prospects of completely weeding out the possibility of sexual impropriety in the workplace. "The reality is you're never gonna get rid of the fact that we are animals and we are sexual beasts," she says. "That's how we make more of our species."

And when it comes to criminal matters, prosecuting offenders is tricky, especially for incidents that occurred far in the past, beyond the reach of statutes of limitations. Slapping meaningful financial penalties on wealthy offenders, especially those who haven't been convicted of a crime, is nearly impossible. Just weeks after Les Moonves was denied a $120 million golden parachute by CBS, he reportedly spent New Year's in St. Barts, vacationing on billionaire

David Geffen's yacht (also said to be on the ritzy island around the same time: Shervin Pishevar and Brett Ratner).[37]

"Unfortunately, we are in a situation where the vast majority of the power in investing is still in the hands of men," Roizen told *Fortune* in late 2018, before hinting at the possibility of a brighter, if not perfect, future. "We are in some hazy days, and we are in a place where there are some difficult situations, but I do think in general, we are moving in the right direction."[38]

CHAPTER 11

Doing Well

Few in Hollywood or Silicon Valley were paying attention in 1986 when a ragtag band of cowboys, hippies, and beatniks launched a music festival in Austin, Texas. Their premise: that the creativity emanating from deep in the heart of the Lone Star State was on par with that of any other city on the planet, if not greater. More than three decades later, it turns out they were on to something. Nowadays, a quarter-million people descend on the city every March—and much like the music business itself, South by Southwest has become a bridge between the worlds of entertainment and technology.

Hop in an Uber at Austin's quickly expanding airport and cruise down Cesar Chavez through the city's east side, clogged with Tesla sedans and pedicabs advertising *Silicon Valley* and Funny Or Die; you could easily be somewhere in California. Hang a left on Rainey Street, and you'll eventually find yourself at the trendy Hotel Van Zandt. On one particularly sunny Saturday, there's a line stretching around the block to see an exclusive performance— not a private concert by local legends Willie Nelson or Gary

Clark Jr. but a startup competition headlined by Ashton Kutcher and Guy Oseary.

On the hotel's fourth-floor pool level, Oseary welcomes the hundreds of guests packed in to catch a glimpse of venture capital in action, as Kutcher sits on a dais alongside an all-star roster of fellow judges: billionaire Marc Benioff, actor Matthew McConaughey, entrepreneurship guru Gary "Vee" Vaynerchuk, and StyleSeat founder Melody McCloskey (a previous recipient of Kutcher's cash). They're here to listen to pitches from five entrepreneurs, with the winner to receive a $100,000 investment from Sound Ventures, the firm Oseary and Kutcher launched after their success with A-Grade.

It's a surreal situation. As each contestant takes the stage, the erstwhile *That '70s Show* star peppers founders with a stream of questions jammed with startup jargon, simultaneously incisive and supportive. "What's your current cost of user acquisition?" he asks the founder of Daymaker, a startup that aims to—wait for it—gamify child-to-child charitable giving. He presses another on the potential size of her market, and the next on privacy implications. When Vaynerchuk hammers a good-natured entrepreneur a little too hard, Kutcher snaps back at his fellow investor: "Gary, he just complimented your fucking shoes."[1]

Of all the options, Kutcher seems particularly interested in a company called LearnLux, which uses online tools to teach personal finance skills to large groups. The model: get corporations to sign up, paying the startup $1 per month per employee in an effort to improve company-wide financial literacy. At one point, cofounder Rebecca Liebman mentions she's in the process of converting a swath of her 250,000 customers from free pilot signees to paid users.

"Have you made that conversion yet?" asks Kutcher.

"We're starting to convert them," she replies.

"And how's that going?"

"Forty percent of millennials opt out of their 401(k) just because they don't know what to do," she explains. "We've seen huge increases in 401(k) opt-in rates."

Meanwhile, Kutcher's own conversion—from actor dabbling in startups to venture capitalist with a thespian habit—is proving similarly successful.

By the mid-2010s, Kutcher's startup activities were outshining his acting career, and his roles continued to reflect his passion for tech. He starred in *Jobs*, a 2013 biopic about Apple's founder, where his performance earned decent feedback even amid lukewarm reviews for the film itself. The *San Francisco Chronicle*, for instance, dubbed his performance "perfectly convincing" while offering a less charitable description of the movie: "Surprisingly, it doesn't fail in the ways some might expect."[2] He managed to find other ways to link his roles as actor and investor, calling attention to one of A-Grade's portfolio companies by annotating a Steve Jobs speech via Genius.[3]

Kutcher also spent the first half of the decade as America's highest-paid television actor, playing an internet billionaire as Charlie Sheen's replacement on *Two and a Half Men*. In his first year, Kutcher displayed the logos of several companies in which he owned a stake in real life—including Foursquare and Flipboard—on the back of his character's laptop on the show. That reportedly caught the attention of the FCC and earned him a ban from doing product placement in the future without proper disclosures.

In 2015, the same year he wrapped up his role on the sitcom, Kutcher joined Oseary in launching Sound Ventures. This time, they parted ways with Burkle, their third musketeer and mentor on A-Grade. When I wrote my cover story on Kutcher and Oseary the following year, Burkle had only nice things to say. "We are as close as we've ever been and our teams continue to look at deals together," he explained. His former partners did the same. "We had a great run," said Oseary. Added Kutcher: "Because we're such good friends, we never wanted different perspectives on the potential market to come into conflict."[4]

So why didn't Burkle stick around? Perhaps the billionaire wasn't interested in having to answer to anyone, including Sound Ventures' institutional backer, Liberty Media. The publicly traded giant made $100 million available for Sound's first fund, announced in 2016, with private equity giant TPG Capital on hand to kick in additional cash for any portfolio company looking for a bigger infusion. Then again, maybe Burkle simply wanted to take a different direction than Kutcher and Oseary, preferring to focus on the sort of biotech companies he did with Inevitable Ventures, which he launched with D. A. Wallach around the same time. Kutcher and Oseary were less specific in their aim.

"We were going, 'Where's the green grass that hasn't been disrupted by this sort of new wave of mobile technology?'" Kutcher told me at the time. "We weren't choosing categories. Then we started looking retroactively at our investments, and we're going, 'You know, we're not really choosing stage either.' We're just investing in things that have great value, that have giant upside, momentum, and are disrupting really interesting spaces. We thought if we want to do this effectively, we need to be a stage-agnostic fund." Oseary knew Liberty Media chief Greg Maffei through Live Nation—Liberty is a large shareholder—and set up a sit-down meeting that laid the groundwork for the new fund. The simplicity of having Liberty as their only investor appealed to Kutcher and Oseary, who'd just been through the multipartner process with A-Grade, where each investor required an individualized set of forms and reports.

Liberty backing Sound represented a massive vote of confidence in Oseary and Kutcher by a major institutional player, giving them a chance to prove their worth—and once again collect fees around 2 percent of assets and 20 percent of profits. It also started off as a paradox: a fund fronted by a Hollywood star buying into unsexy sectors like human resources automation (Zenefits) and household service (Handy). Then there was Cowlar, which Oseary describes as "Fitbit for cows," discovered by the duo at Y Combinator. They became investors along with several other firms, including Joe Montana's Liquid 2 Ventures.

As the startup's name suggests, it provides a bovine collar. But this is a smart one that's capable of spotting an infected hoof by way of changes to an animal's gait or recognizing that a cow is pregnant due to behavioral changes before a typical farmer can tell. The cost: $69 per cow, along with a $3 monthly subscription. By early 2017, Cowlar had 600 cows on its platform and a waitlist of 7,200.[5]

"There's a lot of efficiencies," says Oseary. "If you have a Fitbit for cows, you'll be able to know when they're sick. You'll be able to know when they're pregnant and you can [start] milking a cow that's actually ready to be milked. There'll be less losses."[6]

Even for those who don't need to be convinced of the merits of a company like Cowlar, another question may arise: sure, Kutcher grew up in Iowa and even did a stint as a butcher in his early days, but what sort of value can a movie star have for a company whose customers are mostly farmers in the heartland? Kutcher answered that by appearing on *The Late Show with Stephen Colbert* and discussing a number of his investments.

"I usually like it when, at first, it doesn't land in your ear right...it almost needs to seem nonsensical," Kutcher told Colbert of his favorite startups, before moving on to cite Airbnb as a primary example. "The idea that people are just going to sleep on people's couches, and everyone's going to be cool with that, was kind of crazy."[7]

He also hyped Acorns, which enables people to round up the price of everyday purchases to the nearest dollar and automatically reinvest the difference into index funds. When Colbert didn't immediately understand what the company did, he asked Kutcher to explain it again—leading to a minute-long national television spotlight on the startup. "That was our biggest growth day," says Acorns chief Noah Kerner, who estimated that his company added 15,000 new users in the following twenty-four hours. "We acquire customers for low costs, but that was obviously free."[8]

Similarly, Cowlar got a major boost when Kutcher plugged it in his conversation with Colbert. For such an obscure startup, the 10,000-watt glow generated by the two superstars would have been otherwise unimaginable. "It made a significant difference in website visits and people inquiring about the product," says company founder Umer Adnan of Kutcher's late-night appearance. "I still remember people emailing and calling weeks [and] months later, asking us what our symbol on the stock exchange was. We had to keep telling them that we were not a public company."[9]

Perhaps someday Cowlar will be. After talking to farmers about its first iteration, Adnan and his team realized the main barrier to mass adoption was the inconvenience of having to change batteries on each collar. The process was taking farmers about twenty minutes per cow, a major inconvenience for farmers with herds in the thousands. Raising money from Sound Ventures and others—about $1 million in all—gave Cowlar the flexibility to spend over a year reinventing its core product as a $99 solar-powered collar that can run for ten years, which exceeds the life span of most dairy cows.[10]

Within barely a year of Kutcher's appearance, Cowlar's waitlist more than doubled. Adnan points out farmers aren't the only ones who could use the product: the new collar and its sensors monitor more than twenty-five bovine behaviors, making Cowlar interesting to researchers developing veterinary medications and nutritional supplements. Meanwhile, Kutcher and Adnan have discussed other small-screen tie-ins, including the possibility of featuring Cowlar on Kutcher's Netflix sitcom *The Ranch*. And, as Oseary points out, the cycle feeds on itself.

"A lot of things we ended up doing were not exactly what you and I would be talking about when we get behind a company on day one, but now they're part of our ecosystem," says Oseary, turning his focus to me. "And I'm meeting with you now, and I'm telling you, Mister Writer, about Cowlar."[11]

Around the same time Kutcher started pushing bovine fitness devices on late-night television, Shaquille O'Neal's son asked to go to the Staples Center for a special event. When they arrived at the arena where the elder O'Neal had won three consecutive NBA championships with the Lakers, Shaq found the place nearly unrecognizable, packed with teenagers watching two kids play a video game onstage.

"I was like, 'What the hell is this?'" Shaq recalls asking his son. "He said, 'This is esports.' Never heard of it."[12]

The Hall of Famer quickly familiarized himself with the budding phenomenon wherein teams of professionals—usually not old enough to legally buy a beer—duke it out in a particular video game while audiences look on in person and online. So when former Apple executive Andy Miller called and asked him if he'd like to invest in NRG, an esports organization with squads spread across several different games, Shaq jumped right in. Already a co-owner of the Sacramento Kings with Miller, he saw a chance to get in early on the next big thing. Other stars—including singer Jennifer Lopez, retired baseball players Alex Rodriguez and Ryan Howard, and former NFL standouts Michael Strahan and Marshawn Lynch—followed Shaq into NRG.

"You know those little Cabbage Patch dolls?" he asks. "Once the kids [want them], then parents get involved and it's nothing but a hit. So I knew that esports was gonna go."

But when NRG's first team of gamers made its debut—in the

inaugural match of a league based around the popular multiplayer shooting game *Overwatch*—the results weren't quite what Shaq and his fellow investors may have hoped. Their team's players had never competed together; half of them didn't know each other's real names. More concerned with getting the first kill in league history than winning one for NRG, they lost in a blowout. After the game, Miller brought in Howard to address the team.

"Hey, guys, I just want to introduce you to Ryan," Miller began. "Ryan is a World Series champion, National League MVP, played on good teams, bad teams; he knows what it takes to be a team. Tonight, you guys weren't a team. Take it away, Ryan."[13]

"First thing I wanna say is, any of you think you're not the best in the world?" began Howard.

The players muttered and mumbled but didn't reply.

"That's the door, get out right now," Howard continued. "If you don't think you are the best in the world, or this team can be the best in the world, there's no reason to be here. You know why? 'Cause there's 100,000 kids who want to take your spot."

The team snapped to attention as Miller looked on in amazement.

"You guys have to know each other, you have to love each other, you have to trust each other—if you want to be the best team, then nobody wants to be the hero," said Howard. "You guys all [wanted] the first kill, and it was all exciting.... I could just tell, I didn't have to listen to you guys talk, your communication was terrible. You guys have to learn how to be a team."

Howard's speech got through to the players. "They took it to heart and we improved every stage during the year," says Miller.[14] The teamwork vibe spread to NRG's squads for other games. Howard personally announced the addition of a new *Fortnite* player from Philadelphia to the roster. A-Rod recorded a video introducing NRG's *Gears of War* team. Lopez, Lynch, and Strahan appeared in announcement videos as well. When Miller wanted to recruit one particularly gifted *Overwatch* player who went by the name Seagull,

Shaq goaded him on Twitter: "Time to step it up," Shaq wrote. "Come on ova."[15] Seagull and several others joined soon after, and NRG's value has soared. Though the company hasn't raised a round recently, teams of a similar size and scope have been valued at north of $100 million.[16]

Other entertainers joined the fray. Electronic music star Steve Aoki bought a controlling stake in Rogue, known for its *Overwatch* team, in 2016; two years later, esports giant ReKTGlobal bought a majority stake, with Aoki keeping a double-digit percentage of the company (spokespeople for Aoki and ReKT confirmed the deals but declined to offer detailed figures). The deal was a rare highly publicized piece of business news for Aoki, who's usually as quiet about his financial endeavors as he is rambunctious onstage (now in his early forties, the long-locked DJ spent much of his early career making a tradition of throwing cake in the faces of fans at his spirited live shows).

But after a freewheeling lunch in lower Manhattan—where no cakes were harmed—Aoki told me about his startup portfolio, which stretches far beyond esports. He started thinking about investing in 2006 ("The first time I actually made some money and I was like, 'Wow, I'm out of debt and...when I go to New York I don't have to stay at my dad's house anymore.") But rather than dive into startups, Aoki wanted to impress his father, the late Benihana founder Rocky Aoki, by developing a restaurant portfolio of his own. Steve was offered a chance to invest in Shin, a Korean barbeque restaurant in Hollywood, alongside Julian Casablancas of the Strokes, actor Gerard Butler, and cast members of *That '70s Show* (Aoki doesn't remember if Kutcher was involved).

"What do you think, Dad?" he asked. "It's like thirty grand [for] one point in this restaurant with all these celebrities."[17]

"Do you want my real opinion?" his father asked. "You'll lose all your money....I don't even wanna see the debt, I don't wanna see anything, I'll just tell you right now. If you wanna do it just for vanity, you go ahead and do it, but I'm going to tell you right now you will not make your money back."

Steve ignored his father's advice. *I've gotta show him and show myself I can do it,* he thought. The restaurant closed within just a few years; the younger Aoki didn't try his hand at investing again until 2011, when D. A. Wallach recruited him for Spotify's artist round. The DJ remembers meeting Wallach and Sean Parker at the Peninsula Hotel in Beverly Hills. The duo spent about five minutes pitching him together before Parker flitted off to another table, but Aoki was already sold. He wrote a six-figure check—and sold his stake several years later for about six times what he paid.

Suddenly enamored of startup investing, Aoki helped seed a handful of earlier-stage companies with a combination of sweat and cash. One such outfit, Lily, offered a drone with a built-in camera that would follow and film you wherever you went as long as you wore a tracking device on your wrist. It was meant to appeal to surfers and snowboarders (and perhaps cake-throwing DJs) but found broad support, raising $34 million on Kickstarter in 2015 before adding $15 million from backers including Joe Montana's Liquid 2 and Ron Conway's SV Angel. Aoki helped out by doing appearances at CES and interviews touting the startup. But the company's founders spent so much building Lily that they ran out of money before they could bring their product to market. Aoki lost a six-figure investment, not to mention countless hours spent on promotion.

"It's the nature of the business," he says. "So after a couple of them—that was the big one, the idea was great but execution was always a complete other story—I'm very, very cautious when it comes to really great ideas with low infrastructure. Because at the end of the day, that's why you need investment, you want to build infrastructure, but you need to make sure the person who's running that company can figure it out, can operate."

Aoki shifted to late-stage investments, ones where he already knew the company was viable; he might never get a 50x return that way, but he figured he could easily earn several times what he was putting in. He sat down with his team and wrote out a short list of target companies. Between 2014 and 2017, he found a way into several, including Airbnb and Pinterest.

Often he took a circuitous route. A cold call got him into Uber, where a rambling series of events took him to his next big purchase. In 2016, he found himself at a White House Correspondents' Association dinner, seated with Arianna Huffington, Bill Nye, and DJ Khaled. He followed the crew to a party at the home of a Washington bigwig, where he met an Uber executive who helped him connect with a SpaceX employee looking to sell stock in the privately held company.

"It's a lot of the same people, they're all friends with each other," says Aoki. "They all kind of know who's real [and] go through the vetting process: 'Is this person really going to help us financially or strategically, or are they just talk?'"

Aoki's father never got to see his son's financial labors come to full fruition—the restaurateur passed away in 2009. But Steve knew that Rocky got to at least appreciate his creative career. "He was happy that I was doing my thing," says Aoki. "I'm happy about that."

Even as stars like Aoki piled into the world's top startups, Kutcher and Oseary had something of a head start in the venture capital world—not just when compared to other stars and handlers, but even relative to some of Hollywood's most powerful companies.

CAA spent much of the early 2010s dabbling in startup investing, finding success with Funny Or Die and others. In a typical case, Michael Yanover would receive a call from a major venture firm offering to set aside several hundred thousand dollars' worth of equity in a promising startup for CAA to invest in. He'd knock on his CFO's door and ask permission to take the plunge. Then a back-and-forth would ensue over the agency's overall strategy; often Yanover would have to go back to the venture capitalist and decline to invest.

After one such introduction, Yanover took the founder of a promising photo-sharing service and his partner for lunch at the mall across the street from CAA's Los Angeles headquarters.

"How many people are in this company all together?" asked Yanover after they sat down.[18]

"Four," his lunchmate replied.

"I'm having lunch with half your company right now."

"Yeah, basically."

"Well, how much money are you raising? How much do you need?"

"You should invest $100,000."

"I don't have $100,000 to invest," sighed Yanover. "I wish I could."

The cofounder happened to be Kevin Systrom; his company was Instagram. Within months, Facebook bought the company for $1 billion, widely considered to be one of the bigger bargains in recent Silicon Valley history. But the experience gave Yanover the ammunition he needed to start CAA Ventures, a fund backed by both the talent agency and outside investors looking to profit from its connections.

"The idea was, can we be a value-add?" says Yanover. "When I was asked, 'Do you want to invest on Instagram?' it wasn't because I'm a fun guy to hang out with...it's because they wanted the help of CAA with Instagram. That was why we were being invited to those parties."

CAA Ventures has since invested in dozens of startups, and although it hasn't yet found the next Instagram, good calls include dating app Hinge (eventually bought by Match) and meditation app Calm (which Kutcher and Oseary also invested in). More recently, scores of celebrities have started funds of their own—Kevin Durant, Carmelo Anthony, Jay-Z, Derek Jeter, and Kobe Bryant, to name a few.

Not to be outdone, Kutcher and Oseary forged ahead with their own venture capital careers. In the summer of 2018, an SEC filing revealed a new fund: the $150 million Sound Ventures II. Kutcher, Oseary, and Effie Epstein—the duo had brought her on the prior year to help run Sound—were listed as directors.[19]

"Ashton and Guy have been investing for over a decade and so we had quite a bit of overlap in our networks," says Epstein. "Their reputation on the street was super strong: founder-first mentality and scary smart. We spent almost a year getting to know each other before I joined them at Sound."[20]

Oseary confirms that Liberty Media wasn't an investor in Sound II and that the new fund is "a collective of a few people,"[21] while Epstein describes the investors as "a tight-knit group of LPs including our founders, very large family offices, and corporates."[22] According to Epstein, despite a different sort of investor breakdown, the fund remains in line with the philosophy Kutcher and Oseary have employed over the past decade: invest in the best entrepreneurs, regardless of industry or stage.

"We're family," says Epstein. "Direct, collaborative, and aren't afraid to disagree. All three of us source deals, evaluate deals, and support our entrepreneurs along with the phenomenal team we've built here at Sound."

Neither Epstein nor Oseary would elaborate beyond that as this book went to press. "There's not much more to talk about at this stage," said the latter, pointing out that he and Kutcher hadn't really given an in-depth interview about A-Grade until my *Forbes* cover in 2016. "We waited nine years to do your story!"[23]

Back at the Hotel Van Zandt in Austin, the judges have retreated from the stage to debate the contestants. Onlookers sidle up to the bar or step outside to soak up the Texas sun for a few moments; I try unsuccessfully to bet my neighbor $20 that Rebecca Liebman will win. Finally, Kutcher returns to the stage with Benioff, Vaynerchuk, McConaughey, and McCloskey—and a check the size of an Amazon door desk.

"We've made our decision. Is Rebecca still here?"[24]

An entire row of the audience, all clad in Kɪss Mʏ Assᴇᴛ t-shirts, lets out a collective whoop as Liebman makes her way to the stage.

"Rebecca, we have to have a quick conversation, our due diligence conversation," Kutcher says. "What's the valuation on your company?"

"We're gonna close the round right now?" she asks.

Kutcher nods.

"What do you think your company might be worth?" he inquires.

"Well, if you do it like PayPal, you think about the future."

"I'm talking about today."

"Today, let's do...ten to twelve [million]."

"How would you feel if, instead of having a 'one' here, we just put a 'two' here?" asks Kutcher, indicating the gargantuan check in his hands.

"Amazing."

"All right, LearnLux: two hundred thousand!"

The crowd erupts, and Kutcher congratulates her again. Then Benioff steps forward.

"Can we get another two hundred thousand on there from me?" the billionaire asks.

Liebman enthusiastically accepts, and the audience cheers again.

It's a peak moment for Liebman and her team, but also a telling one for Kutcher, Oseary, and Sound. Whereas they started out by following experienced investors into deals and graduated into a partnership with Burkle, they've now reached such a level of respect on their own that Silicon Valley billionaires are willing to follow *them* into deals.

Liebman's startup is a reminder of one part of the A-List Angel formula—picking up equity in promising companies, sometimes for free—that's actually available to many everyday people. As Liebman noted at the beginning of her presentation, a hefty percentage of workers fail to take advantage of investment programs offered by their employers. Turning down the free money of a 401(k) match is almost akin to a celebrity staying on the sidelines when pre-IPO stakes in Uber are available.

Oseary sees his and Kutcher's role a bit differently.

"We didn't leave money on the table," he says, speaking of the days before he and Kutcher made startup investing de rigueur in Hollywood. "We jumped in here because we are excited about [these] founders and new ideas and ways to better our lives."[25]

CHAPTER 12

Doing Good

The archipelago of Svalbard sits about halfway between the uppermost coast of Norway and the North Pole; with just over 2,000 human inhabitants, there are usually more arctic foxes and polar bears roaming the area than angel investors or television actors. Sophia Bush dented those demographics in 2018 with a visit to the Svalbard Global Seed Vault. The facility is like a backup drive for the world's food supply—in case of disaster, countries can retrieve seeds from Svalbard to reboot their agricultural process. Bush was amazed to find that nations from the United States to Russia to Venezuela to North Korea had made deposits in the same climate-controlled aisles she roamed.

This isn't the only sort of seed investing that interests Bush. Emboldened by her success with Uber, she has expanded her portfolio to include startups such as PenPal Schools, which offers lessons—in everything from Financial Literacy & Money Management to Protecting the Planet—by linking over a quarter million students in 150 countries with teachers and peers around the globe.

"Somebody's out there creating this really incredible space for education that teaches kids about the world, and about the environment, and about each other," Bush tells me over the phone a year after her trip. "That feels like a way forward, and when you see the positive ramifications in classrooms in the way that kids pay better attention, and the way that they become kinder, and the way that their understanding of empathy increases, that feels like a thing that we should all really be focusing on."[1]

Thanks to Bush and several others, PenPal raised over $1 million in its 2017 seed round—a tiny sum compared to Silicon Valley's usual suspects, but a strong start nonetheless. Perhaps more importantly, the startup underscores the notion that philanthropy and moneymaking can go hand in hand. That's been very much on the minds of Bush and her entertainment world peers—and in quite a few cases, their efforts have already yielded some notable results.

"Capitalism is not immoral, but it is amoral," Bono tells me on a warm summer day in lower Manhattan, shortly before getting photographed for the *Forbes* Centennial issue, a special edition highlighting the world's greatest living business minds. "And it requires our instruction. It's a wild beast that needs to be tamed, a better servant than master."[2]

The U2 front man has been following that philosophy for years. On the venture capital side, he invested early in Facebook, Yelp, and Sonos. Even as he's become one of the world's wealthiest musicians—U2 has grossed over half a billion dollars since Guy Oseary took over as manager in 2013—the singer has fixated on using his influence, in tandem with the market economy, for the greater good.

In 2006, at the World Economic Forum in Davos, Bono launched (RED), an organization that teams with corporations to direct swaths of their massive marketing budgets toward combating HIV and AIDS. Boosted by the enormous platform of Bono and his pals, (RED) has spawned some $500 million in funding to fight both.

Bono's next act is occurring at the intersection of entertainment, venture capital, and philanthropy, inspired by a conversation he had several years ago with Sudanese-British billionaire Mo Ibrahim. The telecom tycoon, who established the Ibrahim Prize—a multimillion-dollar award given to African leaders able to both improve their countries and leave office on time at the end of their terms—welcomed Bono and a few "Silicon Valley types" (whom the singer declines to name) to the continent with a challenge.

"He said, 'Look at you, you think of yourselves as brave, but really you paddle around in the shallow water of the Nasdaq,'" Bono remembers the billionaire saying. "Come invest in Africa, that's deep water. If you really believe in us, invest. Not just *in* us, but invest *with* us.' And the beginnings, for me, of Rise started there."[3]

The singer is speaking of TPG's Rise Fund, which he cofounded with executive Bill McGlashan and eBay billionaire Jeff Skoll to invest in Africa and beyond; they were joined by a cast of moguls including Laurene Powell Jobs, Richard Branson, and Ibrahim. Rise aimed to raise $1.5 billion for what John Kerry, a senior advisor to the fund, compared to the beginnings of a privately funded version of the Marshall Plan, the multibillion-dollar U.S.-led effort to rebuild Europe after World War II.[4]

Rise and other initiatives of its ilk are long overdue, arriving at a time when many are understandably questioning whether the very existence of billionaires is a symptom of societal ill rather than a potential force for good. According to a recent Gallup poll, 51 percent of Americans between the ages of 18 and 29 have a positive view of socialism, holding steady over the past decade; only 45 percent view capitalism favorably, a 12-point decline over just two years.[5]

Bono teaming up with John Kerry and a bunch of billionaires to save the world could easily be derided by critics as neoliberal fan fiction at best, and at worst, some unholy mix of white savior thinking and a public relations ploy aimed at papering over the cutthroat side of institutional investing (it's worth noting that, several years after cofounding Rise, McGlashan parted ways with TPG in the wake of his arrest in connection with the 2019 college admissions–fixing scandal).[6]

At the same time, it's hard to deny that the world needs imaginative solutions. Or, as Kerry puts it: "What do you do in an age that demands one hundred Marshall Plans but [has] few constituencies anywhere stepping up to provide them? The answer is, you think differently—and you think creatively."[7]

Perhaps unsurprisingly, some of the more prominent names on the Hollywood–Silicon Valley axis have launched initiatives in the same vein as the Rise Fund. Among them: Andreessen Horowitz's Cultural Leadership Fund, announced in 2018. Led by Chris Lyons, who'd served half a decade as the firm's chief of staff, the fund was conceived to further level the playing field between creators and owners.

"Consumer behavior—in other words, culture—has become central to successfully building, marketing, and selling new technologies," wrote Lyons and Horowitz in a blog post introducing the fund. "African Americans invented all modern forms of music from jazz to blues to rock and roll to hip hop. In the United States, most fashion, dance, and language innovation has come from this relatively small community."[8]

Lyons and Horowitz felt that, although Andreessen Horowitz had invested in many companies founded by black entrepreneurs, from Steve Stoute (UnitedMasters) to Ryan Williams (Cadre), the background of those profiting from cultural trends didn't quite match that of those creating them. As such, the Cultural Leadership Fund raised a reported $15 million from figures including Nas, Shonda Rhimes, Will Smith, Jada Pinkett Smith, Diddy, and Kevin Durant.

The fund invests alongside Andreessen Horowitz itself, offering a way to access some of the best deals in Silicon Valley with the help of the firm's Rolodex—essentially institutionalizing the A-List Angel approach, but with a loftier goal. In order to ensure that the fund was more than a vehicle to simply make rich celebrities wealthy, its creators added a twist: all fees and "carry"—something on the order of 2 percent of assets and 20 percent of profits—would be given to nonprofits focused on helping African Americans join the tech sector. That line of thinking struck a chord with other Silicon Valley investors.

"Consumer technology is more about popular culture than technology these days," says Jeremy Liew, of Lightspeed, who notes that one-third of his firm's portfolio companies have female founders, up from about a quarter a couple of years ago. "The pop culture lead tends to be less white men and more women and people of color."[9]

So, just as Andreessen Horowitz's Cultural Leadership Fund has focused on bringing more black entrepreneurs into the fold, others have tried to address a broader slate of underrepresented groups. Backstage Capital, for example, aims to invest in startups launched by women, people of color, and LGBTQ entrepreneurs—groups that receive only about 20 percent of all venture dollars in aggregate despite accounting for the bulk of the world's population.[10]

Backstage's founder is Arlan Hamilton, a former tour manager and magazine publisher. Her company's website describes her as "a black woman from Texas" who's "hella gay." She never graduated from college or thought she could crack Silicon Valley—until "something happened that sparked a new, unexpected passion . . . she learned that entertainment notables like Ellen [DeGeneres], Ashton Kutcher, Troy Carter were investing in tech startups."

Hamilton raised a fund and in 2015 set a goal of investing in 100 startups helmed by underrepresented entrepreneurs within five years, getting there a year and a half early while spreading $4 million across companies like Kairos, a facial recognition startup, and Mars Reel, a high school sports video-sharing service founded by twentysomething twins Brandon and Bradley Deyo.

"I remember the first time we found out that you could raise money for your business," Bradley said after raising $4.7 million (investors include Drake, LeBron James, and Nas). "Before this we would mow lawns and shovel snow."[11]

In 2018, Hamilton announced Backstage's next effort, a fund aiming to raise $36 million with an even more laser-focused purpose: funding startups founded by black women, $1 million at a time. ("They're calling it a 'diversity fund,'" tweeted Hamilton. "I'm calling it an IT'S ABOUT DAMN TIME fund.")[12] By showing that outsiders with no college degree could become Silicon Valley insiders, figures like Carter helped pave the way for institutions like Backstage, and for people like Hamilton and the Deyo brothers, to engage with the startup world.

"There wasn't a lot of access to deals for people of color or people coming from hip-hop or entrepreneurial backgrounds similar to ours," says Carter, noting that a whole generation will now see examples of success in industries where there are not thousands— but millions—of jobs set to open up in the coming years. "This is part of the vernacular now, and it has expanded beyond being on the stage, or being on the court...there is a much broader world out there in terms of opportunity."[13]

And indeed, many of Carter's peers emphasize that challenging common assumptions about investing is a key to changing some of Silicon Valley's imbalances. Bush, one of the many celebrities who backed Uber alongside Carter, points out that she essentially fell into startup investing as a result of the connections she'd made on the charity circuit.

"When women start making money, they get approached to be philanthropists. When men start making money, they get approached to be investors," she says. "We're not invited to that table...to be a woman in the room at all feels important."[14]

While traditionally underrepresented groups found new ways into the venture world, a fundamental shift was happening in the broader investing landscape. In the United States, outlays with a focus on social responsibility grew more than 33 percent from 2014 to 2016, from $6.57 trillion to $8.72 trillion.[15]

Particularly in the wake of Donald Trump's 2016 election and the accompanying rollback of environmental and social programs, young Americans became increasingly focused on sustainable investing: 28 percent of millennials were "very interested" in such options in 2015; that number surged to 38 percent in 2017. Many impact funds available to the public, however, had hefty minimums: BlackRock, the world's largest asset manager, required a minimum investment of $1,000 for its offerings; cheaper options from other outfits were often just baskets of shares in massive companies like Walmart that happened to give a lot to charities. By 2017, a few plucky newcomers like Motif, which allowed small-scale impact investing, had started to make a dent. But for most of the population, the options were fairly limited.

The front lines of impact investing, as Mo Ibrahim had told Bono, were in places like Africa—and near the privately held companies building the machinery of change. The Rise Fund debuted in 2017, blowing past its initial $1.5 billion capital goal en route to raising $2 billion, investing in companies promoting environmental and social good.[16]

The fund's first set of investments showed the breadth of its goals. Fourth Partner Energy, a solar company in India, has prevented the release of more than 16 million tons of carbon into the atmosphere. Digital House coding school in Latin America has expanded from 60 to more than 8,000 students in just a couple of years. Cellulant, a Kenya-based monetary platform, now processes 12 percent of Africa's digital payments—crucial on a continent where the demands of development often outpace existing traditional banking infrastructure.

The Rise Fund took its efforts a step further than most, creating an analytical arm to quantify impact. Rise measured this through something called the impact multiple of money, or IMM, a metric based on decades of research done by the broader social investing community. The fund's aim: to generate an IMM of at least $2.50 for every $1 invested. Then Rise spun off the outfit, called Y Analytics, so that others could more easily quantify their own efforts.[17]

"Y Analytics will help inform capital in pursuit of change, ensuring that every dollar is used most effectively and providing a common language to pursue positive impact," said TPG in a statement. The goal? "Narrowing the gap to reach the [United Nations'] Sustainable Development Goals and advancing progress toward sustainability and economic inclusion."

Sometimes, the goals of Rise actually overlap with those of investors who aren't exclusively looking for social returns. Perhaps its best-known portfolio company is Acorns, which has raised over $200 million from an array of investors including TPG itself, Liberty Media, and Sound Ventures. "If you don't have a purpose and don't focus on doing things the right way with integrity," says Acorns' Kerner, "then we're not going to be here either because people aren't going to ultimately love the product."[18]

"It's a common theme for the companies we invest in: they better our lives," adds Oseary. "When it all works out, it's just the by-product of the real goal, which is working with the greatest talent in the world. And helping them solve problems."[19]

The broader market continued to chug along through 2018 and 2019, flirting with all-time highs, with indices from the Dow Jones Industrial Average to the tech-heavy Nasdaq up by multiples of their Great Recession lows. In the venture capital world, the numbers have been particularly eye-popping. Global volume soared to roughly 34,000 deals in 2018, up 32 percent year-over-year and nearly 60 percent since 2014—in other words, the average pace of annual growth has been accelerating. According to Crunchbase, $91.4 billion was invested in the fourth quarter of 2018, up 2.4 percent from the third.[20]

Over the course of this bonanza, Hollywood and Silicon Valley have gradually mended an often frayed relationship. "I think that has changed now to 'we have great things we can do together,'" says Bill Gross, whose Idealab incubator continues to churn out promising startups in Pasadena. "You can't have a company that isn't tech anymore. It used to be entertainment companies thought they could be not-tech companies. That's over."[21]

At the same time, giant tech platforms know they can't live without content. Some, like Spotify, lured artists with the promise of musical ubiquity and occasional equity. Others showed stock isn't the only way to compensate creatives: Netflix spent $12 billion on content in 2018, increasing that number by 20 percent for 2019—something few would have predicted in the mid-aughts.[22]

"For five, six years, everyone believed, 'Shit, content is no longer going to be how you make money; it's all about distribution,'" says D. A. Wallach. "So everyone was scurrying to tech, which in media was where distribution was being disrupted. But then that spilled over in their mental model to anything tech. 'Tech's the new entertainment.' And now it's almost gone back...to content being really valuable, because now the distribution platforms are all competing to have differentiated content."[23]

Despite all the hand-wringing in the creative community over not securing stakes in social media platforms—which many felt were built on the backs of entertainers—the controversy over companies like Facebook in recent years complicates matters. Would artists really want to defend directly profiting off a company seen by many as a nefarious hoarder of personal data and an influencer of elections, an outfit without which Donald Trump—not exactly a favorite in Hollywood—might never have been elected?

Indeed, venture capitalist Roger McNamee, a touring musician himself and an early investor in Facebook along with Bono, has strong opinions about the social network. McNamee insists he tried to warn Facebook's leaders that devious types would exploit its audience in 2016 but was ignored. "Move fast, break things, apologize, repeat," said McNamee, characterizing the company's approach following the release of his 2019 book, *Zucked: Waking Up to the Facebook Catastrophe*. "They've been doing it from Day One. It's culturally built in."[24]

And even as shares of certain tech titans soar, dark clouds have gathered around the broader financial world. Wild swings have become the norm as surging debt, trade wars, and unpredictable leadership roil markets. Recently, initial public offerings of some of the world's most desirable startups have fallen flat, while others were scuttled altogether. Some venture capital firms have been cautioning their portfolio companies to prepare for an approaching downturn.

"We wanted to have some fat on our bones for sure," noted the founder of biotech startup Zymergen, which has raised hundreds of millions of dollars, much of it recently. "The time to raise money is when people are giving it to you."[25]

A-List Angels and their allies forged an investment philosophy in the fires of the Great Recession. And, as the likes of Troy Carter point out, one of the lessons learned when the last tech bubble popped is that the best companies find a way to make it through the toughest stretches.

"We went through a period of time where there was a lot of capital out there being allocated to companies who wouldn't necessarily qualify as venture-backed companies; also, founders who maybe shouldn't have been CEOs," says Carter. "Companies being able to figure out how to get to profitability quicker is going to be a key element moving forward. I do think we'll see less companies who are willing to run at a potential loss for as long as companies like Amazon and Spotify...but in terms of great companies, I think they're going to continue to be well funded."[26]

"If it's all just profit, profit, profit, what are we really doing?" asks Sophia Bush as we wind down our interview.

In recent years, other creators have grappled with the same dilemma, joining entrepreneurs in taking lessons learned from the venture capital world and applying them in philanthropic settings. Matt Damon's Water.org, for example, is now working not just to raise money to bring indoor plumbing to the poorest households in the world but also to scale the plan by creating venture funds that generate low-single-digit returns by giving cheap microloans.

Billionaire founders of companies including Airbnb, Facebook, and Uber have committed to donating more than half their wealth to charity as part of what's known as the Giving Pledge. The initiative, launched by Bill and Melinda Gates and Warren Buffett in 2010, now includes some 200 of the richest individuals and couples on the planet. At press time, Rise was in the process of raising a second multibillion-dollar fund.

These gestures, of course, are not going to magically solve all the world's ills. But they are a start. With any luck, the current generation of filmmakers, athletes, musicians—and others they've inspired—will find new, creative ways to make the world in some way better.

"I've never had that clichéd view of commerce and culture being different," says Bono. "Whether it's a song or business or a solution to a problem facing the world's poor...I've always seen what I do as an activist, as an artist, as an investor, as coming from the same place.'"[27]

And already, the next generation of entertainers is using its platform to pick up conversations advanced by the likes of U2's front man.

"To Bono's point, I do think that if we could readjust some of the settings, we could be doing a lot more good," says Bush. "My goal is always to talk about how we can take away the 'philanthropic or business' idea. There's no reason that they can't be both."[28]

ACKNOWLEDGMENTS

This book would not have been possible without the help of an A-list of its own. Major thanks are in order to the impeccable William Clark for his support as both an agent and friend. On the other side of the table, I'm grateful to editor Phil Marino and the folks at Little, Brown for understanding and honing my vision.

Without my sources, I couldn't have written this book; there are too many to mention here, but not for lack of gratitude (though you can catch most of them in the notes section that follows). Non-human sources like Crunchbase Pro and wealth estimates from the pages of *Forbes* helped immensely as well.

I deeply appreciate the support given by a multitude of *Forbes* colleagues past and present—particularly Randall Lane, Michael Noer, Rob LaFranco, Sue Radlauer, Michael Solomon, Natalie Robehmed, Hana Alberts, and Paul Anderson—and the welcome distraction offered by my teammates on the softball field, Bloom Cup or not. Fake sports served as a great way to procrastinate as well, and for that I must applaud the Commish and crew of CABLE misfits who've been diverting my attention for a quarter century now.

ACKNOWLEDGMENTS

Changes of scenery are often helpful for writing and necessary for reporting. This book benefited greatly from the hospitality of the Mosses, Seymours, Adlers, and Blampos on the East Coast; the Bruner-Kerners and Lachmans out West; and the O'Malleys, Pecks, and La Roccos in between. New York friends offered diversions from Central Park visits (Choppy, Madeline Kerner, David Korngold, Sean Pool, Julia King), to covert neckwear enthusiasm (Peter Schwartz, Mike Safir), to karaoke and YouTube (Dan Kato, Anna Zhukovskaya, Mike Seplowitz, Vicky Schussler, and Nathan Griffith—who, when it comes to writing last-minute code for a book cover, is a true "All-Star").

The unsung heroes of every book are the early readers. I was immensely fortunate to have the help of dear friends including startup aficionados Nicole Villeneuve and Andrew Cedotal, who were kind enough to devote much of a Northern California road trip (and random chunks of other time) to discussing my manuscript, even at its most primordial. Jon Bittner gave me invaluable access to the brain of a founder at all hours (Rebecca Blum was kind enough to encourage this while being her awesome self as well), and Cherie Hu made sure I got my facts straight. And, as always, Nick Messitte gave me a ruthless and incisive round of comments that helped me tighten up this book.

Any author would be lucky to have two parents who are gifted writers and editors—I'm fortunate enough to have three. So, a big thanks to my mom, for sending encouragement from deep in the heart of Texas; to my dad, for our long talks over dinner in New York; and to Judith, for taking her science textbook editor's microscope to my drafts, as usual, and helping me zap the rotten parts.

Most of all, I'm thankful to my wonderful wife, Danielle La Rocco. She has been kind enough to put up with four books' worth of: ambient strains of mopey music, forgotten pasta on the stove, weekends and vacations filled with impromptu writing sessions, and

ACKNOWLEDGMENTS

more additional surprises than I can remember (though she may). She has, nevertheless, offered sage advice as a reader of several very rough first drafts, tracked down missing photographs in deepest Brooklyn, and even dreamed up the idea for the cover of this book. Danielle, Shaq may be big, but my love for you is even bigger.

GIVING BACK

Silicon Valley has proven to be the most powerful engine of wealth creation of the twenty-first century, but, as noted throughout this book, the tech world has had a pattern of enriching a cohort that is mostly white and mostly male. Though many A-List Angels helped open some doors for a more diverse set of founders and investors, there's still plenty of work to be done in order to get the startup economy to more closely resemble the makeup of the country, and of the world. And every little bit helps. So, for every copy of this book that's sold, a donation will be made to Black Girls Code, a nonprofit organization that focuses on bringing technology training early to women of color, the most underrepresented group in Silicon Valley. Those skills offer a path to many of the millions of jobs now opening up in the computing world; Black Girls Code aims to train 1 million young women by 2040. To learn more, or to make a donation of your own, visit www.blackgirlscode.com.

GLOSSARY

The intersection of Hollywood and Silicon Valley is a busy place inhabited by scores of stars, startups, entrepreneurs, investors, and handlers. In an effort to simplify this, here's a glossary below to serve as a reference.

A-Grade First venture capital outfit, launched by Ron Burkle, Ashton Kutcher, and Guy Oseary; investments include Airbnb, Uber, Spotify, Warby Parker, and Pinterest

Acorns Southern California company that enables people to round up the price of everyday purchases and automatically reinvest the difference

Umer Adnan Founder of Cowlar, billed as "Fitbit for cows"

Airbnb Home-sharing company posing an existential threat to the hotel industry

Jason Aldean Country singer; Tidal investor

Jessica Alba Star actress; founder of The Honest Company; startup investor

GLOSSARY

Paul Allen Late cofounder of Microsoft; rock music enthusiast; early 1990s connector of tech and entertainment

Marc Andreessen Cofounder of Netscape; cofounder of Andreessen Horowitz with Ben Horowitz, backing the likes of Airbnb, Lyft, and Dropbox

Steve Aoki DJ/producer; investor in companies including Uber and Spotify

Justin Bieber Pop idol; investor in Spotify and others

BlackJet Private jet-sharing startup that crashed despite backing from many Uber investors

Michael Blank CAA agent; Buster Posey guru; driving force behind many creators' apps

Richard Branson Billionaire founder of Virgin (Records, Airlines, Galactic, etc.); investor in unicorns including Ring and Square

Scooter Braun Manager who discovered Justin Bieber; Hollywood power broker; backer of Uber, Spotify, and many others

Ron Burkle Billionaire supermarket mogul turned startup investor; cofounder of A-Grade with Kutcher and Oseary

Troy Carter Music industry veteran; former manager of Lady Gaga; Spotify skeptic turned investor turned executive; backer of companies including Uber, Lyft, and Spotify

Shawn "Jay-Z" Carter Entrepreneur; investor in Uber, BlackJet, and others; occasional rapper

Brian Chesky Cofounder of Airbnb; friend of Kutcher and Oseary; purveyor of canine birthday party office culture

Coinbase Cryptocurrency trading platform backed by several major venture firms and A-List Angels

Sean "Diddy" Combs Bad Boy founder; hip-hop impresario; investing pal of Ron Burkle and Ben Horowitz

Jack Conte One-half of indie duo Pomplamoose; founder of Patreon

202

GLOSSARY

Ron Conway Founder of SV Angel; investor in companies from Twitter to Facebook

Creative Artists Agency (CAA) Hollywood agency cofounded by Michael Ovitz; investor in companies from Patreon to dating service Hinge through its CAA Ventures arm

Mark Cuban Billionaire entrepreneur; owner of the NBA's Dallas Mavericks; *Shark Tank* judge

Robert "RZA" Diggs Ringleader of the Wu-Tang Clan; chess aficionado; startup investor

Dropbox File-hosting service that added investors from Nas to Andreessen Horowitz before becoming a multibillion-dollar publicly traded company

Kevin Durant NBA star; Silicon Valley investor in companies including Postmates and Acorns

Josh Elman Silicon Valley veteran who has worked at Facebook, Twitter, Greylock, and Robinhood

Daniel Ek Swedish cofounder of audio-streaming giant Spotify with Martin Lorentzon

Effie Epstein Sound Ventures partner of Kutcher and Oseary

Facebook Social network founded by Mark Zuckerberg and several others; fast mover, breaker of things; early investors range from Bono to Greylock

Susan Fowler Software engineer; writer; Uber whistleblower; advocate for changing Silicon Valley culture

Bill Gates Microsoft cofounder; philanthropist; longtime richest person in America; not-so-secret *Buffy the Vampire Slayer* fan

Genius Lyrics site originally known as Rap Genius; annotator of the entire internet

Tony Gonzalez NFL legend; investor in Beyond Meat and FitStar (later acquired by Fitbit)

Bill Gross Idealab cofounder; investing mentor of Oseary and Kutcher; early Google shareholder

GLOSSARY

Greylock Silicon Valley firm whose investments include Airbnb, Facebook, Dropbox, and Instagram

Arlan Hamilton Founder of Backstage Capital, a firm dedicated to investing in women and people of color; counts Carter and Kutcher as inspiration

Paul "Bono" Hewson U2 front man; Facebook investor; philanthropist; managed by Oseary

Ben Horowitz Entrepreneur; venture capitalist; hip-hop enthusiast; his firm Andreessen Horowitz backed companies including Airbnb, Lyft, and Dropbox

Idealab Brainchild of Bill Gross; early nexus of entertainment and tech; incubator of several billion-dollar companies

Instagram Photo and video-sharing platform now owned by Facebook

Curtis "50 Cent" Jackson Rapper; entrepreneur; Vitaminwater investor

LeBron James NBA star; backer of companies including Beats by Dr. Dre, Blaze Pizza, and Mars Reel

Nasir "Nas" Jones Rapper; venture capitalist; friend and frequent investment partner of Horowitz; early backer of Genius, Ring, Lyft, Dropbox, and dozens more

Beyoncé Knowles International icon; superstar singer; Uber investor

Ashton Kutcher Actor; longtime business partner of Oseary; cofounder of A-Grade and Sound Ventures; early backer of Airbnb, Uber, Spotify, and many others

Tom Lehman Cofounder and CEO of Genius; ceramics expert

Jared Leto Actor; musician; investor in dozens of startups, including Robinhood

Jeremy Liew Venture capitalist (Lightspeed) specializing in retail

Chris Lighty Late manager of 50 Cent; co-architect of Vitaminwater deal

Adam Lilling Founder of Plus Capital, which links stars with startups

GLOSSARY

Loudcloud Software company founded by Marc Andreessen and Ben Horowitz; later known as Opsware

Martin Lorentzon Swedish cofounder of audio-streaming giant Spotify with Daniel Ek

Lyft Ridesharing app originally known as Zimride; investors include Troy Carter and Nas

Michael Ma Entrepreneur; seed-stage venture capitalist; cofounder of Liquid 2 Ventures with Joe Montana; investor in Cowlar with Oseary and Kutcher

Marshall "Eminem" Mathers Rapper; top-selling act of 2000s; protégé of Dr. Dre

Paul McCartney Legendary former Beatle; music publishing enthusiast

Mahbod Moghadam Estranged cofounder of Genius; provocateur of billionaires

Joe Montana NFL Hall of Famer; investing buddy of Ron Conway; cofounder of Liquid 2 Ventures; backer of Cowlar alongside Kutcher and Oseary

Myspace Forerunning social media startup and music hub

Shaquille O'Neal NBA Hall of Famer; occasional rapper, actor, law enforcement agent; early backer of Google, Ring, Vitaminwater, Uber, and Lyft

Opsware See Loudcloud

Guy Oseary Manager of Madonna and U2; cofounder of A-Grade and Sound Ventures with Ashton Kutcher; early investor in Uber, Airbnb, Spotify, and dozens more

Michael Ovitz CAA founder; modern Hollywood pioneer; advisor to Horowitz

Rohan Oza Marketing guru starting at Coca-Cola/Sprite; Vitaminwater deal co-architect

Amanda Palmer Creator extraordinaire; Dresden Dolls singer; Patreon artist

Gwyneth Paltrow Actress; founder of lifestyle startup Goop

GLOSSARY

Patreon Platform cofounded by Conte that connects creators with their audience, allowing them to monetize their work on a direct-to-subscriber basis

Pinterest Social media startup created to display beautiful images of beautiful things

Shervin Pishevar Venture capitalist; early investor in Uber, Airbnb, and many others

Postmates Food delivery startup that counts Kevin Durant among its backers

Nicole Quinn Venture capitalist (Lightspeed) specializing in retail

Robinhood Commission-free stock-trading platform backed by stars including Jay-Z, Nas, and Kevin Durant

Ring Virtual doorbell startup purchased by Amazon for over $1 billion; prior investors included Shaq and Nas

David S. Rose The guy who actually wrote the book on angel investing—*Angel Investing: The Gust Guide to Making Money and Having Fun Investing in Startups*

Heidi Roizen Veteran executive in Silicon Valley companies spanning tech (Apple) and venture capital (Draper Fisher Jurvetson) over several decades

Howard Rosenman Film producer (*Call Me by Your Name, Buffy the Vampire Slayer*); observer of early attempts to unite Hollywood and Silicon Valley

George Herman "Babe" Ruth Hall of Fame baseball player; A-List Angel prototype

Chris Sacca Retired thirtysomething billionaire investor; founder of Lowercase Capital, early backer of Uber; buddy of Kutcher and Oseary; cowboy shirt aficionado

Anthony Saleh Manager of Nas; investor in Dropbox, Lyft, Genius, Ring, and many more

Robert Schweppe Author; longtime Los Angeles Dodgers executive

Sequoia Capital Silicon Valley venture firm behind companies from Apple to Zappos

Sound Ventures Venture capital outfit launched by Kutcher and Oseary after their success with A-Grade

Jamie Siminoff Founder of Ring, the virtual doorbell startup whose investors included Shaq and Nas before Amazon bought the company for $1 billion in 2018

Spotify Audio-streaming site founded by Daniel Ek and Martin Lorentzon

Steve Stoute Marketing guru; friend and investing buddy of Jay-Z and Horowitz

Sweetgreen Salad-focused fast casual food chain; backers range from giant financial institutions to stars like Jay-Z

Twitter Microblogging site backed by Silicon Valley and popularized by Kutcher and other Hollywood stars

Uber Ride-sharing company founded by Travis Kalanick; investors include A-Grade

Vitaminwater Flavored water brand that added 50 Cent and Shaq as backers before its parent company, Glacéau, got bought by Coca-Cola for $4.1 billion

D. A. Wallach Venture capitalist; musician; college classmate of Mark Zuckerberg; investor in Spotify and more

William Morris Endeavor (WME) Hollywood superagency helmed by Ari Emanuel

Y Combinator Startup accelerator that helped boost companies including Airbnb, Genius, and Coinbase

Michael Yanover CAA agent who helped get the agency into startup investing

Ilan Zechory Cofounder and president of Genius; trained hypnotherapist

Brian Zisk Entrepreneur; venture capitalist; Hawaiian shirt enthusiast

Mark Zuckerberg Facebook founder; Harvard classmate of D. A. Wallach

NOTES

Introduction

1 Ashton Kutcher, conversation with author, October 2016, Boston, Massachusetts.

2 Author's note: This quote originally appeared in my cover story on Kutcher and Guy Oseary, "Eight and a Half X," *Forbes*, March 26, 2016, https://www.forbes.com/sites /zackomalleygreenburg/2016/03/23/how-ashton-kutcher-and-guy-oseary-built-a-250-million-portfolio-with-startups-like-uber-and-airbnb/. Fun fact: this story was published in the 2016 Midas List edition of *Forbes*, which 8.8 million people read—the highest total of any issue in the magazine's first century.

3 Troy Carter, telephone interview by author, February 2019.

4 Nasir "Nas" Jones, interview by author, New York, New York, August 2018.

5 Guy Oseary, interview by author, Los Angeles, California, March 2016.

6   Heidi Roizen, telephone interview by author, April 2018.

7   Troy Carter, telephone interview by author, January 2018.

8   Josh Elman, interview by author, Menlo Park, California, October 2018.

9   Jack Conte, interview by author, San Francisco, California, October 2018.

10 David S. Rose, interview by author, New York, New York, August 2018. Author's note: "There's no official place where [angel investors] hang out," says Rose, author of *Angel Investing: The Gust Guide to Making Money and Having Fun Investing in Startups*. "On the other hand, I've seen enough of this happen: people just luck out. I mean, you could be a hotdog seller on the street and it turns out that the guy who gives you an extra buck tip every day happens to be Mike Bloomberg...and you say, 'I'm going to start a new thing.' And he says, 'Sure, I'll give you $100,000 to go start a new hotdog stand.'"

11 Heidi Roizen, telephone interview by author, April 2018.

12 Ashton Kutcher, interview by author, Los Angeles, California, March 2016.

13 Michael Ma, telephone interview by author, January 2018.

14 D. A. Wallach, interview by author, Los Angeles, California, December 2017.

15 Shaquille O'Neal, interview by author, Atlantic City, New Jersey, July 2018.

16 Joe Montana, telephone interview by author, September 2018.

17 Chris Rock, "Drugs, Donuts and Wealth," *Never Scared*, DreamWorks/Geffen (2004).

NOTES

Chapter 1: Employees Only

1   Shaquille O'Neal, interview by author, Atlantic City, New Jersey, July 2018.

2   "Shaquille O'Neal," Basketball Reference, n.d., https://www.basketball-reference.com/players/o/onealsh01.html#all_all_salaries.

3   Author's note: Shaq also released a compilation album, *The Best of Shaquille O'Neal*, in 1996—after only two studio records. It featured songs including "Shoot Pass Slam" and "I'm Outstanding."

4   Chris Rock, "Drugs, Donuts and Wealth," *Never Scared*, DreamWorks/Geffen (2004).

5   Shaquille O'Neal, interview by author, Atlantic City, New Jersey, July 2018.

6   Rowland E. Prothero, ed., *The Works of Lord Byron* (London: Charles Scribner's Sons, 1904), 285.

7   Walter Isaacson, *The Innovators* (New York: Simon & Schuster, 2014), 27.

8   Charles Musser, interview by author, New Haven, Connecticut, November 2018.

9   Grace Kingsley, "100 Years Ago, Charlie Chaplin Began Work in His New Studio," *Los Angeles Times*, January 26, 2018, http://www.latimes.com/entertainment/movies/la-et-mn-classic-hollywood-archive-chaplin-studio-centennial-20180126-story.html.

10 Charles Musser, interview by author, New Haven, Connecticut, November 2018.

11 John McCabe, *Cagney* (New York: Knopf, 1997), 100–2.

12 Dennis McDougal, *The Last Mogul* (New York: Da Capo Press, 1998), 117.

13 Robert Schweppe, interview by author, Los Angeles, California, February 2018.

14 Robert W. Creamer, *Babe: The Legend Comes to Life* (New York: Simon & Schuster, 1974), 110, 148, 208–12.

15   Author's note: Ruth asked for $10,000 in his next deal and received $7,000—still meager by today's standards, but not bad for an entertainer in the early twentieth century. "I've never paid an actor that much," complained Red Sox owner Harry Frazee, who doubled as a Broadway producer. Frazee famously sold Ruth to the Yankees five years later for $100,000 and a $300,000 loan, which he used in part to keep his theatrical productions afloat, with Fenway Park as collateral to guarantee the note. Before the transaction with Boston was finalized, the Yankees asked Ruth if he could behave himself in New York. The slugger said yes, but only if the Yankees increased his salary to $20,000—and they did. He didn't exactly hold up his end of the bargain.

16   Bill Francis, "Big Star on the Big Screen," National Baseball Hall of Fame website, n.d., https://baseballhall.org/discover-more/stories/short-stops/big-star-on-the-big-screen.

17   Creamer, *Babe: The Legend Comes to Life*, 274.

18   Robert Schweppe, interview by author, Los Angeles, California, February 2018.

19   Creamer, *Babe: The Legend Comes to Life*, 348–51.

20   "Hollywood 'Paid Fortune to Smoke,'" BBC News, September 25, 2008, http://news.bbc.co.uk/2/hi/health/7632963.stm. Author's note: Hollywood icons from Betty Grable to Clark Gable earned up to $10,000 to shill cigarette brands—a low-six-figure sum in today's dollars—somewhat paltry considering the advertisements were often extensive, with stars acting out meticulously scripted testimonials.

21   Horatia Harrod, "45 Things You Didn't Know About Marilyn Monroe," June 1, 2016, https://www.telegraph.co.uk/films/2016/06/01/50-things-you-didnt-know-about-marilyn-monroe/.

22   Mark Potts, "It's a Long and Winding Lawsuit," *Washington Post*, August 9, 1987, https://www.washingtonpost.com/archive/business/1987/08/09/its-a-long-and-winding-lawsuit/17f298c7-a9ea-4d95-8a8e-bf3771832a97.

23 Paul McCartney, as told to author, "On Ownership," *Forbes*, September 28, 2017.

24 Adam Fisher, *Valley of Genius: The Uncensored History of Silicon Valley* (New York: Twelve/Hachette Book Group, 2018), 2.

25 Author's note: As my dear friend Peter Schwartz noted in his book *Baseball as a Road to God*, Ty Cobb checked into an Atlanta-area hospital toward the end of his life with a pistol and $1 million in bonds.

26 Al Stump, "A Money Player," *Los Angeles Times*, July 12, 1991, http://articles.latimes.com/1991-07-12/sports/sp-2097_1_ty-cobb.

27 Emily Chang, *Brotopia* (New York: Portfolio/Penguin, 2018), 17.

28 John Markoff, "Robert Taylor, Innovator Who Shaped Modern Computing, Dies at 85," *New York Times*, April 14, 2017, https://www.nytimes.com/2017/04/14/technology/robert-taylor-innovator-who-shaped-modern-computing-dies-at-85.html.

29 Isaacson, *The Innovators*, 273–74.

30 Fisher, *Valley of Genius*, 20–22.

31 Isaacson, *The Innovators*, 281.

32 Markoff, "Robert Taylor, Innovator Who Shaped Modern Computing, Dies at 85."

33 Isaacson, *The Innovators*, 294.

34 Ben Horowitz, *The Hard Thing About Hard Things* (New York: HarperCollins, 2014), 271.

35 Curt Flood, letter to Bowie Kuhn, Johns Hopkins virtual library, December 24, 1969, https://exhibits.library.jhu.edu/exhibits/show/freedom-papers/curt-flood/letter-to-the-commissioner.

36 Robert Schweppe, interview by author, Los Angeles, California, February 2018.

37 Matt Kelly, "Catfish Hunter Signs Free Agent Contract with New York Yankees," National Baseball Hall of Fame website, n.d., https://baseballhall.org/discover/inside-pitch/catfish-hunter-signs-with-yankees.

38 Author's note: A fascinating exception was Gene Autry,

who parlayed country music success into owning baseball's Anaheim Angels—in 1991, the *Los Angeles Times* reported that the octogenarian's net worth had soared past $300 million.

39   Ahiza Garcia, "These Are the Only Two Owners of Color in the NFL," CNN, May 18, 2018, https://money.cnn.com/2018/05/18/news/nfl-nba-mlb-owners-diversity/index.html.

40   Walter LaFeber, *Michael Jordan and the New Global Capitalism* (New York: W. W. Norton & Company, 2002), 63–65.

41   Nasir "Nas" Jones, interview by author, New York, New York, August 2018.

42   Heidi Roizen, telephone interview by author, April 2018.

43   Fisher, *Valley of Genius*, 7.

44   Isaacson, *The Innovators*, 352–53.

45   Paul Bond, "Apple, Beatles Settle Trademark Dispute," *Hollywood Reporter*, February 6, 2007, https://www.hollywoodreporter.com/news/apple-beatles-settle-trademark-dispute-129482. Author's note: In 1978, Apple and the Beatles reached a settlement in which the former paid the Beatles' holding company $80,000 and promised not to go into the music business; Apple forked over another $26.5 million in 1991 after selling computers with music-playing software, and yet another payment in 2007 for an undisclosed amount following the release of the iPod.

46   Andy Miller, interview by author, Austin, Texas, March 2018.

47   Heidi Roizen, telephone interview by author, April 2018.

48   Chang, *Brotopia*, 8, 23.

49   Karen Langford, telephone conversation with author, July 2013. Author's note: This information originally appeared in my 2014 book *Michael Jackson, Inc.*

50   Paul McCartney, as told to author, "On Ownership."

51   Josh Elman, interview by author, Menlo Park, California, October 2018.

52   Shaquille O'Neal, interview by author, Atlantic City, New Jersey, July 2018.

Chapter 2: Crash Course

1 Guy Oseary, interviews by author, Los Angeles, California, December 2017 and March 2016.

2 Bill Gross, interview by author, Pasadena, California, February 2018.

3 Al Duncan, electronic message to author on behalf of Bill Gross, February 2018.

4 Bill Gross, interview by author, Pasadena, California, February 2018.

5 Author's note: Representatives for Douglas did not reply to a request for comment.

6 Howard Rosenman, interview by author, New York, New York, April 2018.

7 Heath Evans, "'Content Is King'—Essay by Bill Gates 1996," Medium, January 29, 2017, https://medium.com /@HeathEvans/content-is-king-essay-by-bill-gates-1996-df7 4552f80d9.

8 James Bates, "Investor to Put $500 Million in New Studio," March 20, 1995, *Los Angeles Times*, March 20, 1995, http://articles .latimes.com/1995-03-20/news/mn-45009_1_paul-allen.

9 Author's note: Spielberg, contacted through a spokesperson, ultimately did not respond to interview requests for this book; a request to speak with Allen was pending when he passed away.

10 Howard Rosenman, interview by author, New York, New York, April 2018.

11 Heidi Roizen, telephone interview by author, April 2018.

12 Howard Rosenman, interview by author, New York, New York, April 2018.

13 Guy Oseary, interview by author, Los Angeles, California, December 2017.

14 Bill Gross, interview by author, Pasadena, California, February 2018.

15 Guy Oseary, interview by author, Los Angeles, California, December 2017.

16 Bill Gross, interview by author, Pasadena, California, February 2018.

17 Mike Tarsala, "Pets.com Killed by Sock Puppet," MarketWatch, November 8, 2000, https://www.marketwatch.com/story/sock-puppet-kills-petscom.

18 "Priceline.com Soars on First Trading Day," Marketwatch.com, March 30, 1999, https://www.marketwatch.com/story/ipo-report-pricelinecom-soars-on-first-trading-day.

19 Bill Gross, interview by author, Pasadena, California, February 2018. Author's note: Google did not respond to a request for comment for this book.

20 Ashton Kutcher, interview by author, Los Angeles, California, March 2016.

21 Matthew J. Belvedere, "No Megabucks for Shatner on Priceline Stock: CEO," CNBC, November 8, 2013, https://www.cnbc.com/2013/11/08/no-mega-bucks-for-shatner-on-priceline-stock-ceo.html.

22 Michael Yanover, interview by author, Los Angeles, California, December 2017.

23 Brad Stone, *The Upstarts* (New York: Little, Brown, 2017), 114–15.

24 Adam Fisher, *Valley of Genius: The Uncensored History Of Silicon Valley* (New York: Twelve/Hachette Book Group, 2018), 285–86. Author's note: Eileen Richardson also served as Napster's first CEO.

25 Josh Elman, interview by author, Menlo Park, California, October 2018.

26 Author's note: An entertainment attorney once told me a musician he represented turned in an album during the late 1990s and was informed by the record label that there were too many hits—some of them should be saved for the next album—and more filler was needed.

27 "U.S. Recorded Music Revenues by Format," RIAA.com, https://www.riaa.com/u-s-sales-database/.

28   Brad Stone, *The Upstarts* (New York: Little, Brown, 2017), 116.

29   Steven Bertoni, "Sean Parker: Agent of Disruption," *Forbes*, September 21, 2011, https://www.forbes.com/sites/stevenbertoni/2011/09/21/sean-parker-agent-of-disruption/.

30   Author's note: I admit that, as teenagers, several of my friends and I fell into this group, often spending lunch breaks day-trading tech stocks from computers in our high school library. Like most amateurs in the late 1990s, we did very well despite a near total lack of knowledge—until the bottom fell out.

31   Nate Lanxon, CNET, "The Greatest Defunct Web Sites and Dotcom Disasters," November 18, 2009, https://www.cnet.com/uk/news/the-greatest-defunct-web-sites-and-dotcom-disasters/.

32   Bill Gross, interview by author, Pasadena, California, February 2018.

33   Al Duncan, electronic message to author, March 2019. Author's note: Idealab had actually sold part of its stake in eToys following its IPO. Gross subsequently plowed hundreds of millions in proceeds into new companies in robotics, artificial intelligence and cleantech. According to Idealab, the total return was among the best in its history, topping 10,000 percent in ROI.

34   Michael Yanover, interview by author, Los Angeles, California, December 2017.

35   Bill Gross, interview by author, Pasadena, California, February 2018.

36   Guy Oseary, interview by author, Los Angeles, California, March 2016.

37   Author's note: Burkle's relationship with Clinton seemed to fizzle after the former president's unremarkable post–White House partnership with Yucaipa.

38   Guy Oseary, interview by author, Los Angeles, California, March 2016.

Chapter 3: Liquid Gold

1 Ben Horowitz, telephone interview by author, October 2012. Author's note: This quote originally appeared in my story "Inside Andreessen Horowitz's $15 Million Investment in Rap Genius," *Forbes*, October 3, 2012, https://www.forbes.com/sites/zackomalleygreenburg/2012/10/03/inside-andreessen-horowitz-15-million-investment-in-rap-genius.

2 David Streitfeld, "One Family, Many Revolutions: From Black Panthers, to Silicon Valley, to Trump," *New York Times*, https://www.nytimes.com/2017/07/22/technology/one-family-many-revolutions-from-black-panthers-to-silicon-valley-to-trump.html.

3 Miguel Helft, "Silicon Valley's Stealth Power," *Fortune*, February 27, 2014, http://fortune.com/2014/02/27/silicon-valleys-stealth-power/.

4 Streitfeld, "One Family, Many Revolutions: From Black Panthers, to Silicon Valley, to Trump."

5 Ben Horowitz, *The Hard Thing About Hard Things* (New York: HarperCollins, 2014), 36.

6 Bill Gross, interview by author, Pasadena, California, February 2018. Author's note: Shaq's team would not comment on the Big.com proposal.

7 Shaquille O'Neal, interview by author, Atlantic City, New Jersey, July 2018.

8 Miguel Helft, "Ron Conway Is a Silicon Valley Startup's Best Friend," *Fortune*, February 10, 2012, http://fortune.com/2012/02/10/ron-conway-is-a-silicon-valley-startups-best-friend/.

9 Ron Conway, electronic message to author, September 2018.

10 Bill Gross, interview by author, Pasadena, California, February 2018.

11 Al Duncan, electronic message to author, March 2019.

12 "If You Had Invested Right After Google's IPO," Investopedia, August 13, 2015, https://www.investopedia.com/

articles/active-trading/081315/if-you-would-have-invested-right-after-googles-ipo.asp.

13 Shaquille O'Neal, interview by author, Atlantic City, New Jersey, July 2018.

14 Lea Goldman, "Capitalist Rap," *Forbes*, June 17, 2006, https://www.forbes.com/forbes/2006/0703/138.html#3eeefd426b5e.

15 Ray Latif, "Strand Equity Acquires Minority Stake in Bai Brands," *BevNet*, June 27, 2013, https://www.bevnet.com/news/2013/strand-equity-acquires-minority-stake-in-bai-brands/.

16 Rohan Oza, telephone interview by author, January 2017.

17 Shaquille O'Neal, interview by author, Atlantic City, New Jersey, July 2018.

18 Horowitz, *The Hard Thing About Hard Things*, 197–99.

19 "The Difference Between Good and Bad Organizations," *Farnam Street* (blog), January 2015, https://fs.blog/2015/01/ben-horowitz-good-and-bad-organizations/.

20 Streitfeld, "One Family, Many Revolutions: From Black Panthers, to Silicon Valley, to Trump."

21 Horowitz, *The Hard Thing About Hard Things*, 145.

22 David Carr, "Suddenly, an Affinity for Teenagers," *New York Times*, October 17, 2005, https://www.nytimes.com/2005/10/17/technology/suddenly-an-affinity-for-teenagers.html.

23 Troy Carter, telephone interview by author, January 2018.

24 Michael Arrington, "Stories from the Tell-All MySpace [*sic*] Book," TechCrunch, January 24, 2009, https://techcrunch.com/2009/01/24/myspacebook.

25 Steven Bertoni, "Sean Parker: Agent of Disruption," *Forbes*, September 21, 2011, https://www.forbes.com/sites/stevenbertoni/2011/09/21/sean-parker-agent-of-disruption/.

26 Roger McNamee, *Zucked: Waking Up to the Facebook Catastrophe* (New York: Penguin Press, 2019), 13–18. Author's note: In 2009, Elevation itself reportedly poured $90 million into Facebook, adding another $120 million the following year; from 2009 to 2011, the social network's valuation soared from $10 billion to $50 billion.

27 Heidi Roizen, telephone interview by author, April 2018.

28 Martinne Geller, "Coca-Cola to Buy Glacéau for $4.1 Billion," Reuters, May 25, 2007, https://www.reuters.com /article / us-coke-Glaceau /coca-cola-to-buy-Glaceau-for-4-1 -billion-idUSN2544359220070525.

29 Guy Oseary, interview by author, Los Angeles, California, March 2016.

30 50 Cent, interview by author, New York, New York, August 2018. Author's note: This quote first appeared in my story "The 50 Cent Machine," *Forbes*, August 18, 2008, https://www. forbes.com / 2008 / 08 / 15 / music-50cent-hiphop-biz-media-cz_ zog_0818fifty.html.

31 David Gelles, "Vita Coco Sells Stake to Owner of Red Bull China," *New York Times*, July 14, 2014, https://dealbook. nytimes.com/2014/07/14/vita-coco-sells-stake-to-owner-of-red-bull-china/.

32 Bill Gross, interview by author, Pasadena, California, February 2018.

33 Horowitz, *The Hard Thing About Hard Things*, 270.

Chapter 4: Dude, Where's My Startup?

1 Ashton Kutcher and Guy Oseary, interview by author, Los Angeles, California, March 2016. Author's note: This quote and a few others in this chapter originally appeared in my story "Eight and a Half X," *Forbes*, March 26, 2016, https://www .forbes.com /sites /zackomalleygreenburg /2016 /03 /23/how-ashton-kutcher-and-guy-oseary-built-a-250-million-portfolio-with-startups-like-uber-and-airbnb/.

2 Chris Sacca, electronic message to author, March 2016.

3 Ashton Kutcher, interview by author, Los Angeles, California, March 2016.

4 Marc Andreessen, telephone interview by author, March 2016.

5 Ashton Kutcher, interview by author, Los Angeles, California, March 2016.

6   Daniel Kreps, "Nipple Ripples," *Rolling Stone,* January 30, 2014, https://www.rollingstone.com/culture/culture-news/nipple-ripples-10-years-of-fallout-from-janet-jacksons-halftime-show-122792/.

7   Michael Yanover, interview by author, Los Angeles, California, December 2017.

8   Paul Sawyers, "Google Acquired YouTube 10 Years Ago Today," VentureBeat, October 9, 2016, https://venturebeat.com/2016/10/09/google-acquired-youtube-10-years-ago/.

9   Michael Yanover, interview by author, Los Angeles, California, December 2017.

10   Josh Elman, interview by author, Menlo Park, California, October 2018.

11   Guy Oseary, interview by author, Los Angeles, California, December 2017.

12   Ashton Kutcher, interview by author, Los Angeles, California, March 2016.

13   Marc Andreessen, telephone interview by author, March 2016.

14   Robert "RZA" Diggs, telephone interview by author, April 2018.

15   Dylan Loeb McClain, "Martial Art of Chess, Promoted by a Rapper," *New York Times,* June 7, 2008, https://www.nytimes.com/2008/06/07/arts/music/07clan.html.

16   Author's note: I wrote the story that revealed the existence of the Wu-Tang Clan's secret album in 2014 for *Forbes,* traveling all the way to Morocco to become the first civilian to hear it. For the full story, visit this improbable URL: www.forbes.com/wu-tang.

17   Brian Zisk, telephone interview by author, November 2018.

18   McClain, "Martial Art of Chess, Promoted by a Rapper."

19   Brian Zisk, telephone interview by author, November 2018.

20   Robert "RZA" Diggs, telephone interview by author, April 2018.

21 Brian Zisk, telephone interview by author, November 2018.

22 Robert "RZA" Diggs, telephone interview by author, April 2018.

23 Guy Oseary, interview by author, Los Angeles, California, March 2016.

24 Ashton Kutcher, interview by author, Los Angeles, California, March 2016.

25 Brian Chesky, as told to author, "On Zig Zagging," *Forbes*, September 28, 2017.

26 Brad Stone, *The Upstarts* (New York: Little, Brown, 2017), 136.

27 Guy Oseary, interview by author, Los Angeles, California, December 2017.

28 Stone, *The Upstarts*, 148–49.

29 Ibid, 150.

30 Guy Oseary, interview by author, Los Angeles, California, December 2017.

31 Mark Cuban, electronic message to author, March 2016.

32 David Geffen, electronic message to author, March 2016.

33 Ashton Kutcher, interview by author, Los Angeles, California, March 2016.

34 Michael Yanover, interview by author, Los Angeles, California, December 2017.

Chapter 5: From Gaga to Google

1 Troy Carter, telephone interview by author, January 2018.

2 Bob Lefsetz, "Troy Carter," *The Bob Lefsetz Podcast*, July 2018, https://soundcloud.com/bob-lefsetz/troy-carter-31.

3 Troy Carter, interview by author, Los Angeles, California, November 2015.

4 Lefsetz, "Troy Carter."

5 Ibid.

6 Josh Elman, interview by author, Menlo Park, California, October 2018.

NOTES

7   Andrew Hampp, "How Miracle Whip, Plenty of Fish Tapped Lady Gaga's 'Telephone,'" *AdAge*, March 13, 2010, http://adage.com/article/madisonvine-news/miracle-whip-plenty-fish-tap-lady-gaga-s-telephone/142794/.

8   Danielle Sacks, "Troy Carter: Fired by Lady Gaga and Loving It," *Fast Company*, January 13, 2014, https://www.fastcompany.com/3024171/step-up-troy-carter.

9   Josh Elman, interview by author, Menlo Park, California, October 2018.

10 Troy Carter, telephone interview by author, January 2018.

11 Justin Bieber, interview by author, Los Angeles, California, April 2012. Author's note: Some quotes and insights from this chapter originally appeared in my story "Justin Bieber, Venture Capitalist," *Forbes*, May 16, 2012, https://www.forbes.com/sites/zackomalleygreenburg/2012/05/16/justin-bieber-venture-capitalist-the-forbes-cover-story.

12 Scooter Braun, interview by author, Los Angeles, California, April 2012.

13 Josh Elman, interview by author, Menlo Park, California, October 2018.

14 Scooter Braun, interview by author, Los Angeles, California, April 2012.

15 Jon Russell, "Viddy, Once Touted as 'The Instagram for Video,' Will Shut Down on December 15," TechCrunch, November 4, 2014, https://techcrunch.com/2014/11/04/viddy-once-touted-as-the-instagram-for-video-will-shut-down-on-december-15/.

16 Justin Bieber, interview by author, Los Angeles, California, April 2012.

17 Scooter Braun, interview by author, Los Angeles, California, April 2012.

18 Russell, "Viddy, Once Touted as 'The Instagram for Video,' Will Shut Down on December 15."

19 Troy Carter, telephone interview by author, January 2018.

20 Josh Elman, interview by author, Menlo Park, California, October 2018.

21 Troy Carter, telephone interview by author, January 2018.

22 Erin Griffith, "Ouch: Universal Music Group Sold Back Valuable Uber Shares," *Fortune*, June 4, 2014, http://fortune.com/2014/06/04/universal-music-group-sold-uber-domain/. Author's note: During the early aughts, Universal Music Group invested in a blogging platform called Uber.com. Kalanick decided to shorten his startup's name from UberCab years later after a spat with San Francisco authorities, who demanded the company stop marketing itself as a cab company in deference to city-approved drivers picking up street hails. Strapped for cash, he bought the domain from Universal in exchange for equity. The 2 percent of Uber he coughed up is now worth well over $1 billion, but Universal sold its shares early for a far more modest sum.

23 Shervin Pishevar, electronic message to author, March 2019.

24 Bruce Upbin, "Hyperloop Is Real," *Forbes*, February 11, 2015, https://www.forbes.com/sites/bruceupbin/2015/02/11/hyperloop-is-real-meet-the-startups-selling-supersonic-travel/.

25 Brad Stone, *The Upstarts* (New York: Little, Brown, 2017), 173.

26 Shervin Pishevar, electronic message to author, March 2019.

27 Troy Carter, telephone interview by author, January 2018.

28 Stone, *The Upstarts*, 174–78.

29 Ashton Kutcher, interview by author, Los Angeles, California, March 2016.

30 Sophia Bush, telephone interview by author, July 2019.

31 Guy Oseary, interview by author, Los Angeles, California, December 2017.

32 Sophia Bush, telephone interview by author, July 2019.

33 Troy Carter, telephone interview by author, January 2018.

Chapter 6: Nasdaq Dough

1   Ilan Zechory, interview by author, Brooklyn, New York, February 2018.

2   Nasir "Nas" Jones, interview by author, New York, New York, August 2018.

3   Ben Horowitz, telephone interview by author, October 2012. Author's note: This quote originally appeared in my story "Inside Andreessen Horowitz's $15 Million Investment in Rap Genius," *Forbes*, October 3, 2012, https://www.forbes.com/sites/zackomalleygreenburg/2012/10/03/inside-andreessen-horowitz-15-million-investment-in-rap-genius/.

4   Nasir "Nas" Jones, interview by author, New York, New York, August 2018.

5   Department of the Treasury staff, "Certificate of Release of Federal Tax Lien," Internal Revenue Service filing, October 13, 2009, retrieved via https://static.hiphopdx.com/2017/01/nas-tax-debt-1.jpg. Author's note: In a 2018 video, Nas's ex-wife accused him of physical and emotional abuse during their relationship a decade earlier; he denied the claims and was never charged.

6   Anthony Saleh, telephone interview by author, February 2019.

7   Steve Stoute, telephone interview by author, October 2018.

8   Nasir "Nas" Jones, interview by author, New York, New York, August 2018.

9   David S. Rose, interview by author, New York, New York, August 2018.

10 Nasir "Nas" Jones, interview by author, New York, New York, August 2018.

11 Guy Oseary, telephone interview by author, February 2019.

12 David S. Rose, interview by author, New York, New York, August 2018.

13 Ilan Zechory, interview by author, Brooklyn, New York, February 2018.

14 Anthony Saleh, telephone interview by author, February 2019.

15 Nasir "Nas" Jones, telephone interview by author, October 2012.

16 Anthony Saleh, telephone interview by author, February 2019.

17 Ilan Zechory, interview by author, Brooklyn, New York, February 2018.

18 Ben Sisario, "Rap Genius Website Agrees to License with Music Publishers," *New York Times,* May 6, 2014, https://www.nytimes.com/2013/11/12/business/media/in-music-piracy-battles-lyrics-demand-respect-too.html.

19 Genius founders, "Rap Genius Is Back on Google," Genius.com, n.d., https://genius.com/Genius-founders-rap-genius-is-back-on-google-annotated.

20 Tom Lehman, interview by author, Brooklyn, New York, February 2018.

21 Tom Lehman, "A Statement About Mahbod's Annotations on Elliot Rodger's Manifesto," Genius, May 26, 2014, https://genius.com/tom-lehman-a-statement-about-mahbods-annotations-on-elliot-rodgers-manifesto-annotated.

22 Ilan Zechory, telephone interview by author, January 2017.

23 Dan Gilbert, "I'm Hoping It's 'Smart' to Invest in 'Genius,'" Genius.com, n.d., https://genius.com/Dan-gilbert-im-hoping-its-smart-to-invest-in-genius-annotated.

24 Anthony Saleh, telephone interview by author, February 2019.

25 Nasir "Nas" Jones, interview by author, New York, New York, August 2018.

26 Anthony Saleh, telephone interview by author, February 2019.

27 Author's note: One insider claims Ben Horowitz flew Nas out on a private jet to meet Coinbase's founders to help seal the

deal for both his firm and the rapper's. Saleh disputes this account but wouldn't explain more about what took place, saying only: "It's so fucking legendary that...Ben wants to save it." (A spokesperson for Horowitz wouldn't comment on the story.)

28 Drew Houston, conversation with author, Jersey City, New Jersey, October 2018.

29 Anthony Saleh, telephone interview by author, February 2019.

30 Brad Stone, *The Upstarts* (New York: Little, Brown, 2017), 246.

31 Clifford "T. I." Harris, interview by author, New York, New York, June 2018.

32 Peter Holslin, "Chamillionaire Wants to Be a Chabillionaire," Noisey, April 28, 2015, https://noisey.vice.com/en_us/article/ryzv45/chamillionaire-wants-to-be-a-chabillionaire.

33 David S. Rose, interview by author, New York, New York, August 2018.

34 Anthony Saleh, telephone interview by author, February 2019.

35 Nasir "Nas" Jones, interview by author, New York, New York, August 2018. Author's note: Jay-Z showed his respect for Nas's investing blueprint more through actions than words. In 2018, Beyoncé's husband launched a venture outfit of his own, calling it MVP, short for Marcy Venture Partners. As had been the case with Nas, the namesake was his childhood housing project home.

36 Ilan Zechory, interview by author, Brooklyn, New York, February 2018.

37 Ilan Zechory, electronic message to author, August 2019.

38 Author's note: Myriad startups have raised oodles of cash without generating any revenue.

39 Ilan Zechory, electronic message to author, February 2019, and interview by author, Brooklyn, New York, February 2018.

40 Mahbod Moghadam, electronic message to author, March 2018.

41 Ilan Zechory, interview by author, Brooklyn, New York, February 2018.

42 Nasir "Nas" Jones, interview by author, New York, New York, August 2018.

43 Peter Bittenbender, interview by author, New York, New York, August 2018.

44 Nasir "Nas" Jones, interview by author, New York, New York, August 2018.

45 Anthony Saleh, telephone interview by author, February 2019.

46 "Viacom Acquires Nas-Invested Company PlutoTV for $340 Million," *Vibe*, January 24, 2019, https://www.vibe.com/2019/01/nas-invested-company-acquired-by-amazon.

47 Nasir "Nas" Jones, interview by author, New York, New York, August 2018.

Chapter 7: Spotify Spotter

1 D. A. Wallach, interview by author, Los Angeles, California, December 2017. Author's note: Representatives for Apple, Facebook, and Spotify did not reply to requests for comment.

2 Jimmy Iovine, opening remarks at Beats reception, New York, New York, October 2011. Author's note: This quote was originally published in my story "HTC Hasn't Forgotten About Dre," *Forbes*, October 12, 2011, http://www.forbes.com/sites/zackomalleygreenburg/2011/10/12/htc-hasnt-forgotten-about-dr-dre-or-jimmy-or-monster/.

3 Steven Bertoni, "Spotify's Daniel Ek: The Most Important Man in Music," *Forbes*, January 4, 2012, http://www.forbes.com/sites/stevenbertoni/2012/01/04/spotifys-daniel-ek-the-most-important-man-in-music/.

4 Guy Oseary, telephone interview by author, February 2019.

5 D. A. Wallach, interview by author, Los Angeles, California, December 2017.

6   Author's note: Chester French was a duo consisting of Wallach and Maxwell Drummey by the time they signed their record deal—but its larger, original lineup also included Damien Chazelle, writer and director of *La La Land*, and Justin Hurwitz, who created the film's score.

7   D. A. Wallach, interview by author, Los Angeles, California, December 2017.

8   Author's note: Kutcher also starred in an ill-advised 2012 Popchips commercial in which he played four different people looking for love, including a Bollywood producer named Raj, in brownface; Popchips pulled the spot from its Facebook and YouTube pages after a public outcry.

9   D. A. Wallach, interview by author, Los Angeles, California, December 2017.

10 D. A. Wallach, electronic message to author, February 2019.

11 D. A. Wallach, interview by author, Los Angeles, California, December 2017.

12 Andrew Hampp, "Guy Oseary, Scooter Braun and Troy Carter: The Billboard Cover Story, Power Trio," *Billboard*, April 11, 2013, https://www.billboard.com/articles/business/1557311/guy-oseary-scooter-braun-and-troy-carter-the-billboard-cover-story-power.

13 Brian Zisk, telephone interview by author, November 2018.

14 Brian Dunn, telephone interview by author, December 2016. Author's note: This quote first appeared in my book *3 Kings*, which Little, Brown published in 2018.

15 Troy Carter, interview by author, Los Angeles, California, November 2015.

16 Kjetil Sæter, interview by author, Oslo, Norway, January 2017.

17 Hasit Shah, "Poor Lonely Computer: Prince's Misunderstood Relationship with the Internet," NPR, March 8, 2016, https://www.npr.org/sections/therecord/2016/03/08/469627962/poor-lonely-computer-princes-misunderstood-relationship-with-the-internet.

18   Garth Brooks, interview by author, Austin, Texas, March 2017. Author's note: This quote was originally published in my story "Why Garth Brooks Went to SXSW—And Amazon Music," *Forbes*, March 17, 2017, https://www.forbes.com/sites/zackomalleygreenburg/2017/03/17/why-garth-brooks-went-to-sxsw-and-amazon-music.

19   Jason Aldean, interview by author, Hartford, Connecticut, May 2015.

20   Tidal, "TIDAL | #TIDALforALL" video, YouTube, March 30, 2015, https://www.youtube.com/watch?v=cYYGdcLbFkw.

21   Kjetil Sæter and Gunnar Sellæg, interviews by author, Oslo, Norway, January 2017.

22   Noah Yoo, "The Full Transcript of Jay-Z's Tidal Q&A," *The Fader*, April 1, 2015, https://www.thefader.com/2015/04/01/the-full-transcript-of-jay-zs-qa-at-the-clive-davis-institute-of-recorded-music.

23   D. A. Wallach, telephone interview by author, December 2016.

24   Troy Carter, telephone interview by author, January 2018.

25   Ashton Kutcher, interview by author, Los Angeles, California, March 2016.

26   D. A. Wallach, interview by author, Los Angeles, California, December 2017.

27   Brian Zisk, telephone interview by author, November 2018.

28   D. A. Wallach, interview by author, Los Angeles, California, December 2017.

29   Erin Griffith, "Start-Ups Ask, 'Are We Making Money for Saudi Arabia?'" *New York Times*, November 1, 2018, https://www.nytimes.com/2018/11/01/technology/start-ups-venture-capital-saudi-arabia.html.

30   D. A. Wallach, interview by author, Los Angeles, California, December 2017.

NOTES

Chapter 8: New Ownership

1 Jack Conte, interview by author, San Francisco, California, October 2018; Jack Conte, "Pedals Behind the Scenes," May 7, 2013, https://www.youtube.com/watch?v=lHJkI UEONL8.

2 Adam Lilling, interview by author, New York, New York, July 2018.

3 Amanda Groves, interview by author, New York, New York, July 2018.

4 Adam Lilling, interview by author, New York, New York, July 2018.

5 Clare O'Connor, "How Jessica Alba Built a $1 Billion Company, and $200 Million Fortune, Selling Parents Peace of Mind," *Forbes*, May 27, 2015, https://www.forbes.com/sites/clareoconnor/2015/05/27/how-jessica-alba-built-a-1-billion-company-and-200-million-fortune-selling-parents-peace-of-mind/.

6 Author's note: One could argue crowdfunding dates back many centuries, to everything from war bonds to subscription-based book series.

7 Jack Conte, interview by author, San Francisco, California, October 2018.

8 Taryn Arnold, "These 34 Creators Earned over $150,000 Each on Patreon in 2016," *Patreon*, January 6, 2016, https://blog.patreon.com/top-earners-2016.

9 Amanda Palmer, electronic message to author, March 2019.

10 Jack Conte, interview by author, San Francisco, California, October 2018.

11 Jeremy Liew, interview by author, Menlo Park, California, October 2018.

12 O'Connor, "How Jessica Alba Built a $1 Billion Company, and $200 Million Fortune, Selling Parents Peace of Mind."

NOTES

13 Nicole Quinn, interview by author, Menlo Park, California, October 2018.

14 Gwyneth Paltrow, panel at Upfront Summit, Los Angeles, California, January 2019.

15 Author's note: A spokesperson for Paltrow did not respond to multiple interview requests for this book.

16 Jeremy Liew, interview by author, Menlo Park, California, October 2018.

17 Jack Conte, interview by author, San Francisco, California, October 2018.

18 Lorenzo Franceschi-Bicchierai, *Motherboard*, "Crowdfunding Site Patreon Gets Hacked," October 1, 2015, https://motherboard.vice.com/en_us/article/xywedn/crowdfunding-site-patreon-gets-hacked.

19 Crunchbase data; Josh Constine, "Patreon Raises Big Round at ~$450M," TechCrunch, September 14, 2017, https://techcrunch.com/2017/09/14/patreon-series-c/.

20 Jack Conte, "We Messed Up," *Patreon*, December 13, 2017, https://blog.patreon.com/not-rolling-out-fees-change.

21 Amanda Palmer, electronic message to author, March 2019.

22 Jack Conte, interview by author, San Francisco, California, October 2018.

23 "Scary Pockets," https://www.youtube.com/channel/UC-2JUs_G21BrJ0efehwGkUw.

24 Jack Conte, interview by author, San Francisco, California, October 2018.

25 *Brad Buonasera v. The Honest Company*, United States District Court Southern District of New York, No. 7:16-cv-01125, June 12, 2017, accessed via https://www.truthinadvertising.org/wp-content/uploads/2016/02/Buonasera-v-The-Honest-Co-joint-notice-of-settlement.pdf; and *Candace Hiddlestone and Julie Hedges v. The Honest Company*, United States District Court Central District of California, September 16, 2016, accessed via https://www.courtlistener.com/recap/gov.uscourts.cacd.658704.1.0.pdf.

26 Serena Ng, "No Longer a Unicorn, Jessica Alba's Honest

Co. Struggles to Grow," *Wall Street Journal*, January 5, 2018, https://www.wsj.com/articles/no-longer-a-unicorn-jessica-albas-honest-co-faces-growth-challenges-1515157203.

27 *People of the State of California v. Goop*, Superior Court of the State of California, September 4, 2018, accessed via https://www .truthinadvertising.org/wp-content/uploads/2018/09/Goop-California-Signed-Judgment.pdf.

28 Ashley Cullins, "Gwyneth Paltrow's Goop Settles False Advertising Suit," *Hollywood Reporter*, September 5, 2018, https:// www.hollywoodreporter.com/thr-esq/gwyneth-paltrows-goop -settles-false-advertising-suit-1139977. Author's note: The suit called out items like a $66 vaginal "jade egg" intended to boost women's sexual energy; in the settlement, Goop admitted to no wrongdoing but was forced to curtail advertising claims of health benefits associated with its products.

29 Jack Conte, interview by author, San Francisco, California, October 2018.

Chapter 9: Stocks for Jocks

1 Georgie Moskowitz, electronic message to author, October 2019.

2 Tony Gonzalez, telephone interview by author, March 2018.

3 Georgie Moskowitz, electronic message to author, October 2019.

4 Tony Gonzalez, telephone interview by author, March 2018.

5 *United States of America v. Scilabs Nutraceuticals, Inc., and Paul P. Edalat*, United States District Court Central District of California, No. SACV 14-01759-JLS, November 12, 2014, accessed via https://www.docketbird.com/court-documents/USA-v-Kelly /CONSENT-DECREE-OF-PERMANENT-INJUNCTION -by-Judge-Josephine-L-Staton-against-Defendants-Paul-Edalat -and-Scilabs-Nutraceuticals-Inc-MD-JS-6-Case-Terminated/ cacd-8:2014-cv-01759-00007.

6 Michael Blank, interview by author, Los Angeles, California, December 2017.

7 Ibid.

8 Tony Gonzalez, telephone interview by author, March 2018.

9 Chris Dufresne, "Montana: After a Miraculous Recovery from Back Surgery, Joe's Play Has Been Less Than a Miracle," *Los Angeles Times*, December 17, 1986, http://articles.latimes.com /1986-12-17/sports/sp-3146_1_joe-montana.

10 Joe Montana, telephone interview by author, September 2018.

11 Edward Robinson, "Winning Super Bowl Lets Former 49ers Fumble Investing," *Bloomberg Markets*, February 9, 2011, https://www.bloomberg.com/news/articles/2011-02 -02/winning-super-bowls-lets-montana-teammates-fumble-handling-elite-investor.

12 Michael Ma, telephone interview by author, January 2018.

13 Michael Ma, electronic message to author, February 2019.

14 Joe Montana, telephone interview by author, September 2018.

15 Michael Ma, telephone interview by author, January 2018; electronic message to author, February 2019.

16 Joe Montana, telephone interview by author, September 2018.

17 Jamie Siminoff, interview by author, Santa Monica, California, December 2018.

18 Author's note: Siminoff posits that one of the best ways to turn your children into inventors is to leave them alone. "A lot of times, parents are like, 'Hey, build this, we'll help you,'" he says. "It's like, 'Oh, my kid built this!' And I'm like, 'No, you built that, and your kid likes it.' My dad was just like, 'Oh, I don't know what to do. There's tools in the basement.' You know? And my mom was like, 'You need to eat your vegetables.' No one gave a shit about what I was doing. They certainly weren't pushing me to a life of invention, [but] my parents let me continue to build anything I wanted."

19 Jamie Siminoff, interview by author, Santa Monica, California, December 2018.

20 Jamie Siminoff, electronic message to author, February 2019.

21 David S. Rose, interview by author, New York, New York, August 2018.

22 Troy Carter, telephone interview by author, January 2018.

23 Jamie Siminoff, interview by author, Santa Monica, California, December 2018.

24 Shaquille O'Neal, interview by author, Atlantic City, New Jersey, July 2018.

25 Author's note: Also instrumental in the Ring deal was ABG, the brand management group that had earlier signed O'Neal to a fascinating deal. According to the company's founder, Jamie Salter, the arrangement called for ABG to manage Shaq's brand as a joint venture—in exchange for an eight-figure chunk of cash, much of which Shaq reinvested into ABG itself. That stake is already worth many times what Shaq paid for it, though his team wouldn't comment on specifics, saying only that he was among the largest stakeholders in the $4 billion company.

26 Jamie Siminoff, interview by author, Santa Monica, California, December 2018.

27 Mark Harris, "Video Doorbell Firm Ring Says Its Devices Slash Crime—But the Evidence Looks Flimsy," *MIT Technology Review*, October 19, 2018, https://www.technologyreview.com/s/612307/video-doorbell-firm-ring-says-its-devices-slash-crimebut-the-evidence-looks-flimsy.

28 Jamie Siminoff, interview by author, Santa Monica, California, December 2018.

29 Shaquille O'Neal, interview by author, Atlantic City, New Jersey, July 2018.

30 Jamie Siminoff, interview by author, Santa Monica, California, December 2018.

31 Georgie Moskowitz, electronic message to author, October 2019.

32 Kurt Badenhausen, "Inside Serena Williams' Plan to Ace Ven-

ture Investing," *Forbes*, June 3, 2019, https://www.forbes.com/sites/kurtbadenhausen/2019/06/03/inside-serena-williams-plan-to-ace-venture-investing/. Author's note: Williams's team did not respond to an interview request for this book.

33 Tony Gonzalez, telephone interview by author, March 2018.

Chapter 10: Icarus, Inc.

1   Heidi Roizen, telephone interview by author, April 2018.
2   Emily Chang, *Brotopia* (New York: Portfolio/Penguin, 2018), 7.
3   Ibid, 93, 100.
4   Heidi Roizen, telephone interview by author, April 2018.
5   Colleen Taylor, "BlackJet, the Uber for Private Jet Travel, Appoints Shervin Pishevar as Its Chairman," TechCrunch, February 14, 2013, https://techcrunch.com/2013/02/14/BlackJet -the-uber-for-private-jet-travel-appoints-shervin-pishevar-as-its-chairman/.
6   Monica Smith, "BlackJet SF Launch Event Recap," ABCey, n.d., http://abcey.com/BlackJet-sf-launch-event-recap/.
7   Taylor, "BlackJet, The Uber For Private Jet Travel, Appoints Shervin Pishevar As Its Chairman." Author's note: Rotchin did not respond to interview requests for this book in early 2019.
8   Shervin Pishevar, electronic message to author, March 2019.
9   Troy Carter, electronic message to author, January 2019.
10 Green Jets, "Notice of Exempt Offering of Securities," United States Securities and Exchange Commission, May 7, 2012, https://www.sec.gov/Archives/edgar/data/1549428/00015 4942812000001/xslFormDX01/primary_doc.xml.
11 Sarah Mitroff, "Startup Offers Private Jet Ride-Sharing, but Cost Is Still Sky-High," *Wired*, October 27, 2012, https://www.wired.com/2012/10/BlackJet/.
12 Author's note: There was a certain only-in-showbiz irony to the moment. Timberlake and Janet Jackson's infamous "wardrobe malfunction" had inspired the creation of

YouTube while making her an eternal enemy of Leslie Moonves, the chief of CBS, which had aired the Super Bowl that year; he reportedly became intent on ruining her career after deciding Jackson hadn't been "sufficiently repentant." In a remarkable exhibition of a double standard, Timberlake was invited back to perform the halftime show at Super Bowl LII, while Jackson remains in something of an NFL exile.

13   "Social Commerce Company BeachMint Launches HomeMint with Justin Timberlake and Interior Designer Estee Stanley," PR Newswire, April 17, 2012, https://www.prnewswire.com/news-releases/social-commerce-company-beachmint-launches-homemint-with-justin-timberlake-and-interior-designer-estee-stanley-147710985.html.

14   Author's note: In a footnote to a footnote, Myspace shuffled along for years after the sale to Time Inc., with most observers unaware of its continued existence until the service reportedly lost some 50 million user-uploaded songs in 2019.

15   Rohan Oza, telephone interview by author, January 2017.

16   Eli Blumenthal, "Dr. Pepper Buys Bai Brands for $1.7B to Expand into Health-Oriented Drinks," *USA Today*, November 22, 2016, https://www.usatoday.com/story/money/business/2016/11/22/dr-pepper-snapple-buys-bai-brands/94283000.

17   Anna Gaca, "Justin Timberlake Wants to Say Bai Bai Bai to This Beverage Lawsuit," *Spin*, June 25, 2018, https://www.spin.com/2018/06/justin-timberlake-bai-lawsuit/.

18   *Kevin Branca vs. Bai Brands*, United States District Court Southern District of California, No. 3:18-cv-00757-BEN-KSC, March 7, 2019, via https://www.proskaueronadvertising.com/files/2019/04/Branca-v.-Bai.pdf.

19   Bruce Upbin, "Hyperloop Is Real," *Forbes*, February 11, 2015, https://www.forbes.com/sites/bruceupbin/2015/02/11/hyperloop-is-real-meet-the-startups-selling-supersonic-travel/.

20   Nitasha Tiku, "Celeb-Backed BlackJet Is Officially Fucked," Valleywag, December 20, 2013, http://valleywag.gawker.com/celeb-backed-blackjet-is-officially-fucked-1487131322.

21   Shervin Pishevar, electronic message to author, March 2019.

22   Green Jets, "Notice of Exempt Offering of Securities," United States Securities and Exchange Commission, May 7, 2012.

23   Emily Chang, "Uber Investor Shervin Pishevar Accused of Sexual Misconduct by Multiple Women, *Bloomberg*, November 30, 2017, https://www.bloomberg.com/news/articles/2017-12-01/uber-investor-shervin-pishevar-accused-of-sexual-misconduct-by-multiple-women.

24   Sam Shead, "Shervin Pishevar Defender Reportedly Says Investor Couldn't Have Engaged in Sexual Misconduct at Uber Party Because He Had a 'Pony's Leash in One Hand and a Drink in the Other,'" *Business Insider*, December 1, 2017, https://www.businessinsider.com/shervin-pishevar-defender-he-couldnt-have-touched-austin-geidt-because-pony-leash-drink-report-2017-12.

25   Author's note: In February 2019, a representative from Sherpa Capital told me that Pishevar is "no longer affiliated" with the company.

26   Marcus Baram, "The Shervin Pishevar Sexual-Assault Legal Saga Is Getting Even Crazier," *Fast Company*, December 6, 2017, https://www.fastcompany.com/40504774/the-shervin-pishevar-sexual-assault-legal-saga-is-getting-even-crazier. Author's note: In December 2017, reports emerged that Pishevar had been detained but not charged on suspicion of rape in London (in addition to denying these allegations, Pishevar—a prominent Democratic donor—sued a conservative research firm that he claimed had been hired by one of his competitors to "destroy his career.")

27   Ronan Farrow, "From Aggressive Overtures to Sexual Assault: Harvey Weinstein's Accusers Tell Their Stories," *The New*

Yorker, October 10, 2017, https://www.newyorker.com/news/news-desk/from-aggressive-overtures-to-sexual-assault-harvey-weinsteins-accusers-tell-their-stories.

28 Audrey Carlsen, Maya Salam, Claire Cain Miller, Denise Lu, Ash Ngu, Jugal K. Patel, and Zach Wichter, "#MeToo Brought Down 201 Powerful Men. Nearly Half of Their Replacements Are Women," *New York Times*, October 29, 2018, https://www.nytimes.com/interactive/2018/10/23/us/metoo-replacements.html.

29 Sheelah Kolhatkar, "The Tech Industry's Gender-Discrimination Problem," *The New Yorker*, November 20, 2017, https://www.newyorker.com/magazine/2017/11/20/the-tech-industrys-gender-discrimination-problem

30 Heidi Roizen, telephone interview by author, April 2018.

31 Susan Fowler, "Reflecting on One Very, Very Strange Year at Uber," SusanJFowler.com, February 19, 2017, https://www.susanjfowler.com/blog/2017/2/19/reflecting-on-one-very-strange-year-at-uber. Author's note: An Uber spokesperson, reached via email, would not comment on this incident, or more generally for the book.

32 Sophia Bush, telephone interview by author, July 2019.

33 Heidi Roizen, telephone interview by author, April 2018.

34 Theodore Schleifer, "Steve Jurvetson Was Pushed Out of His Firm as the Lines Between Personal And Professional Crossed," *Recode*, November 18, 2017, https://www.recode.net/2017/11/18/16647078/steve-jurvetson-dfj-women-silicon-valley-tech-allegations-fired.

35 Steve Jurvetson, untitled post, Facebook, November 14, 2017, https://www.facebook.com/jurvetson/posts/10159616207180611?pnref=story.

36 Heidi Roizen, telephone interview by author, April 2018.

37 Emily Smith, "Les Moonves Wasn't Only One Escaping Scandal on St. Barts," *New York Post*, January 2, 2019, https://pagesix.com/2019/01/02/les-moonves-wasnt-only-one-escaping-scandal-on-590m-yacht/.

38   Polina Marinova, "DFJ Partner Heidi Roizen: Sexual Harassment Allegations Are a 'Wake-Up Call to Any Firm,'" *Fortune*, December 5, 2018, http://fortune.com/2018/12/05/heidi-roizen-dfj/.

Chapter 11: Doing Well

1   Ashton Kutcher, panel conversation, Austin, Texas, March 2018.

2   Mick LaSalle, "*Jobs* Review: Kutcher's Fine, but Film's Timing Is Off," *San Francisco Chronicle*, August 15, 2013, https://www.sfchronicle.com/movies/article/Jobs-review-Kutcher-s-fine-but-film-s-timing-4735382.php.

3   Ilan Zechory, telephone interview by author, February 2018.

4   Ashton Kutcher and Guy Oseary, interview by author, Los Angeles, California, March 2016. Author's note: Some of these quotes initially appeared in my cover story "Eight and a Half X," *Forbes*, March 26, 2016, https://www.forbes.com/sites/zackomalleygreenburg/2016/03/23/how-ashton-kutcher-and-guy-oseary-built-a-250-million-portfolio-with-startups-like-uber-and-airbnb/.

5   Josh Constine, Ryan Lawler, and Sarah Buhr, "The 52 Start-ups That Launched at Y Combinator W17 Demo Day 1," TechCrunch, March 20, 2017, https://techcrunch.com/2017/03/20/yc-demo-day-winter-2017.

6   Guy Oseary, interview by author, Los Angeles, California, December 2017.

7   Ashton Kutcher, interview by Stephen Colbert, "Ashton Kutcher Examines President Trump's Tweeting Style," *The Late Show with Stephen Colbert*, July 14, 2017, https://www.youtube.com/watch?time_continue=2&v=gYD07kGeNAM.

8   Noah Kerner, telephone interview by author, October 2019.

9   Umer Adnan, electronic message to author, February 2019.

10   Umer Adnan, telephone interview by author, February 2019.

11   Guy Oseary, telephone interview by author, February 2019.

12 Shaquille O'Neal, interview by author, Atlantic City, New Jersey, July 2018.

13 Andy Miller, interview by author, Austin, Texas, March 2018.

14 Andy Miller, electronic message to author, February 2019.

15 Shaquille O'Neal, electronic message, Twitter, July 24, 2016, https://twitter.com/shaq/status/757289366003658752?lang=en.

16 Andy Miller, electronic message to author, February 2019.

17 Steve Aoki, telephone interview by author, January 2019.

18 Michael Yanover, interview by author, Los Angeles, California, December 2017.

19 United States Securities and Exchange Commission, "Notice of Exempt Offering of Securities," Form D, July 11, 2018, https://www.sec.gov/Archives/edgar/data/1744008/00017 4400818000001/xslFormDX01/primary_doc.xml.

20 Effie Epstein, electronic message to author, February 2019.

21 Guy Oseary, telephone interview by author, February 2019.

22 Effie Epstein, electronic message to author, February 2019.

23 Guy Oseary, telephone interview by author, February 2019.

24 Ashton Kutcher, Marc Benioff, and Rebecca Liebman, panel conversation, Austin, Texas, March 2018.

25 Guy Oseary, telephone interview by author, February 2019.

Chapter 12: Doing Good

1 Sophia Bush, telephone interview by author, July 2019.

2 Bono, as told to author, "On Advocacy," *Forbes*, September 28, 2017.

3 Bono, interview by author, New York, New York, June 2017.

4 Adam Lewis, "TPG Adds John Kerry to $2B Rise Fund," *Pitch-Book*, April 26, 2018, https://pitchbook.com/news/articles/tpg-adds-john-kerry-to-2b-rise-fund.

5 Frank Newport, "Democrats More Positive About Socialism Than Capitalism," Gallup, August 13, 2018, https://news.gallup.com/poll/240725/democrats-positive-socialism-capitalism.aspx.

6   Author's note: McGlashan issued a statement at the time, declaring, "I will be focused on addressing the allegations that have been presented, and there are aspects of the story that have yet to emerge that I wish I could share."

7   John Kerry, "We Live in Extraordinary Times," *Medium*, April 26, 2018, https://medium.com/@JohnKerry/we-live -in-extraordinary-times-but-in-too-many-ways-its-a-global- version-of-a-tale-of-two-fe139f0c4089.

8   Ben Horowitz and Chris Lyons, "Introducing the Cultural Leadership Fund," *Andreessen Horowitz* (blog), August 22, 2018, https://a16z.com/2018/08/22/introducing-the- cultural-leadership-fund.

9   Jeremy Liew, interview by author, Menlo Park, California, October 2018.

10   Backstage Capital, "#Backstage100," https://backstagecapital .com/100/.

11   Hayley Cuccinello, "Sure Shots: These Twin 27-Year-Olds Are Building a Seven-Figure Business on High School Sports," *Forbes*, December 31, 2018, https://www.forbes.com/ sites/hayleycuccinello/2019/12/31/sure-shots-these-twin-27 -year-olds-are-building-a-seven-figure-business-on-high-school -sports.

12   Arlan Hamilton, Twitter posts, personal Twitter account, May 5–6, 2018, https://twitter.com/ArlanWasHere/status/9929 04943773208576 and https://twitter.com/ArlanWasHere/ status/993138674475843585; author's note: Hamilton didn't reply to interview requests.

13   Troy Carter, telephone interview by author, February 2019.

14   Sophia Bush, telephone interview by author, July 2019.

15   Morgan Stanley, "Sustainable Signals," Institute for Sustainable Investing, 2017, https://www.morganstanley.com/ pub/content/dam/msdotcom/ideas/sustainable-signals/pdf /Sustainable_Signals_Whitepaper.pdf.

16   Adam Lewis, "TPG Adds John Kerry to $2B Rise

Fund," *PitchBook*, April 26, 2018, https://pitchbook.com/news/articles/tpg-adds-john-kerry-to-2b-rise-fund.

17   Abby Schultz, "The Rise Fund Spin-Off Marks Growth of Impact Investing," *Barron's*, January 24, 2019, https://www.barrons.com/articles/the-rise-fund-spin-off-marks-growth-of-impact-investing-01548368130.

18   Noah Kerner, telephone interview by author, October 2019.

19   Guy Oseary, telephone interview by author, February 2019.

20   Jason D. Rowley, "Q4 2018 Closes Out a Record Year for the Global VC Market," Crunchbase, January 7, 2019, https://news.crunchbase.com/news/q4-2018-closes-out-a-record-year-for-the-global-vc-market.

21   Bill Gross, interview by author, Pasadena, California, February 2018.

22   Todd Spangler, "Netflix Spent $12 Billion on Content in 2018," *Variety*, January 18, 2019, https://variety.com/2019/digital/news/netflix-content-spending-2019-15-billion-1203112090.

23   D. A. Wallach, interview by author, Los Angeles, California, December 2017.

24   Margaret Sullivan, "An Early Facebook Investor Throws Up His Hands: We've Been 'Zucked,'" *Washington Post*, February 7, 2019, book-investor-throws-up-his-hands-weve-been-zucked/2019/02/07/1e7bdfd2-2ad0-11e9-b011-d8500644dc98_story.html?utm_term=.dab7ca34de40.

25   Jonathan Shieber, "Amid Plummeting Stocks and Political Uncertainty, VCs Urge Their Portfolios to Prepare for Winter," TechCrunch, December 25, 2018, https://techcrunch.com/2018/12/25/amid-plummeting-stocks-and-political-uncertainty-vcs-urge-their-portfolios-to-prepare-for-winter/amp.

26   Troy Carter, telephone interview by author, February 2019.

27   Bono, as told to author, "On Advocacy," *Forbes*, September 28, 2017, p. 117.

28   Sophia Bush, telephone interview by author, July 2019.

INDEX

INDEX

INDEX

INDEX

INDEX

INDEX

ABOUT THE AUTHOR

Zack O'Malley Greenburg is the senior editor of media and entertainment at *Forbes* and the author of four books, including the Jay-Z biography *Empire State of Mind*. His work has also appeared in the *New York Times,* the *Washington Post,* the *Hollywood Reporter,* *McSweeney's,* and the Library of Congress. Greenburg has served as an expert source for NPR, the BBC, MTV, and CBS's *60 Minutes.* He has appeared as a speaker at SXSW, CES, TEDx, Harvard, and Yale. He lives in New York with his wife and cats.